30°E 60° 90° 120° 150°

Europe-Asia Boundary

A S I A
118-139

U R O P E
80-99

F R I C A
100-117

AUSTRALIA
NEW ZEALAND
OCEANIA
140-153

N T A R C T I C A
154-159

Winkel Tripel Projection

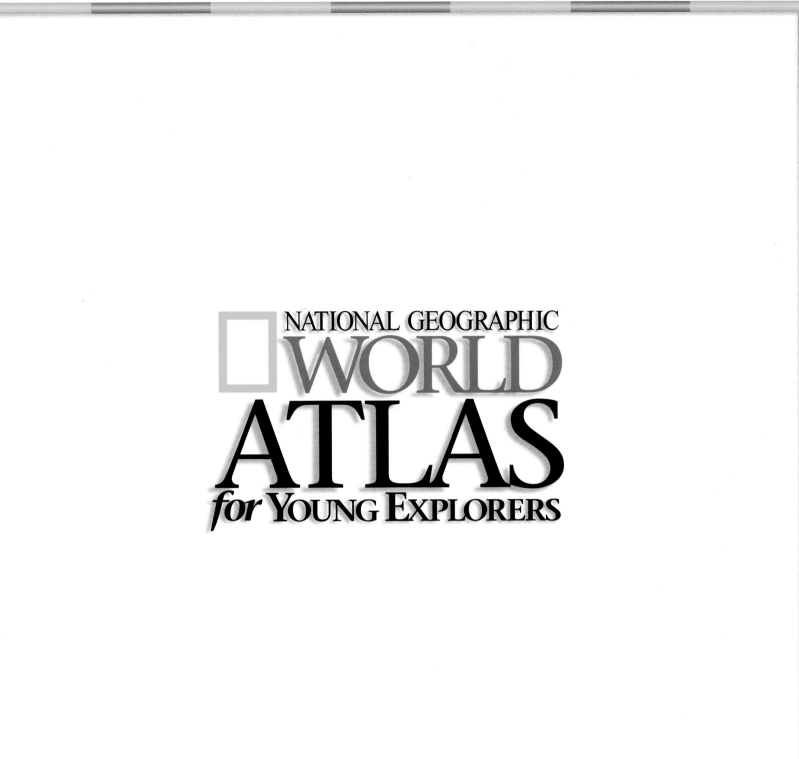

NATIONAL GEOGRAPHIC

WORLD

ATLAS

for YOUNG EXPLORERS

From North America (near right) to Antarctica (far right), the *National Geographic World Atlas for Young Explorers* covers the earth's seven continents in words, maps, and photographs.

NATIONAL GEOGRAPHIC
WORLD
ATLAS
for YOUNG EXPLORERS

NATIONAL GEOGRAPHIC SOCIETY
WASHINGTON, D.C.

Photographs from Tony Stone Images

Contents

KINDS OF MAPS:
PAGE 10

Planet Earth

The World

AFRICA: CHEETAH, PAGE 106

North America 32

NORTH AMERICA:
GRAND CANYON,
PAGE 38

SOUTH AMERICA:
MACHU PICCHU,
PAGE 68

South America 64

Europe 80

Africa 100

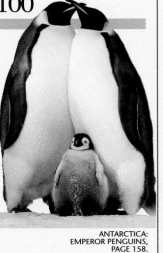

ANTARCTICA: EMPEROR PENGUINS, PAGE 158.

Asia 118

ASIA: GREAT WALL OF CHINA, PAGE 122

Australia
New Zealand, and Oceania 140

AUSTRALIA: BOY WITH KANGAROO, PAGE 145

Antarctica 154

FACTS & FIGURES 160

EUROPE: SOCCER PLAYERS, PAGE 84

How To Use This Atlas

You can use this atlas for all kinds of exploration. To learn about maps, read the first section, Understanding Maps. Some basic facts about the earth appear in the second part, Planet Earth. The world maps that follow will give you an overall picture of the planet. After that, the maps are arranged by continent. You can get an understanding of a continent's culture and people by reading the photographic essay. You can find cities, mountains, and rivers on the continent and regional maps. Or, you can just browse, and see where you end up!

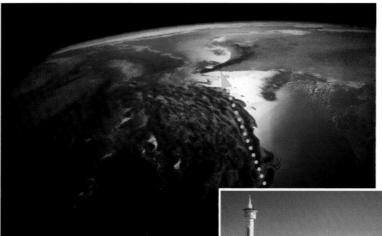

Connections: Planet to Map

Each continent section in this atlas opens with a large photograph (like the one of Asia, above). This picture shows one part of a continent seen from space. In most cases, the photos were taken from the space shuttle. Can you make the connection? Look for these places on the maps.

▲ *Every continent photo is accompanied by a smaller photo. This one is the city of Dubayy. The small photo shows a close-up part of the land in the big picture.*

Projections

Every map in this atlas is drawn to a particular projection. The projection determines how—and how much— land shapes are stretched. Our world political and physical maps use the Winkel Tripel projection (right), which gives a good overall picture of the continents' shapes. Many of our regional maps use an azimuthal equidistant projection, which shows accurate sizes on large-scale maps.

Flags and Stats

Each regional map has a box that shows the flag for each country or U.S. state featured. The box also lists each country's area, population, capital, and official or most common languages. Territories of other countries are listed at the end of the box.

"You Are Here"

Locator globes help you find a map area on the planet. On regional maps, the area covered by the m is yellow on the globe and the continent it belongs to is green. On continent maps, the whole continer is yellow. All the other land is brown.

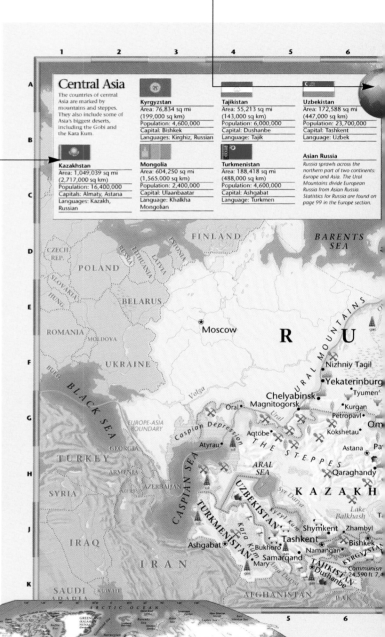

Index and Grid

Use the Index to find any place on these maps. It's arranged alphabetically. Look for the place-name you want. Next to it is a page number, a letter, and another number. Go to the page. Draw imaginary lines from the letter along the left edge and the number along the top of the map. Your place will be close to where the lines meet.

Baghdad, Iraq **134** G8
Bahamas (islands) **61** D11; 60
Bahia Blanca, Argentina **79** E9
Bahr el Arab (river), Sudan **113** J10
Bahrain **135** E10
Baikal, Lake, Russia **129** G11

Corner Tabs

Every section in this atlas has its own color. Look for the color on the Contents pages and in the top right-hand corner of every page. Within that colored corner tab you'll see the name of the section and the title for each topic or map. These corner tabs give you a handy way to find the map you want.

North America
South America
Europe
Africa
Asia
Australia
Antarctica

Map Icons

Our regional maps have little pictures, or icons, that tell you what kinds of crops, farm animals, industries, and other economic activities are common in each region. Sometimes the icon has a label that identifies it more specifically. Below is the key to those icons.

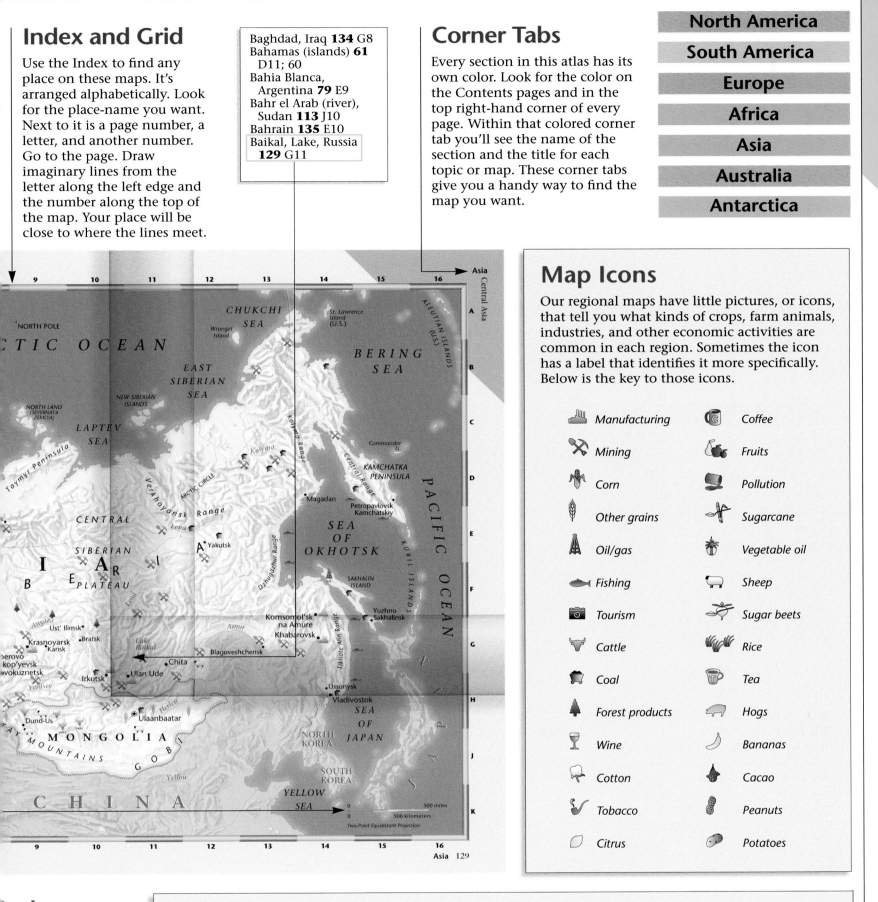

Manufacturing
Mining
Corn
Other grains
Oil/gas
Fishing
Tourism
Cattle
Coal
Forest products
Wine
Cotton
Tobacco
Citrus

Coffee
Fruits
Pollution
Sugarcane
Vegetable oil
Sheep
Sugar beets
Rice
Tea
Hogs
Bananas
Cacao
Peanuts
Potatoes

Scales

If you want to find out how far it is from one place on a map to another, use the bar scale. A scale appears on every map. It shows how distance on paper corresponds to distance in the real world.

Map Key

Our maps use symbols to stand for many political and physical features. At right is the key to these symbols. If you're wondering what you're looking at on a map, come back here and check.

✪ ◉ Capitals
• • • Towns
+ + Elevations
⊢⊣ Waterfall
• Depressions
∴ Ruin
▼▼▼▼ Ice shelf

Defined boundary
Undefined boundary
Claimed boundary
Offshore boundary
Rivers
Canal
National Park

Dry salt lake
Swamp
Sand
Lava
Tundra
Below sea level
Glacier

From Local to World

About a hundred years ago, scientist Philip Henry Gosse taught his son Edmund about maps. He had Edmund stand on a stool in the middle of the living room and draw every curlicue of the Oriental rug's pattern onto a piece of paper. Then he had him add the furniture to his drawing, also as seen from the stool, and so on. Edmund learned these things about maps: A map is a drawing of a place as seen from above. It is flat. And it is smaller than the place it shows, shrinking all places and objects by the same amount.

Edmund grew up to be a writer with a passion for maps. Like many others who have grown up to be explorers, scientists, and dreamers of all kinds, he knew that maps could take him places in his imagination and, later, in reality. Maps not only describe places—the shape of a country or location of mountains—they can reveal an astonishing range of information, from inches of rainfall by state to puppy ownership by county. And yet, maps are still the same flexible tool Gosse introduced to his son. They are a way of organizing information in a universal language that you can fold up and stick in your pocket.

Downtown
Looking at maps is lik[e] looking at land from the sky. When you're close to the ground, you see a lot of detail but not much area— as in this view from above downtown Salt Lake City.

City
Zooming out from downtown lets you see the grid of surrounding streets.

State
Many miles up, you can see the whole state of Utah, but not much detail. The city and lake look small.

Country
Higher yet, you notice that Utah is one piece of a larger country, the United States.

World
From space, you can see that a country is just part of a continent, the largest kind of landmass on the round earth.

Make It Flat

To make a map—let's say, of your neighborhood—you need to know what to leave out. Maps show places from above, not from the ground. Objects in a map look flat. Your map will show only unchanging things, such as houses and streets. It won't show the dog that's walking by today.

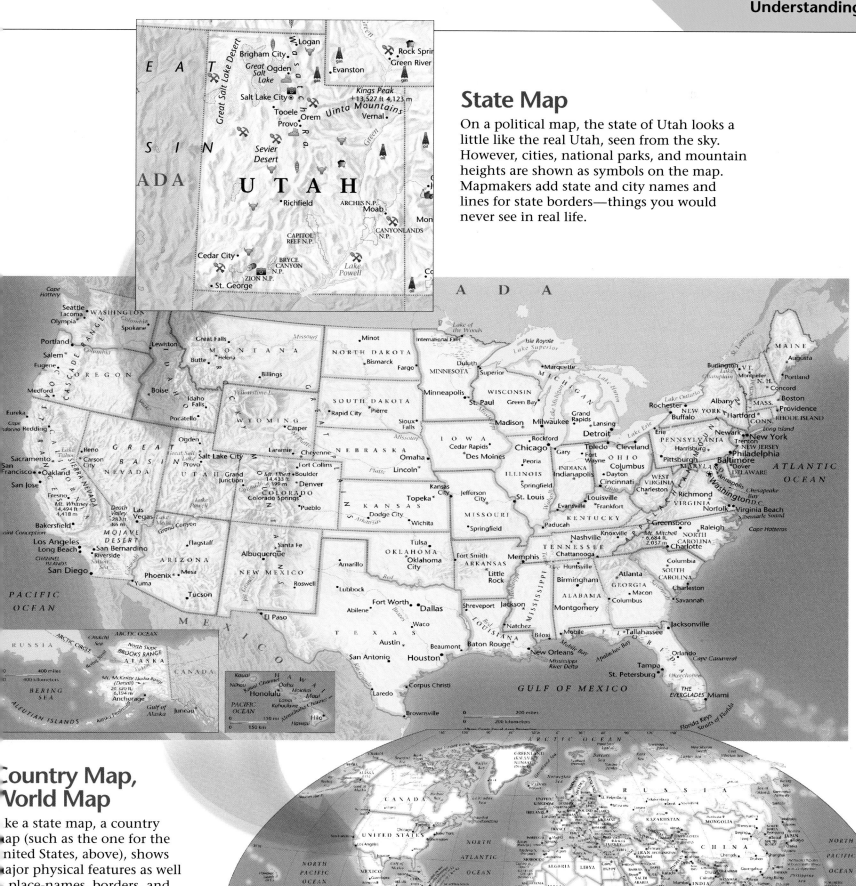

State Map

On a political map, the state of Utah looks a little like the real Utah, seen from the sky. However, cities, national parks, and mountain heights are shown as symbols on the map. Mapmakers add state and city names and lines for state borders—things you would never see in real life.

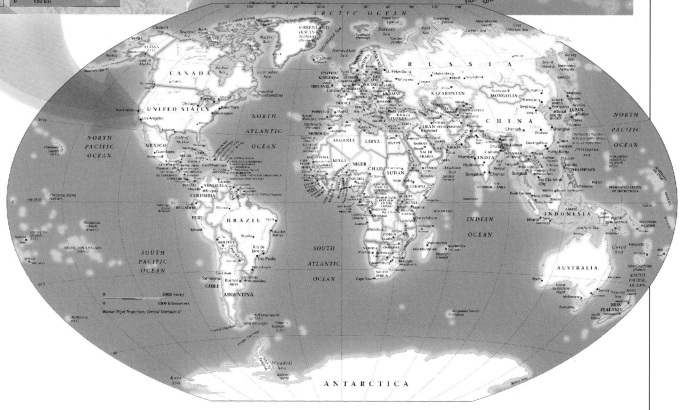

Country Map, World Map

Like a state map, a country map (such as the one for the United States, above), shows major physical features as well as place-names, borders, and other information. Some maps, such as the one above, also have insets: boxes that contain their own maps, showing areas that can't be seen on the main map because they are too small or too far away. A world map, such as the one at right, shows even more area but less detail. This is called a small-scale map.

Kinds of Maps

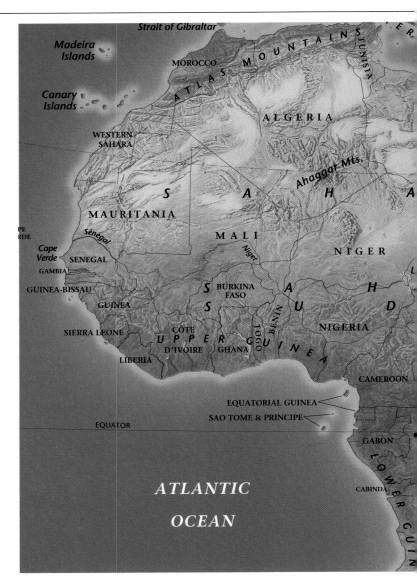

Maps are amazingly useful tools. We use them to preserve information, to display data, and to reveal relationships between seemingly unrelated things. For instance, in the 19th century, Dr. John Snow mapped deaths from cholera in London compared to the locations of public water pumps. His map showed that victims lived only near certain pumps. Snow's map helped to prove that cholera is a disease carried by water.

One thing maps can't do is gather information. Humans have to do that themselves through exploration and by collecting data. Computers sort the data and then cartographers go to work, making an incredible variety of maps.

Projections

Because the earth is round, its surface is best shown on a globe. But a globe can't show you the whole world at one time. Instead, cartographers project the round earth onto a flat surface. Unfortunately, when the earth's surface is peeled off and flattened (below), big gaps open up. To fill in the gaps, mapmakers usually stretch parts of the earth, choosing to show either the correct shapes of places or their correct sizes; it is impossible to show both. The map shape that results is called a projection. There are more than a hundred kinds of projections.

Physical Map

A physical map names landforms and water features rather than cities. This physical map of northwestern Africa identifies rivers, lakes, mountains, and deserts. As on many physical maps, color identifies both elevation—the height of the land—and vegetation regions.

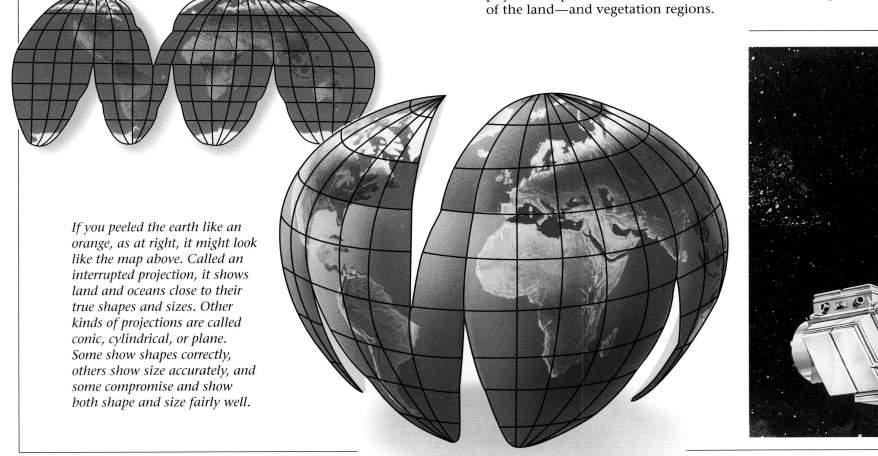

If you peeled the earth like an orange, as at right, it might look like the map above. Called an interrupted projection, it shows land and oceans close to their true shapes and sizes. Other kinds of projections are called conic, cylindrical, or plane. Some show shapes correctly, others show size accurately, and some compromise and show both shape and size fairly well.

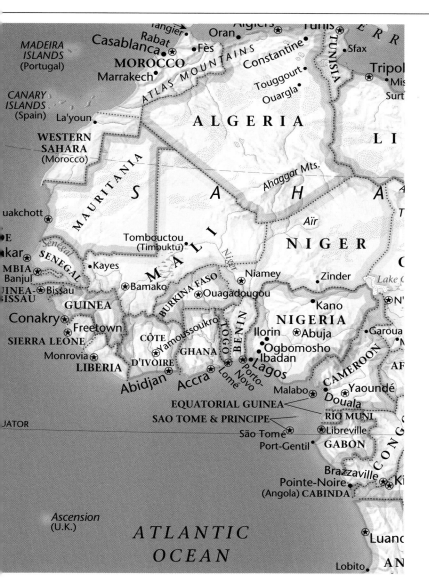

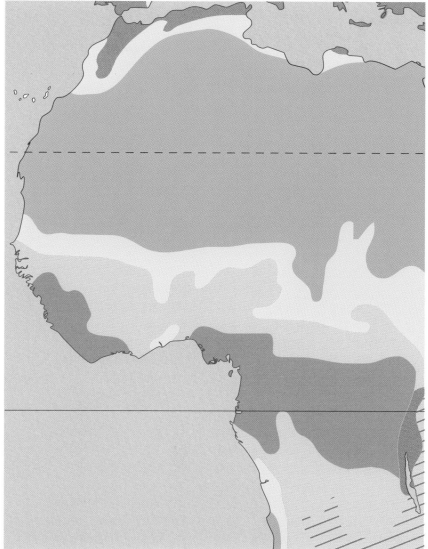

Political Map

A political map shows the names and boundaries of countries and identifies only major physical features. This political map shows countries in northwestern Africa. Dots mark cities. The larger the dot and the city name, the more populous the city. Stars in circles identify capital cities.

Thematic Map

Thematic maps display patterns, usually emphasizing one subject, or theme. This thematic map shows northwestern Africa's climates, with each climate zone marked by a color. Dark green means the area is tropical and wet. Yellow shows semiarid, meaning fairly dry. Orange is arid, or desert.

How Maps Are Made

The main reason we create maps—to organize our knowledge of the world—hasn't changed in 4,000 years of mapping. But the tools have. Today, most cartographers use computers with a program called Geographic Information Systems (GIS). Each kind of information on a map is kept as a separate "layer" in the map's digital files. This allows cartographers to make maps—and change them—more quickly and easily.

Eyes in Space

Monster mappers in the sky, satellites (left) collect data on what they "see" below. Landsat maps are the product of satellites surveying the earth from 22,300 miles (35,887 kilometers) up. Equipment records sunlight reflecting from earth's surface, converting it to numbers. Transmitters beam the numbers to earth.

▲ *Mouse and monitor have replaced pen and paper for modern mapmakers. Here, due to political changes in Africa, a cartographer alters a country's name: Zaire becomes Democratic Republic of the Congo.*

How To Read a Map

A map is more than just a diagram of a place from above. Encoded on an ordinary map is all sorts of information. Learn that code, and you can make any kind of map reveal its secrets.

Take latitude and longitude. These are imaginary measurement lines on a map or globe that form a grid—like tic-tac-toe lines that come together at the North and South Poles. You won't find these lines on the ground because they don't exist in nature. They are simply an invention that helps us pinpoint location, or where a place is on the earth's surface.

Not all maps are drawn with north at the top. On many maps, a directional arrow or a compass rose directs a reader to north on the map.

Every map should have a scale, usually a bar scale. This little code tells you how to measure distances on the map. And many maps also offer a key. The key lists the symbols the cartographer has used on the map and tells what they stand for. Learn to read a key, translate scale, find a direction, and determine a location, and a map will keep no secrets from you.

Latitude and Longitude

Lines of latitude run around the globe horizontally, east and west (below left). Because latitude measures parts of a sphere, it is written in degrees, abbreviated as °. The Equator is 0° latitude. About 60 miles (111 km) north is 1° N latitude. At the same distance south of the Equator is 1° S latitude, and so on, all the way up to 90° N and 90° S—the Poles.

Longitude runs vertically, north and south (below right). Zero degrees longitude, the prime meridian, runs through Greenwich, England. There are 180 degrees east and west. Lines of latitude, or parallels, never meet. Lines of longitude, or meridians, meet at the Poles. The exact location of a place is where its lines of latitude and longitude meet.

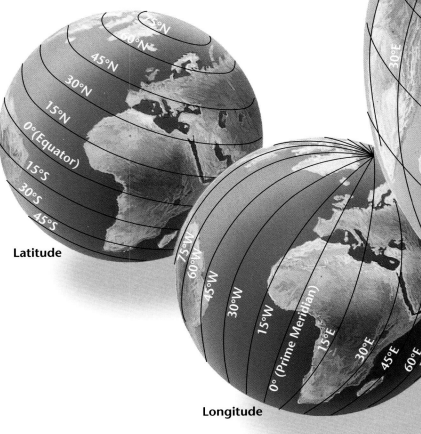

Latitude

Longitude

Zeroing In

Spot has run away. Fortunately, you had him outfitted with a radio tracking collar, and the satellite positioning service tells you he's at 30° S, 60° W. Two clues are obvious. S means Spot is south of the Equator. West means he is west of the prime meridian. On a map, find 30° latitude running across the Southern Hemisphere. Trace it with your finger until you reach longitude 60° W. Hmm. Spot must be visiting cousin Ricardo in Argentina.

◀ *Lines of latitude and longitude form an imaginary grid that helps us locate places on a map. Here, the lines for 30° S, 60° W meet in Argentina near the Paraná River.*

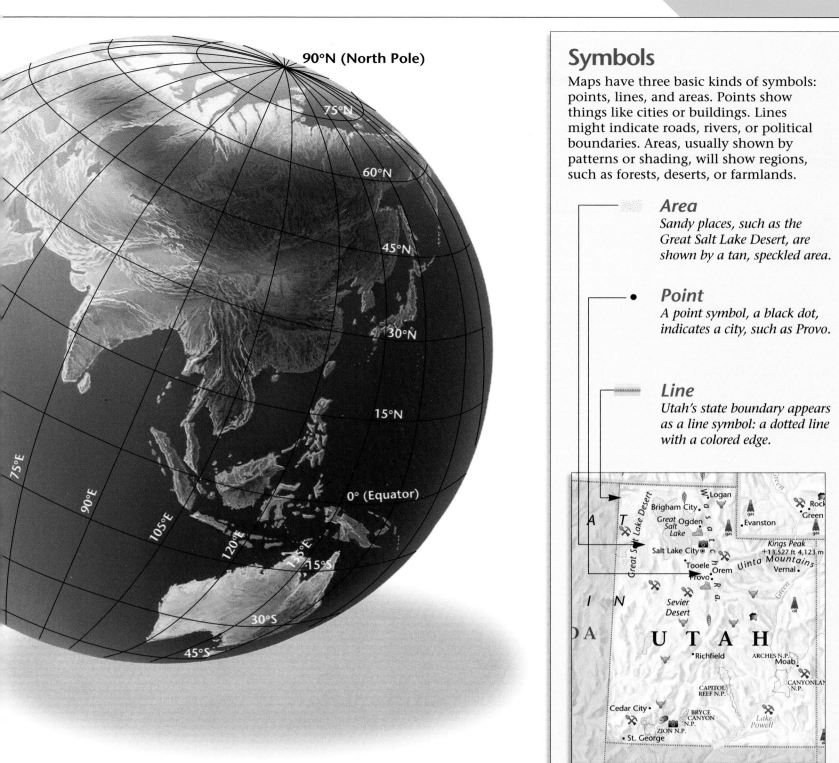

90°N (North Pole)

75°N

60°N

45°N

30°N

15°N

0° (Equator)

15°S

30°S

45°S

75°E

90°E

105°E

120°E

135°E

Symbols

Maps have three basic kinds of symbols: points, lines, and areas. Points show things like cities or buildings. Lines might indicate roads, rivers, or political boundaries. Areas, usually shown by patterns or shading, will show regions, such as forests, deserts, or farmlands.

Area
Sandy places, such as the Great Salt Lake Desert, are shown by a tan, speckled area.

Point
A point symbol, a black dot, indicates a city, such as Provo.

Line
Utah's state boundary appears as a line symbol: a dotted line with a colored edge.

Scale and Direction

A distance scale is a line or a bar that compares distance on the map to distance in the real world. Scales are often accompanied by the name of the map projection. Many maps also have arrows that point to north on the map; some will show all four directions. Maps in this atlas are oriented toward the north, so they do not use arrows.

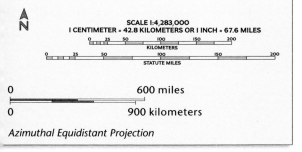

N

SCALE 1:4,283,000
1 CENTIMETER = 42.8 KILOMETERS OR 1 INCH = 67.6 MILES

0 25 50   100   150   200
KILOMETERS

0   25   50   100   150   200
STATUTE MILES

0   600 miles

0   900 kilometers

Azimuthal Equidistant Projection

Quick Look

▶ Looking for Luanda, but don't know where it is? Maps often use a grid around their edges that can help you. Look up the place-name in the index for the atlas or map. Our atlas tells you that Luanda, Angola, is on page 116, B2. Find the letter down the side of the map, then find the number along the top. Draw straight lines down and across the map with your finger. You will find Luanda near the spot where the lines meet.

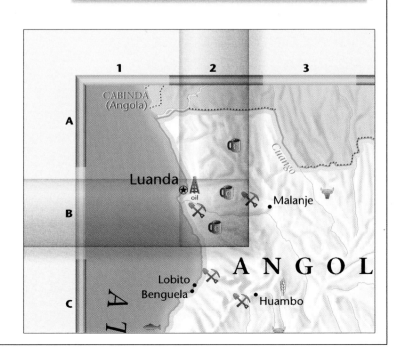

The Earth in Space

Earth, alone, seems vast and varied, with its continents, oceans, and polar caps. But earth is part of a much larger system, and it is the workings of this system that dictate the rhythms of our days, seasons, and years.

Ours is one of nine planets that revolve around a star we call the sun, in a kind of cosmic family we call a solar system. Life on earth depends on the sun for light, warmth, energy, and food. Our year is defined by the sun. The sun's gravity locks earth onto an invisible, oval track around it that takes roughly 365 days to complete.

The sun also defines our day. As earth revolves around the sun, it also rotates on its axis—an invisible line through the Poles—like a spinning top. Thus every place on the planet whirls to face the sun, turns past, and returns every 24 hours. When Africa faces the sun, it is day there. As it turns away, night falls.

Earth's Family

Earth is the third planet of nine orbiting the sun. It is dwarfed by the gas giants Jupiter, Saturn, Uranus, and Neptune. The planets, in turn, are tiny compared to the sun, which contains 99 percent of the matter in the solar system. The painting at right shows the planets' sizes compared to one another and to the sun. Distances are not to scale.

Time Zones

In olden times it was noon when the sun was overhead wherever you happened to be. Then, in the late 1800s, countries recognized the need to divide the earth into 24 standard time zones. Time is counted from the prime meridian Greenwich, England, shown as no on the art at left. For each 15 degrees you travel eastward, the time is one hour later.

Air Cover

Earth's atmosphere surrounds the planet with a life-giving blanket of nitrogen, oxygen, and other gases. Within it, all earth's weather takes place, driven by the sun's energy, the earth's rotation, and ocean currents. Great rafts of air heated at the Equator rise and spin away north and south toward the Poles as polar air flows south, creating weather systems. Powerful currents of air called jet streams, 5 to 9 miles (8 to 15 kilometers) above the planet's surface, move this weather around the globe, unleashing storms and bringing in sunny days.

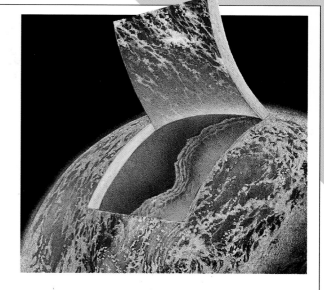

▲ *About 300 miles from top to bottom, earth's atmosphere is thin compared to the planet it covers. All weather occurs in the lowest layer, about 10 miles (16 kilometers) thick.*

▲ *Storm clouds hang low over the Great Plains of the United States. Hot and cold air masses often collide violently over the flat lands of the Plains, producing anything from a thundershower to a deadly tornado.*

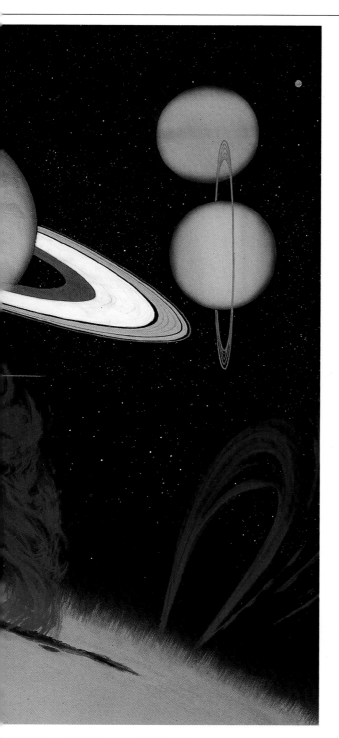

...e Seasons

...e the famous tower ...Pisa, the earth leans. ...s tilt brings us our ...sons of winter, spring, ...mer, and fall. Here's ...w: The hemisphere (the ...th or south half of the ...th) that is tipped ...ard the sun gets lots of ...ct sunlight. It's ...mer there. Six months ...r the hemisphere has ...ched the other side ...ts orbit. It is tilted away ...n the sun and receives ...ch less sunlight, so the ...son there is winter. ...fway between these ...extremes lie spring ...fall.

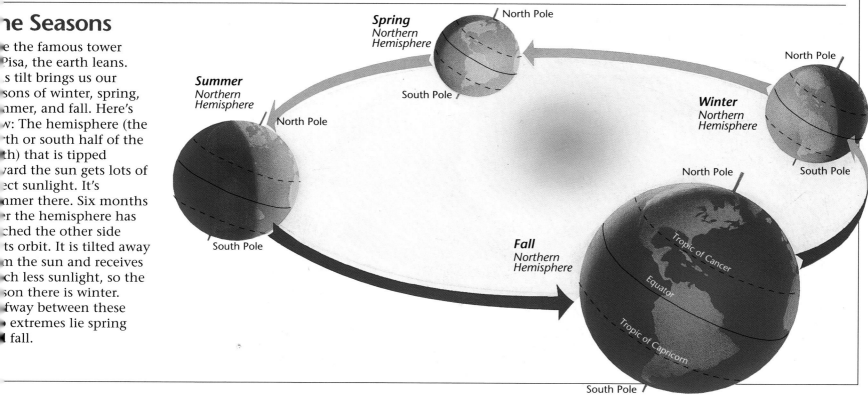

Spring
Northern Hemisphere
North Pole
South Pole

Summer
Northern Hemisphere
North Pole
South Pole

Winter
Northern Hemisphere
North Pole
South Pole

Fall
Northern Hemisphere
North Pole
Tropic of Cancer
Equator
Tropic of Capricorn
South Pole

The Earth in Motion

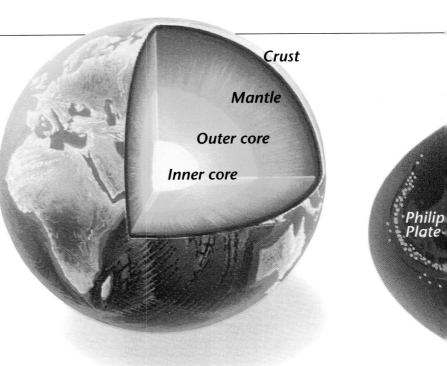

Crust
Mantle
Outer core
Inner core

Philip Plate

If ancient astronauts had photographed the planet as it was 500 million years ago, the earth as seen from space would not be anything we'd recognize. We wouldn't see North America as we know it today. We couldn't find Australia, Asia, or Africa. Most of the landmasses that make up our present-day continents were part of one large supercontinent called Pangaea. Over millions of years, this supercontinent has broken apart into continents, which in turn have drifted and recombined, all at a pace slower than a snail's.

What causes such solid things as continents to wander about? The earth's crust—its thin, rocky outer shell—forms a rigid puzzle of plates floating on partially molten rock in the upper mantle. Heat and currents in the molten rock shove the plates around. These movements still shape the earth.

Into the Core

If you could slice into the earth (above), you would see that its outer layer, the crust, is thin—only 2 miles (3 kilometers) in some spots. Beneath it lie the rocky mantle, a liquid outer core, and a hot, solid, inner core.

Giant Plates

Red lines on the map at right show the boundaries between earth's largest plates. Yellow dots mark the locations of volcanoes. Always on the move, plates collide, grind past each other, or spread apart, releasing molten material from inside the earth.

Continents on the Move

1 Pangaea *About 240 million years ago, earth's continents had collided in a giant pile-up called Pangaea, stretching from Pole to Pole.*

EURASIA
PANGAEA
NORTH AMERICA
PANTHALASSIC OCEAN
SOUTH AMERICA
TETHYS OCEAN
GONDWANA

2 Drifting Apart *By 94 million years ago, Pangaea had been pulled apart into smaller continents. In the warm climate, dinosaurs evolved into earth's most extensive animal group.*

NORTH AMERICA
EURASIA
ATLANTIC OCEAN
PACIFIC OCEAN
TETHYS OCEAN
PACIFIC OCEAN
SOUTH AMERICA
AFRICA
AUSTRALIA

3 Disaster *Continents were moving toward their current position by 65 million years ago. The impact of an asteroid in the Gulf of Mexico may have extinguished half of the world's species.*

NORTH AMERICA
EUROPE
ASIA
ATLANTIC OCEAN
PACIFIC OCEAN
SOUTH AMERICA
AFRICA
PACIFIC OCEAN
AUSTRALIA

4 Deep Freeze *By 18,000 years ago, the continents had close to their modern shapes, but a great ice age had the far north and south locked under glaciers.*

NORTH AMERICA
EUROPE
ASIA
NORTH PACIFIC OCEAN
NORTH AMERICA
NORTH ATLANTIC OCEAN
AFRICA
SOUTH AMERICA
SOUTH PACIFIC OCEAN
SOUTH ATLANTIC OCEAN
NORTH PACIFIC OCEAN
AUSTRALIA
ANTARCTICA

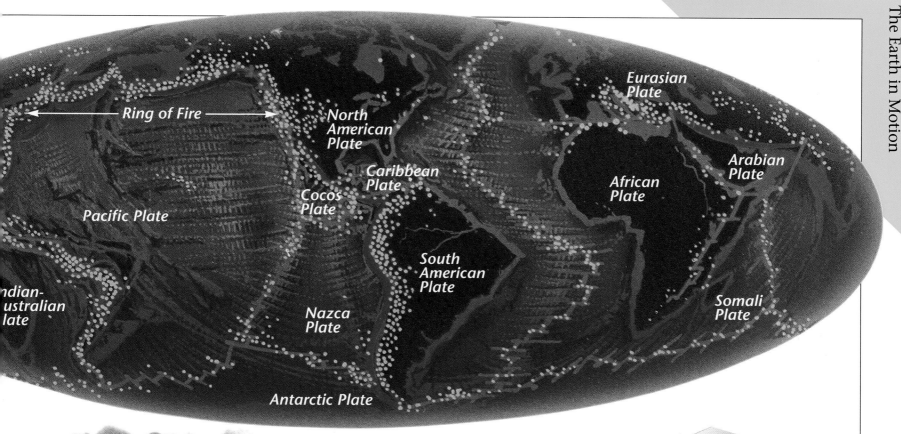

Ring of Fire

Eurasian Plate

North American Plate

Arabian Plate

Caribbean Plate

African Plate

Cocos Plate

Pacific Plate

South American Plate

Somali Plate

Indian-Australian Plate

Nazca Plate

Antarctic Plate

Earth Shapers

The planet's biggest features—its continents, oceans, and mountain ranges—are formed by moving plates. Where plates collide, they push up mountains. Where they pull apart, lava wells out, creating new land. Lifted by plates underneath, land rises to become plateaus. Eruptions and earthquakes accompany this slow movement.

◄ Volcanoes *Most volcanoes form where one plate dives beneath another (as in the Ring of Fire in the map above). The rocky plate melts as it moves downward. Its molten rock, called magma, rises to the surface through the volcano's funnel.*

▼ Faulting *Sometimes plates grind past each other, creating cracks called faults. One famous fault is the San Andreas, in California. Tension builds up along faults as plates stick. When the plates suddenly shift, an earthquake may begin.*

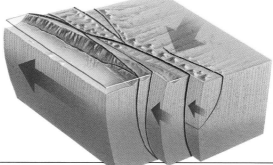

▲ Spreading *Where plates move apart, the crust cracks and molten rock rises up in the rift. Spreading occurs down the middle of the Atlantic Ocean's floor, pulling Europe away from North America.*

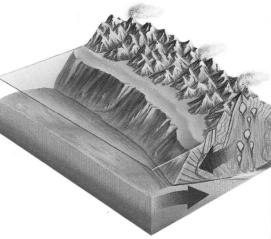

▲ Subduction *When one plate dives beneath another, the process is called subduction. Deep trenches appear where heavy oceanic plates plunge beneath lighter continental plates.*

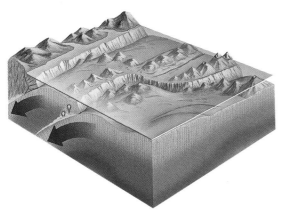

▲ Accretion *In accretion, pieces of crust join each other as two plates collide, causing the pieced-together landscape seen on Alaska's coast.*

The Land

Mesa. Butte. Lagoon. Archipelago. The names humans have given earth's physical features make an intriguing language. Not only do they name the land, but they also distinguish between similar shapes. Take mesa and butte, both steep-sided hills found in deserts. A mesa has a table top—mesa means 'table' in Spanish. A butte has the mesa's steep sides but is smaller and has a bumpy top.

You can find the same kinds of shapes all the world over. That's because similar forces shaped them—either the internal forces of plate movement or the external forces of wind and water. Water and ice are powerful earth movers. Rivers cut valleys and canyons. Glaciers scoop wide, U-shaped mountain valleys, pushing rocks ahead like icy bulldozers. The ace of earth-movers is the ocean, which with one mighty wave can strip away an entire beach—or deposit a new one. The ocean floor itself displays features as varied as those on dry land, including trenches six times as deep as the Grand Canyon and mountains that make Everest look small.

The Dry Earth
▼*People once believed the ocean floor was a seamless basin. Not at all! Drain off the water and you'll expose mountains and canyons. Dominating the oceans is the Mid-Ocean Ridge, a 46,000-mile (75,000-kilometer) crack in the seafloor through which lava rises, creating new crust. In the southwestern Pacific, the Challenger Deep is the lowest spot on earth at 35,840 feet (10,924 meters) below sea level.*

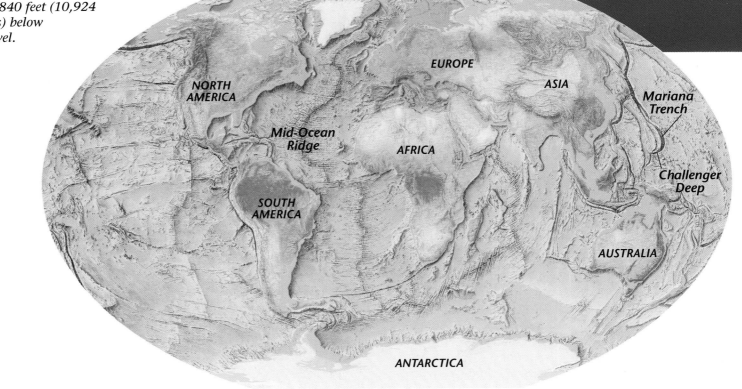

Mountain range

Mountain peak

Glacier

Iceberg

Desert

Mesa

Basin

Oasis

Divide

Plateau

Waterfall

Escarpment

Valley

Lake

Canyon

Canal

Lagoon

Plain

Fork

Delta

Hills

River

Harbor

Breakwater

Tributary

A Name for Every Feature

Land has a vocabulary all its own, each name identifying a specific feature of the landscape. A cape, for example, is a broadish chunk of land extending out into the sea. It is not pointed, however, for then it would be a point. Nor does it have a narrow neck. A sizable cape or point with a narrow neck would be a peninsula. The narrow neck, of course, is an isthmus. Such specific identifiers have proven useful over the centuries. In the early days of exploration, even the simplest maps showed peninsulas, bays, and straits. Sailors used these landmarks to reach safe harbor.

◄ *The landscape at left is an imaginary one that contains many of earth's major landforms and features. Definitions for these terms and others can be found in the Glossary on page 161.*

Desert *Deserts can be hot or cold, sandy or rocky—but they are always dry. The one above, with its tall cactuses, is typical of the American Southwest.*

River *As a river flows downhill, the slope gradually flattens and the river winds from side to side—as seen in England's Thames, above.*

Mountain *Mountains are the highest landforms. Everest, in Asia's Himalaya, is highest of all at 29,028 feet (8,848 meters) above sea level.*

Valley *Valleys come in all shapes. Wide, U-shaped, steep-sided valleys like this one in the Peruvian Andes show geologists where glaciers once passed.*

The Physical World

Look at a physical map of the world, such as the one at right, and you will see one key fact right away. We live on an ocean planet. Water covers more than two-thirds of the earth's surface. Although we give four different names to the four biggest bodies of water—the Pacific, Atlantic, Indian, and Arctic Oceans—in fact they all form one interconnected ocean. We also define the largest landmasses as continents. Geographers usually recognize seven of them: in order of size they are Asia, Africa, North America, South America, Antarctica, Europe, and Australia.

On the Surface

The world physical map, right, shows natural features of the land such as river systems, mountain ranges, deserts, and plains. Certain landforms stand out. Long mountain belts run along the western coasts of North and South America and east-west across Europe and Asia. In the middle of most continents are large flat areas called plains or plateaus. Massive rivers, such as the Amazon, Congo, or Ganges, create green and fertile areas on the land.

A R

Queen Elizabeth Islands
North Magnetic Pole +
Melville Island
Ellesmere Island

Chukchi Sea
Beaufort Sea
Victoria Island
Baffin Island
Baffin Bay

SIBERIA
Brooks Range
ALASKA
Bering Sea
Yukon
Alaska Range (Denali)
+ Mt. McKinley
20,320 feet
6,194 meters
Mackenzie
Great Bear Lake
Great Slave Lake

Hudson Bay

Labrador Sea

Kodiak I.
Alexander Archipelago
Queen Charlotte Islands
Vancouver Island
Coast Mountains
Cascade Range
Canadian Shield
Nelson
Lake Winnipeg
Labrador

Aleutian Islands

NORTH PACIFIC OCEAN

NORTH
AMERICA
ROCKY MOUNTAINS
Great Plains
Missouri
Great Lakes
Appalachian Mountains
Island of Newfoundl
Nova Scotia

NORT
ATLANT
OCEA

Great Salt Lake
Colorado
Death Valley
-282 feet
-86 meters
Central Lowland
Mississippi
Rio Grande
Sierra Madre Oriental

Hawaiian Islands
Kauai
Hawaii

Baja California
Sierra Madre Occidental
Gulf of Mexico
West Indies
Cuba
Greater Antilles
Jamaica
Hispaniola
Bahama Islands
Lesser Antilles
Trinidad

CENTRAL AMERICA
Caribbean Sea

P O L Y N E S I A

Line Islands

Galápagos Islands

Llanos
Orinoco
Negro
Guiana Highlands
Amazon
Amazon
Madeira
Tocantins
São Francisco

Marquesas Islands

Basin
ANDES
SOUTH AMERICA
Brazilian Highlands

Samoa Is.
Cook Islands
Society Is.
Tahiti
Tuamotu Archipelago
Fiji Is.
Tonga Is.
Austral Islands

Lake Titicaca
Mata Grosso Plateau
Atacama Desert
Gran Chaco
Paraguay
Paraná

Easter Island

Cerro Aconcagua +
22,834 feet
6,960 meters
Pampas

SOUTH PACIFIC OCEAN

Isla Grande de Chiloé
Patagonia
Valdés Peninsula
-131 feet
-40 meters

Falkland Islands
Tierra del Fuego
Scoti
Strait of Magellan

South Shetland Islands

ANTA
PEN

Bellingshausen Sea
Ellsworth Land
Ron

Ross Sea
Marie Byrd Land
Vinson Massif
16,067 feet
4,897 meters
Ross Ice Shelf
TRANSANTARCTIC

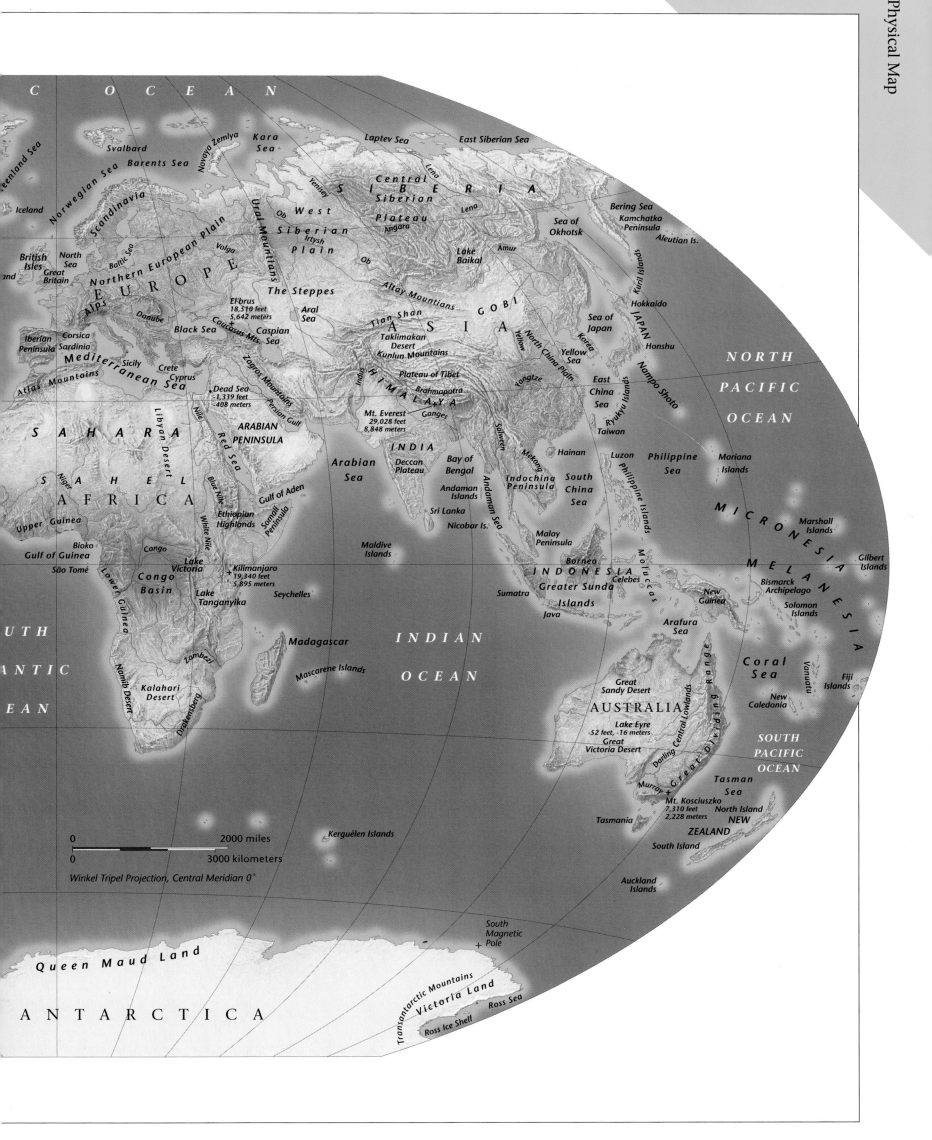

OCEAN

Greenland Sea

Svalbard

Iceland

Norwegian Sea Barents Sea

Novaya Zemlya

Kara Sea

Laptev Sea

East Siberian Sea

Bering Sea

Kamchatka Peninsula

Aleutian Is.

British Isles

North Sea

Great Britain

Scandinavia

Baltic Sea

Northern European Plain

EUROPE

Alps

Ural Mountains

Ob

West Siberian Plain

Irtysh

Yenisey

Central Siberian Plateau

Lena

Angara

Ob

Lena

Amur

Lake Baikal

Sea of Okhotsk

Kuril Islands

Hokkaido

Sea of Japan

JAPAN

Honshu

NORTH

PACIFIC

OCEAN

Volga

The Steppes

Aral Sea

Altay Mountains

A S I A

GOBI

Iberian Peninsula

Corsica

Sardinia

Danube

Black Sea

Caucasus Mts.

El'brus 18,510 feet 5,642 meters

Caspian Sea

Tian Shan

Taklimakan Desert

Kunlun Mountains

North China Plain

Yellow

Korea

Yellow Sea

Nampo Shoto

Sicily

Crete

Cyprus

Mediterranean Sea

Atlas Mountains

Zagros Mountains

Dead Sea -1,339 feet -408 meters

Plateau of Tibet

HIMALAYA

Brahmaputra

Yangtze

East China Sea

Ryukyu Islands

Taiwan

SAHARA

LIBYAN DESERT

Red Sea

Nile

Persian Gulf

ARABIAN PENINSULA

Mt. Everest 29,028 feet 8,848 meters

Ganges

Indus

INDIA

Arabian Sea

Deccan Plateau

Bay of Bengal

Andaman Islands

Andaman Sea

Indochina Peninsula

Mekong

Hainan

South China Sea

Luzon

Philippine Sea

Philippine Islands

Mariana Islands

MICRONESIA

S A H E L

Niger

AFRICA

Blue Nile

White Nile

Gulf of Aden

Ethiopian Highlands

Somali Peninsula

Sri Lanka

Nicobar Is.

Malay Peninsula

Marshall Islands

Upper Guinea

Bioko

Gulf of Guinea

São Tomé

Congo

Lower Guinea

Congo Basin

Lake Victoria

Kilimanjaro 19,340 feet 5,895 meters

Lake Tanganyika

Seychelles

Maldive Islands

Borneo

Celebes

INDONESIA

Greater Sunda Islands

Sumatra

Java

Moluccas

New Guinea

MELANESIA

Bismarck Archipelago

Solomon Islands

Gilbert Islands

Madagascar

Mascarene Islands

INDIAN

OCEAN

Arafura Sea

Coral Sea

Vanuatu

Fiji Islands

SOUTH ATLANTIC OCEAN

Namib Desert

Zambezi

Kalahari Desert

Drakensberg

Kerguélen Islands

Great Sandy Desert

AUSTRALIA

Lake Eyre -52 feet, -16 meters

Great Victoria Desert

Central Lowlands

Great Dividing Range

Darling

New Caledonia

SOUTH

PACIFIC

OCEAN

Tasman Sea

0 ——— 2000 miles

0 ——— 3000 kilometers

Winkel Tripel Projection, Central Meridian 0°

Murray

Tasmania

Mt. Kosciuszko 7,310 feet 2,228 meters

North Island

NEW ZEALAND

South Island

Auckland Islands

South Magnetic Pole

Queen Maud Land

ANTARCTICA

Transantarctic Mountains

Victoria Land

Ross Ice Shelf

Ross Sea

Climate
and Vegetation

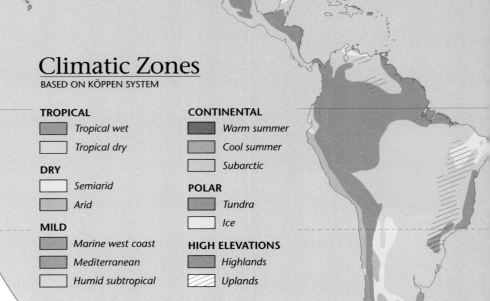

Climate means all the weather that occurs in one place over a long time. Many factors work together to give a place its characteristic climate. These include latitude, height above sea level, distance from the ocean, amount of vegetation, and location within a continent. In general, climate changes slowly over thousands of years. Some things can cause it to change more quickly, however. One agent of change is warming of the atmosphere caused by pollution. Most experts agree that people need to cut back on producing harmful gases such as carbon dioxide to help stop this global warming.

World Climate

The large map (right) shows the system for naming climates invented by Russian-born meteorologist Wladimir Köppen. It divides climates into six groups: tropical, dry, mild, continental, polar, and that of high elevations. The groups then split into types, such as tropical wet and tropical dry.

Climatic Zones
BASED ON KÖPPEN SYSTEM

TROPICAL
- Tropical wet
- Tropical dry

DRY
- Semiarid
- Arid

MILD
- Marine west coast
- Mediterranean
- Humid subtropical

CONTINENTAL
- Warm summer
- Cool summer
- Subarctic

POLAR
- Tundra
- Ice

HIGH ELEVATIONS
- Highlands
- Uplands

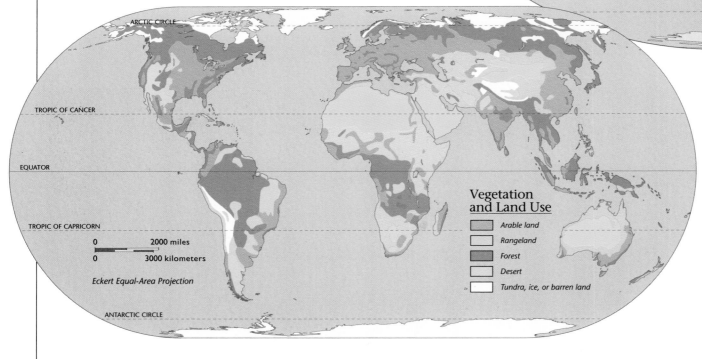

Vegetation and Land Use
- Arable land
- Rangeland
- Forest
- Desert
- Tundra, ice, or barren land

0   2000 miles
0   3000 kilometers

Eckert Equal-Area Projection

Vegetation and Land Use

Compare the two maps on these pages and you can see that vegetation—plant life in a place—is tied to climate. Vegetation and land use falls into five broad categories: arable (suitable for farming); rangeland (an open region where livestock can be kept); forest; desert; and tundra, icy, or barren.

El Niño

El Niño (meaning "The Child" because it typically begins at Christmas) is an occasional warming of the surface water of the Pacific Ocean that affe[c]world climate. During El Niñ[o] warm surface water cuts off nutrient-rich cool water belo[w] pulling fish away from their normal grounds. Warm water brings rainfall eastward, causing flooding in Peru and drought in Australia. Wind patterns shift all over the world. The image at right, made from satellite data, shows unusually warm sea-surface temperatures (red) near the west coast of South America during the severe El Niño of 1997–1998.

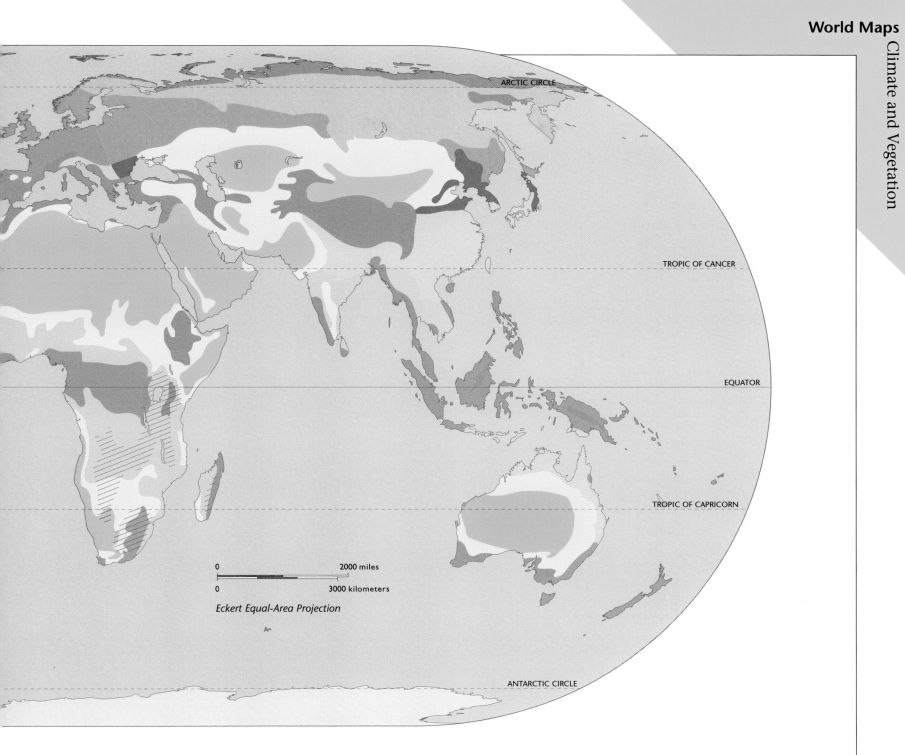

ARCTIC CIRCLE

TROPIC OF CANCER

EQUATOR

TROPIC OF CAPRICORN

0   2000 miles

0   3000 kilometers

Eckert Equal-Area Projection

ANTARCTIC CIRCLE

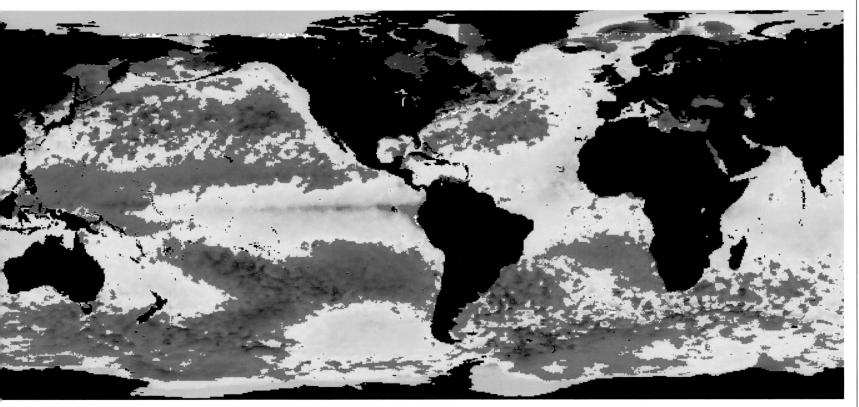

Environment
and Endangered Species

The environment is the sum of all the conditions surrounding a plant or animal. The map at right shows just a few ways in which human activities are changing—and threatening—the world's environments. In tropical and subtropical regions, ranchers, farmers, loggers, and miners have cleared nearly half of the world's original rain forests. About a fifth of the world's population lives in dry lands near deserts. Farming and other activities in these lands may hurt them so much that they will turn into true deserts.

Throughout the world, over 600 species of animals and plants that once were thriving are now threatened with extinction. The map shows just a few of the most threatened animals around the world.

▼ *Pollution from a nearby paper mill threatens wetland wildlife in the state of Georgia. Soil, air, and water pollution are global problems.*

Environment

- ▉ Present rain forest
- ☐ Former rain forest
- ▨ Hyperarid lands
- ☐ Dry lands susceptible to desertification
- • Most polluted cities

▼ *Hunted for its highly decorative shell, the hawksbill turtle is endangered throughout its range in tropical and subtropical waters. Although the turtle is protected by international law, illegal hunting continues to threaten its existence.*

◄ *Africa's black rhinoceros was once numerous in the continent's savannas. Now it is endangered because of demand for its horn, ground up for use in Asian medicines.*

▶ *Loss of habitat due to human settlement has brought the giant panda's population down to a mere 1,000 to 2,000, all in western China.*

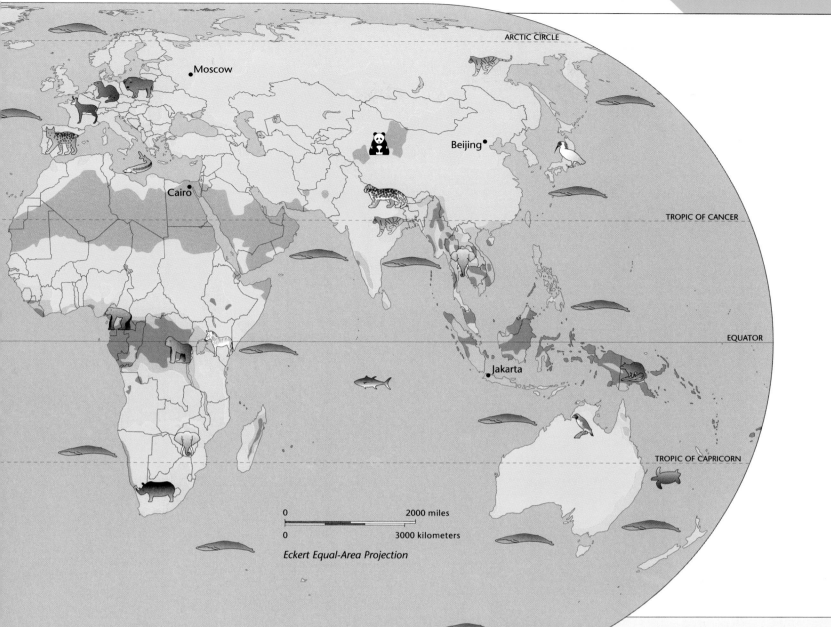

ARCTIC CIRCLE

Moscow

Beijing

Cairo

TROPIC OF CANCER

Jakarta

EQUATOR

TROPIC OF CAPRICORN

```
0                    2000 miles

0                    3000 kilometers
```

Eckert Equal-Area Projection

ANTARCTIC CIRCLE

Car exhaust adds to the smog
Bangkok, Thailand. Burning
fossil fuels is the main source
air pollution.

A logger cuts through an African
mahogany tree in a Congo rain
forest. This logging is illegal, but
the law is hard to enforce.

▲ When the 20th
century began, about
100,000 tigers lived in
Asia. Now humans
have taken over so
much of their land that
the big cats are down to
about 5,000 animals
in the wild.

Key to Endangered Species

- Crested ibis
- Goodfellow's tree kangaroo
- Grevy's zebra
- European bison
- Mountain tapir
- Snow leopard
- Chimpanzee
- Mountain gorilla
- African elephant
- Asian elephant
- Black-footed ferret
- Blue whale
- Southern bluefin tuna

- Gouldian finch
- Giant armadillo
- Spanish lynx
- Chartreuse chamois
- European mink
- American crocodile
- Whooping crane
- California condor
- Beluga sturgeon
- Hawksbill turtle
- Tiger
- Giant panda
- Black rhino

The Political World

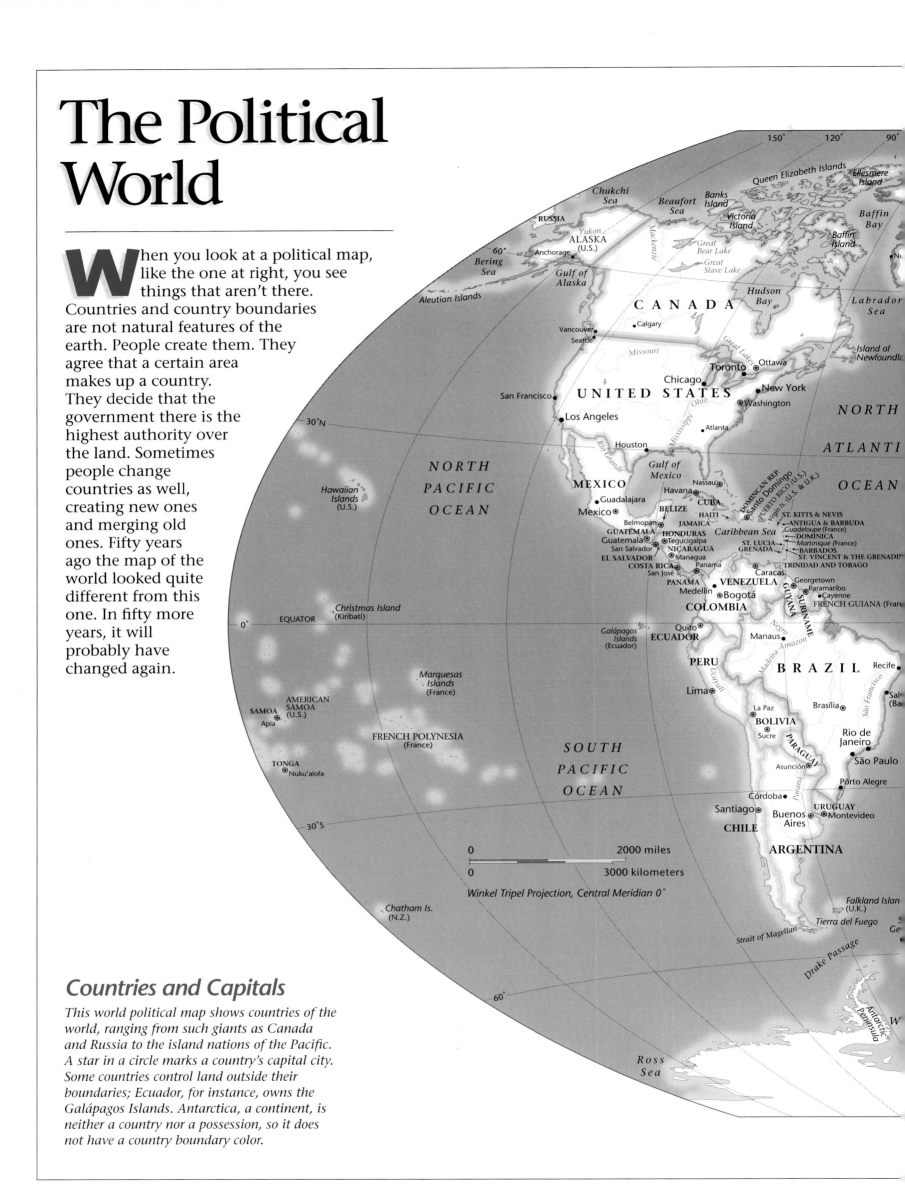

When you look at a political map, like the one at right, you see things that aren't there. Countries and country boundaries are not natural features of the earth. People create them. They agree that a certain area makes up a country. They decide that the government there is the highest authority over the land. Sometimes people change countries as well, creating new ones and merging old ones. Fifty years ago the map of the world looked quite different from this one. In fifty more years, it will probably have changed again.

Countries and Capitals

This world political map shows countries of the world, ranging from such giants as Canada and Russia to the island nations of the Pacific. A star in a circle marks a country's capital city. Some countries control land outside their boundaries; Ecuador, for instance, owns the Galápagos Islands. Antarctica, a continent, is neither a country nor a possession, so it does not have a country boundary color.

ARCTIC OCEAN

Greenland Sea

Norwegian Sea

Barents Sea

Svalbard (Norway)

Franz Josef Land

Novaya Zemlya

Kara Sea

Severnaya Zemlya

New Siberian Islands

Laptev Sea

East Siberian Sea

Bering Sea

ICELAND
Reykjavik

UNITED KINGDOM
IRELAND
Dublin
London

NORTH Sea
DENMARK
Copenhagen

NORWAY
SWEDEN
Oslo
Stockholm
Helsinki
FINLAND
St. Petersburg

Moscow
Minsk
BELARUS

Yekaterinburg
Omsk
Novosibirsk

Lake Baikal

Yakutsk

Sea of Okhotsk

Kamchatka Peninsula

Sakhalin

R U S S I A

Volga
Ural
Ob
Irtysh
Yenisey
Lena
Amur

PORTUGAL
Lisbon
SPAIN
Madrid

FRANCE
Paris

GERMANY
Berlin
Warsaw
POLAND

NETH.
BELG.
LUX.
SWITZ.
AUSTRIA
CZECH. REP.
SLOVAKIA
HUNG.
ROMANIA
MOLD.
UKRAINE
Kiev

SLOV.
CRO.
YUG.
BULGARIA
ITALY
Rome
ALBANIA
MACED.
GREECE
Athens

Black Sea
GEORGIA
ARM.
AZERB.

Astana
KAZAKHSTAN
Aral Sea
Caspian Sea
UZBEKISTAN
Tashkent
Almaty
Bishkek
KYRGYZSTAN
TURKMENISTAN
Ashgabat
TAJIKISTAN
Dushanbe

MONGOLIA
Ulaanbaatar

Harbin
Shenyang
Beijing
Tianjin
NORTH KOREA
Pyongyang
SOUTH KOREA
Seoul

Hokkaido
Sapporo
Honshu
JAPAN
Tokyo
Osaka
Kyushu

NORTH PACIFIC OCEAN

Tunis
TUNISIA
Algiers
Rabat
Casablanca
MOROCCO

MAURITANIA
Nouakchott
GAMBIA
Bamako
MALI

SENEGAL
GUINEA
GUINEA-BISSAU
SIERRA LEONE
LIBERIA
CÔTE D'IVOIRE
Abidjan
GHANA
Accra
Lomé
TOGO
BENIN
Porto-Novo
Niamey
BURKINA FASO
Ouagadougou

Niger

Mediterranean Sea
CYPRUS
LEBANON
ISRAEL
SYRIA
TURKEY
Istanbul
Ankara

IRAQ
Baghdad
IRAN
Tehran
Kabul
AFGHANISTAN

Islamabad
PAKISTAN
Lahore
Delhi
New Delhi

NEPAL
Kathmandu
Thimphu
BHUTAN
Brahmaputra

Chengdu
C H I N A
Yellow
Wuhan
Yangtze
Shanghai

Guangzhou
Hong Kong
Taipei
TAIWAN
Hainan
South China Sea

The People's Republic of China claims Taiwan as its 23rd province.

Philippine Sea

NORTHERN MARIANA ISLANDS (U.S.)

ALGERIA
LIBYA
EGYPT
Cairo
Nile

JORDAN
KUWAIT
QATAR
BAHRAIN
Riyadh
U.A.E.
SAUDI ARABIA
Muscat
OMAN

Red Sea

Karachi
INDIA
Mumbai
Hyderabad
Bangalore
Chennai
Calcutta
Dhaka
BANGLADESH
MYANMAR (BURMA)
Yangon

LAOS
Hanoi
Vientiane
THAILAND
Bangkok
VIETNAM
CAMBODIA
Phnom Penh
Ho Chi Minh City

Luzon
Manila
PHILIPPINES
Mindanao

PALAU

FEDERATED STATES OF MICRONESIA

CHAD
N'Djamena
NIGER
NIGERIA
Abuja
Lagos
CAMEROON
Yaoundé

Khartoum
SUDAN
ERITREA
Asmara
DJIBOUTI
ETHIOPIA
Addis Ababa
YEMEN
Sanaa
Socotra (Yemen)

Arabian Sea
SRI LANKA
Colombo
MALDIVES

Bay of Bengal

Kuala Lumpur
MALAYSIA
BRUNEI
Bandar Seri Begawan
SINGAPORE
Borneo
Sumatra

MARSHALL ISLANDS

KIRIBATI

NAURU

CENTRAL AFRICAN REPUBLIC
Bangui
EQ. GUINEA
SAO TOME AND PRINCIPE
GABON
Libreville
CONGO
DEMOCRATIC REPUBLIC OF THE CONGO
Brazzaville
Kinshasa
CABINDA (Angola)
Luanda
ANGOLA

UGANDA
Kampala
RWANDA
Kigali
BURUNDI
Bujumbura
KENYA
Nairobi
Lake Victoria
TANZANIA
Dar es Salaam

SOMALIA
Mogadishu

SEYCHELLES

COMOROS
Moroni

INDIAN OCEAN

Jakarta
Java
Surabaya
I N D O N E S I A
Celebes

New Guinea
PAPUA NEW GUINEA
Port Moresby

SOLOMON ISLANDS
Honiara

TUVALU

ZAMBIA
Lusaka
MALAWI
Lilongwe
Harare
ZIMBABWE
MOZAMBIQUE
NAMIBIA
Windhoek
BOTSWANA
Gaborone
Pretoria
Johannesburg
Maputo
SWAZILAND
LESOTHO
SOUTH AFRICA
Cape Town
Orange
Zambezi

MADAGASCAR
Antananarivo
MAURITIUS
Port Louis
Réunion (France)

Arafura Sea
Darwin

A U S T R A L I A
Great Australian Bight
Perth
Darling
Murray
Melbourne
Sydney
Canberra

Coral Sea

VANUATU
Port-Vila

New Caledonia (France)

FIJI
Suva

SOUTH PACIFIC OCEAN

Tasman Sea
North Island
Auckland
NEW ZEALAND
Wellington
South Island
Tasmania

SOUTH ATLANTIC OCEAN

Kerguélen Islands (France)

A N T A R C T I C A

Ross Sea

Population Density

Population means all the people in a given area. A map of population density, such as the one at right, shows where people live and how closely crowded they are. Compare it to the physical world map or the climate map and you can see that densely populated places share certain features. They usually have plenty of rain, moderate temperatures, relatively level land, and fertile soil. People tend to live in river valleys and along coasts. In some parts of the world, the crush of people living in limited space is straining the environment.

NORTH AMERICA

Least populous countr
Vatican City (1,00

Most populous city in
North America:
Mexico, Mexico (16.9 million)

SOUTH
AMERICA

Population Density

INHABITANTS PER SQUARE MILE	INHABITANTS PER SQUARE KILOMETER
Under 2	Under 1
2–25	1–10
25–60	10–25
60–125	25–50
125–250	50–100
Over 250	Over 100

Most popu
in South A
São Paulo
(16.8 m

Where People Live

About six billion people now live on earth, inhabiting roughly 30 percent of the planet's land (right). Europe and Asia are the most densely populated; Asia alone contains more than 60 percent of the world's people. Migration from rural areas to cities is building huge urban areas across the world. Sixteen cities now have more than ten million inhabitants.

City Lights

Lights across the earth form the ghostly outline of the continents in this image put together from nighttime satellite photographs. Densely populated areas are bright with city lights; sparsely populated places are dark. In the Persian Gulf (center right), flares from burn-offs of oil and natural gas light the sky. In the Sea of Japan (far right), a well-lit fleet of squid-fishing ships forms a triangular shape. The cloudy light at the top of the image is natural: the northern lights, or aurora borealis.

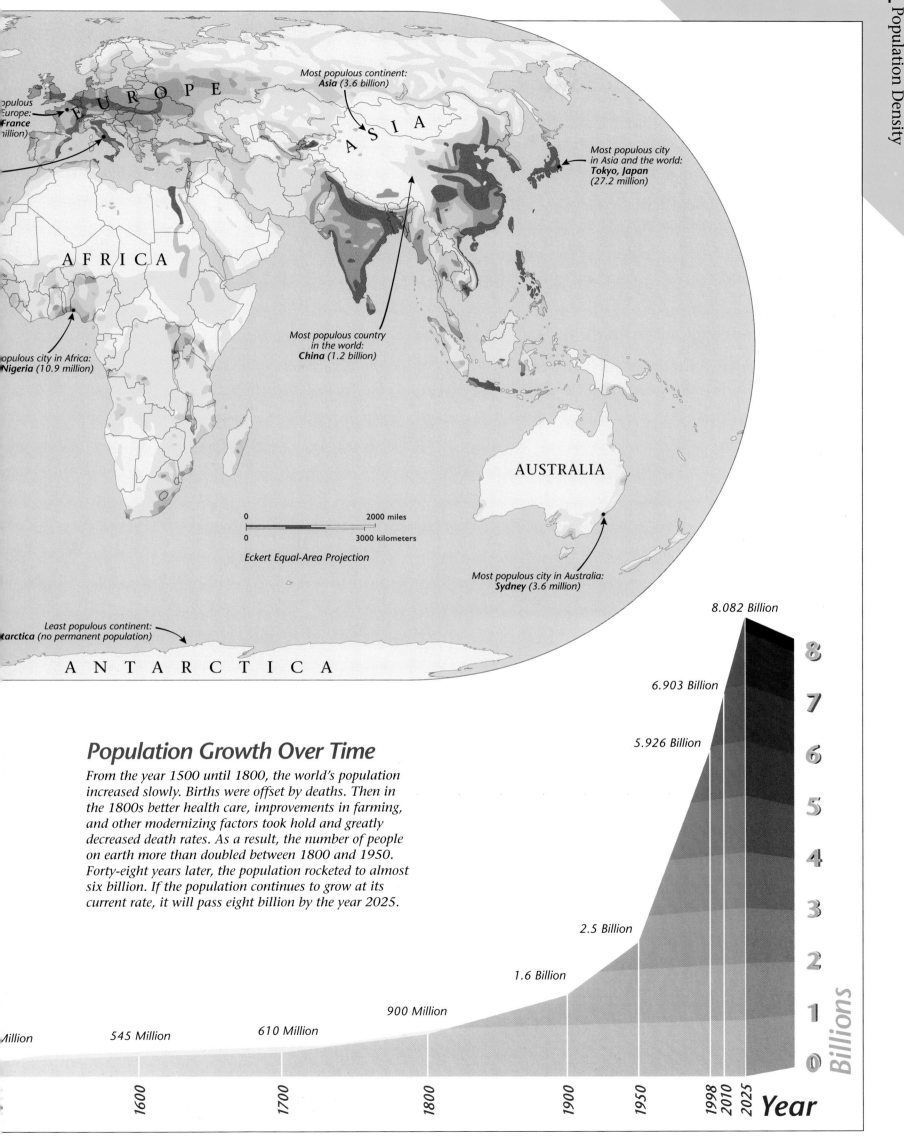

Most populous continent:
Asia (3.6 billion)

...populous
...Europe:
France
...illion)

Most populous city
in Asia and the world:
Tokyo, Japan
(27.2 million)

AFRICA

Most populous country
in the world:
China (1.2 billion)

...opulous city in Africa:
Nigeria (10.9 million)

AUSTRALIA

0   2000 miles

0   3000 kilometers

Eckert Equal-Area Projection

Most populous city in Australia:
Sydney (3.6 million)

Least populous continent:
...tarctica (no permanent population)

ANTARCTICA

Population Growth Over Time

From the year 1500 until 1800, the world's population increased slowly. Births were offset by deaths. Then in the 1800s better health care, improvements in farming, and other modernizing factors took hold and greatly decreased death rates. As a result, the number of people on earth more than doubled between 1800 and 1950. Forty-eight years later, the population rocketed to almost six billion. If the population continues to grow at its current rate, it will pass eight billion by the year 2025.

8.082 Billion

6.903 Billion

5.926 Billion

2.5 Billion

1.6 Billion

900 Million

610 Million

545 Million

...Million

8
7
6
5
4
3
2
1
0

Billions

1600   1700   1800   1900   1950   1998 2010 2025   **Year**

Transportation
and Communication

There are not many truly remote areas left in the world. Roads and rail lines reach into all but the most inaccessible regions. Ships carry vast loads across the oceans, particularly to and from the countries of the Pacific Rim. Airplanes fly over mountains and seas. The map at right shows how the largest land and sea routes connect the world.

Satellite communications shrink the world even more. The chart at far right shows the countries and domains that have the greatest presence on the Internet.

Supplying the World

Trucks, trains, and container ships (right) carry most of the world's freight. Hundreds of millions of tons of raw materials and manufactured goods travel the earth each year.

Transportation

— Railroads
— Roads
— Shipping routes
■ Major port

Air Routes

— Air route

```
0           2000 miles
0        3000 kilometers
Winkel Tripel Projection
```

Air Routes Around the World: A Complex Network

From its beginnings as a sport for dashing aviators early in the 20th century, air travel has become a necessity for most of the world. The United States alone has more than 14,000 airports serving millions of passengers each year. Military operations rely on huge planes to move troops and cargo. Commercial aviation, including overnight package services, is booming. The map above shows the world's major air routes and airfields.

▲ *Air traffic controllers study radar screens at Chicago's O'Hare Airport, one of the world's busiest airfields.*

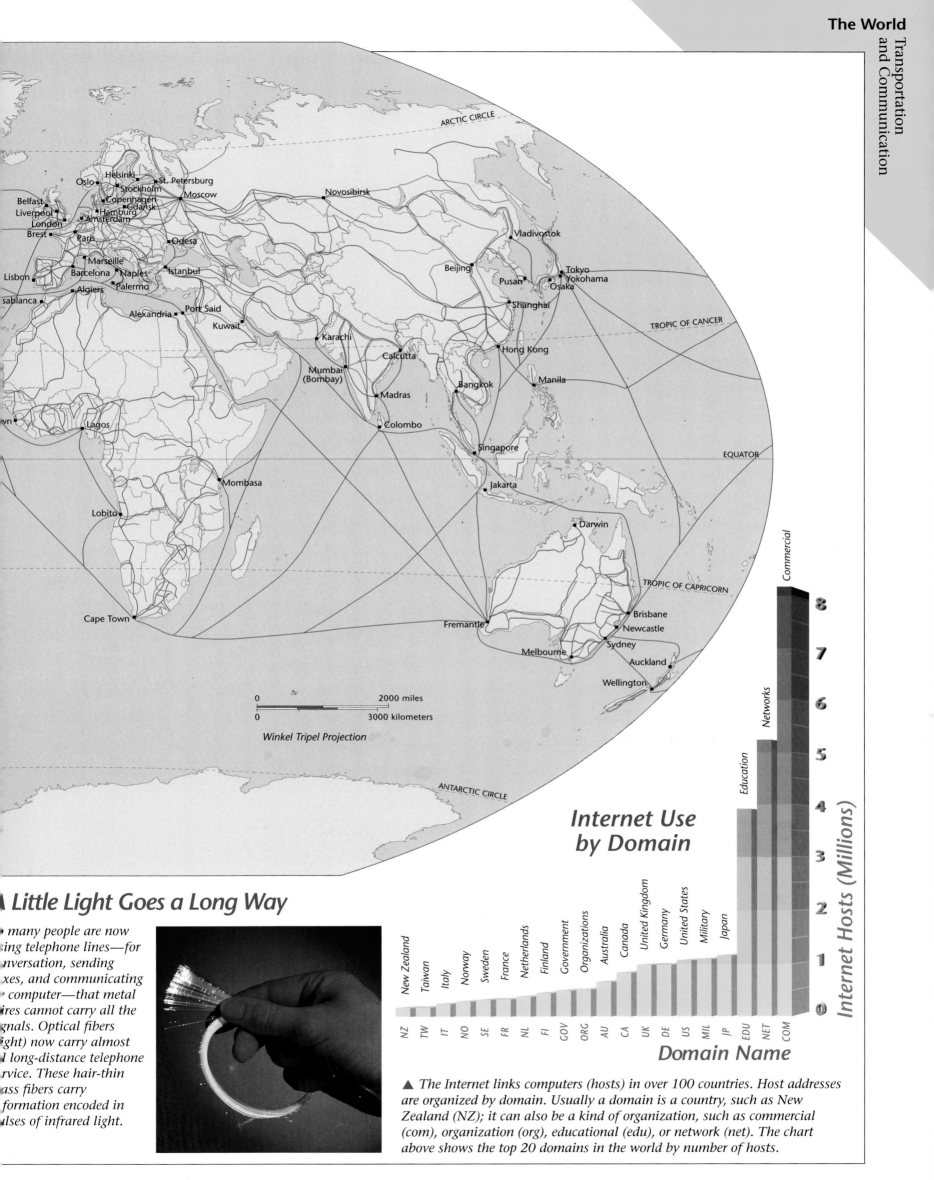

ARCTIC CIRCLE

Oslo   Helsinki   St. Petersburg
Belfast   Stockholm   Moscow   Novosibirsk
Liverpool   Copenhagen   Gdansk
London   Hamburg
Brest   Amsterdam
Paris   Odesa   Vladivostok
Marseille   Istanbul   Beijing   Tokyo
Lisbon   Barcelona   Naples   Pusan   Yokohama
sablanca   Algiers   Palermo   Shanghai   Osaka
Alexandria   Port Said   TROPIC OF CANCER
Kuwait   Karachi
Calcutta   Hong Kong
Mumbai   Bangkok   Manila
(Bombay)   Madras
Lagos   Colombo
Singapore   EQUATOR
Mombasa   Jakarta
Lobito   Darwin
TROPIC OF CAPRICORN
Cape Town   Brisbane
Fremantle   Newcastle
Sydney
Melbourne   Auckland
Wellington

0   2000 miles
0   3000 kilometers

Winkel Tripel Projection

ANTARCTIC CIRCLE

Internet Use by Domain

▲ Little Light Goes a Long Way

many people are now
ing telephone lines—for
nversation, sending
xes, and communicating
computer—that metal
ires cannot carry all the
gnals. Optical fibers
ght) now carry almost
l long-distance telephone
rvice. These hair-thin
ass fibers carry
formation encoded in
lses of infrared light.

Internet Hosts (Millions)

8 7 6 5 4 3 2 1 0

Commercial
Networks
Education
Japan
Military
United States
Germany
United Kingdom
Canada
Australia
Organizations
Government
Finland
Netherlands
France
Sweden
Norway
Italy
Taiwan
New Zealand

COM NET EDU JP MIL US DE UK CA AU ORG GOV FI NL FR SE NO IT TW NZ

Domain Name

▲ The Internet links computers (hosts) in over 100 countries. Host addresses
are organized by domain. Usually a domain is a country, such as New
Zealand (NZ); it can also be a kind of organization, such as commercial
(com), organization (org), educational (edu), or network (net). The chart
above shows the top 20 domains in the world by number of hosts.

High mountains and winding rivers define the western regions of North America, a continent that has been the goal of immigrants since at least the last ice age, 25,000 years ago. Spanish settlers gave names to features in much of the southwestern United States and Mexico, including the Colorado River, shown flowing into the picture from the lower left. You can see the Gulf of California where the river ends at right. The Colorado provides water to farms and towns from Wyoming to Baja California, Mexico. Little of its torrent remains by the time it trickles into the gulf. Most of the land here is pale desert. Rivers and streams support trees and crops—the darker greenish brown in the photo.

Rafters enjoy a wild ride on the roaring Colorado River (below). The river cuts through six states, carving out the Grand Canyon on the way.

CONNECTION: *You can find the lower Colorado on the maps on pages 52–53 and 60–61.*

erica

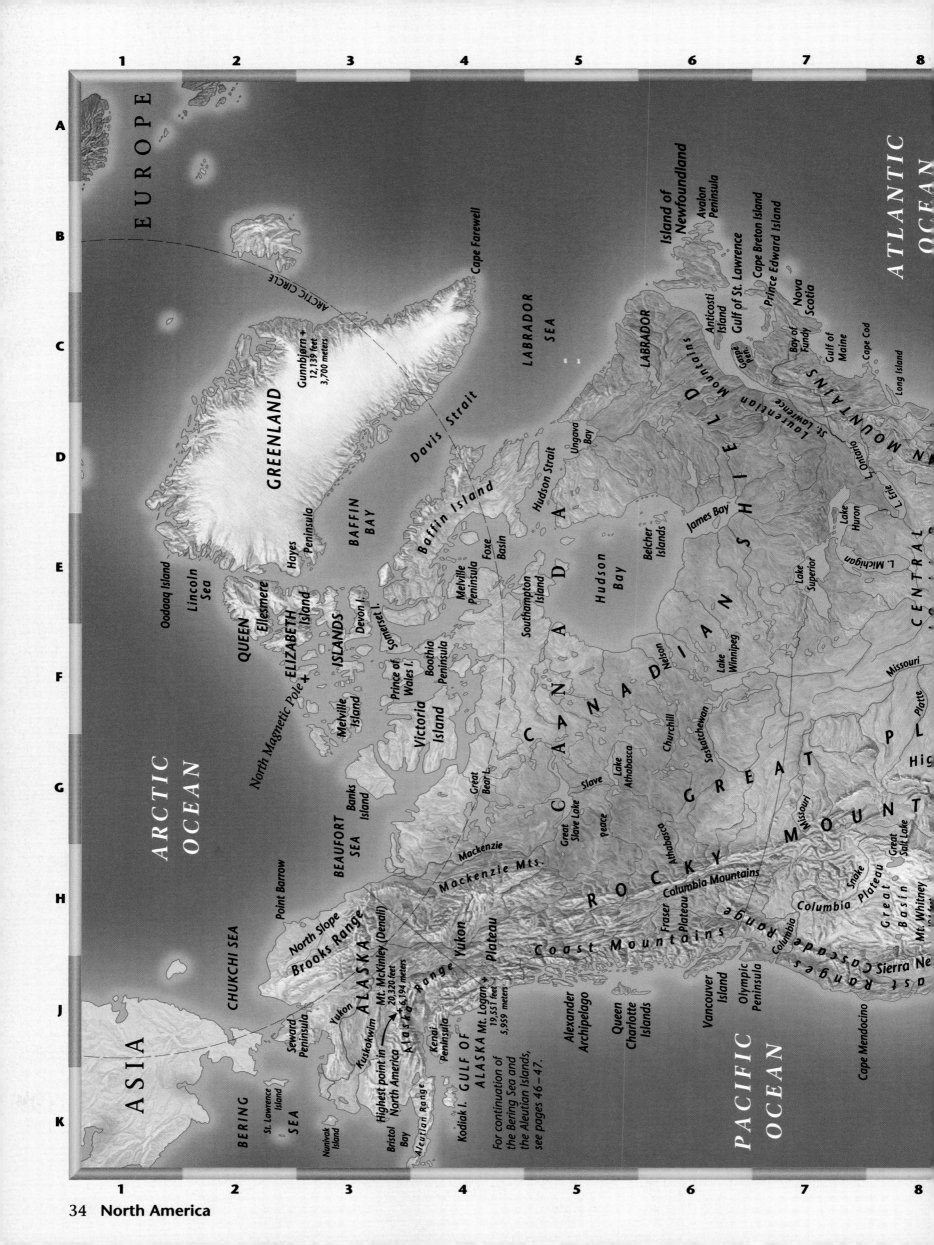

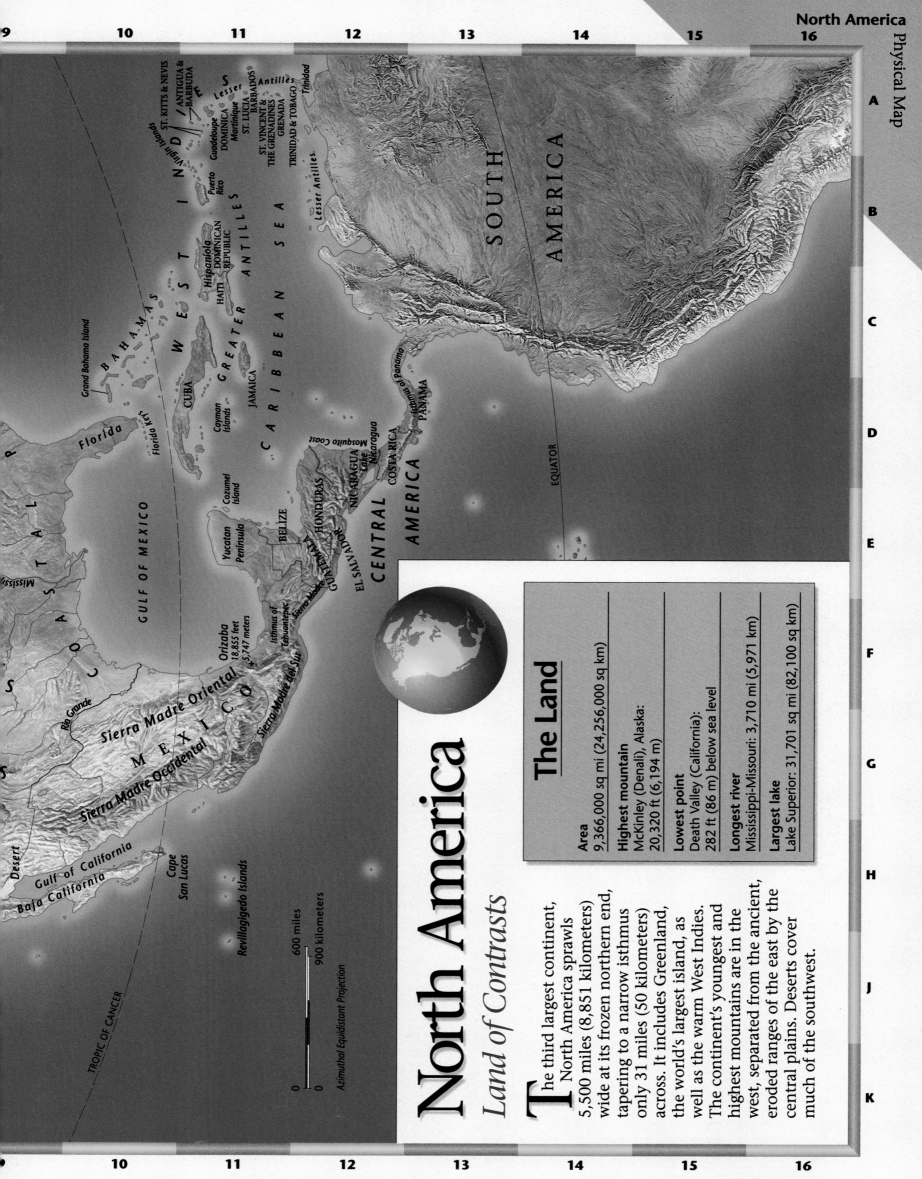

North America
Land of Contrasts

The third largest continent, North America sprawls 5,500 miles (8,851 kilometers) wide at its frozen northern end, tapering to a narrow isthmus only 31 miles (50 kilometers) across. It includes Greenland, the world's largest island, as well as the warm West Indies. The continent's youngest and highest mountains are in the west, separated from the ancient, eroded ranges of the east by the central plains. Deserts cover much of the southwest.

The Land

Area
9,366,000 sq mi (24,256,000 sq km)

Highest mountain
McKinley (Denali), Alaska:
20,320 ft (6,194 m)

Lowest point
Death Valley (California):
282 ft (86 m) below sea level

Longest river
Mississippi-Missouri: 3,710 mi (5,971 km)

Largest lake
Lake Superior: 31,701 sq mi (82,100 sq km)

600 miles
900 kilometers

Azimuthal Equidistant Projection

North America

Continental Melting Pot

North America is a land of immigrants. The first people may have come to the continent 25,000 years ago from Asia. Their path was a wide land bridge between Siberia and the Alaskan Peninsula, long since covered by the rising sea. Vikings visited North America next, settling briefly in Newfoundland around 1,000 A.D. Then, in 1493 Italian explorer Christopher Columbus returned to Europe with word of lands he'd seen. In Central America and the Caribbean, European countries such as Spain and England established plantation colonies. Europeans began to settle across North America, followed by people from South America and Asia. The flow of immigrants has never really stopped.

The immigrant's story is not always a happy one. From the 1500s to the 1800s Africans were brought to North America against their will as enslaved people. Native Americans, the first people here, were displaced by settlers moving onto their lands. Nevertheless, immigrants are still drawn to the United States and Canada because the countries offer personal freedom, stable governments, and opportunities for earning a good living.

▶ **AN ANCIENT STONE** *temple of the El Tajín civilization rises from the Mexican lowlands. Square openings represent the 365 days of the year.*

▲ **MOUNT MCKINLEY'S MISTY BEAUTY** *thrills a hiker. Alaska's McKinley is the highest peak in North America. It is also known as Denali, an Inuit word meaning "High One."*

◄ **THE BRIGHT** *lights of a big city illuminate Times Square in New York's famous theater district. With more than 16 million people in its metropolitan area, the city is the largest in the U.S.*

▶ **NATURALISTS** *credit the beaver with helping to shape much of North America. Felling trees and damming streams, beavers create ponds, which become swamps, then meadows.*

▶ **STEPPING LIGHTLY,** *a young girl dances along one of Antigua's many beaches. The islands of Antigua and Barbuda make up one Caribbean country.*

▼ **POLLUTION** *and overcrowding plague Los Angeles, the largest city on the Pacific coast. The city's strong Hispanic heritage is reinforced by many Mexican immigrants.*

▼ **GOLDEN TOADS,** *gleaming symbols of Costa Rica's rain forest, may be in trouble. Once numerous, the toads have mysteriously vanished from their usual habitat.*

▶ **ARIZONA'S PRIDE,** *the Grand Canyon is the world's largest gorge at 1 mile (1.6 kilometers) from North Rim to river. Its rock walls, carved by the Colorado River, reveal the region's geologic history.*

▶ **AGAINST THE BACKDROP** *of the Twin Butte mountains, bales of hay rest on the fertile soil of Alberta, one of Canada's Prairie Provinces.*

▼ THE BRIGHT BEAUTY
*of autumn leaves brings tourists
to Vermont every year. The
forested slopes of the northern
Appalachian Mountains cover
much of New England.*

▼ IN THE NARROWEST PLACE
*on the continent, a canal cuts
through the Isthmus of Panama.
The canal is a shortcut between
the Atlantic and Pacific Oceans.*

▲ THE CHÂTEAU FRONTENAC *hotel
presides over Québec, Canada's oldest city.
Two official languages—French and
English—reflect Canada's colonial heritage.*

▼ A PUEBLO INDIAN ARTIST *in New
Mexico's Nambe Pueblo shapes a stone.
Native Americans throughout the continent
struggle to retain their identity and culture.*

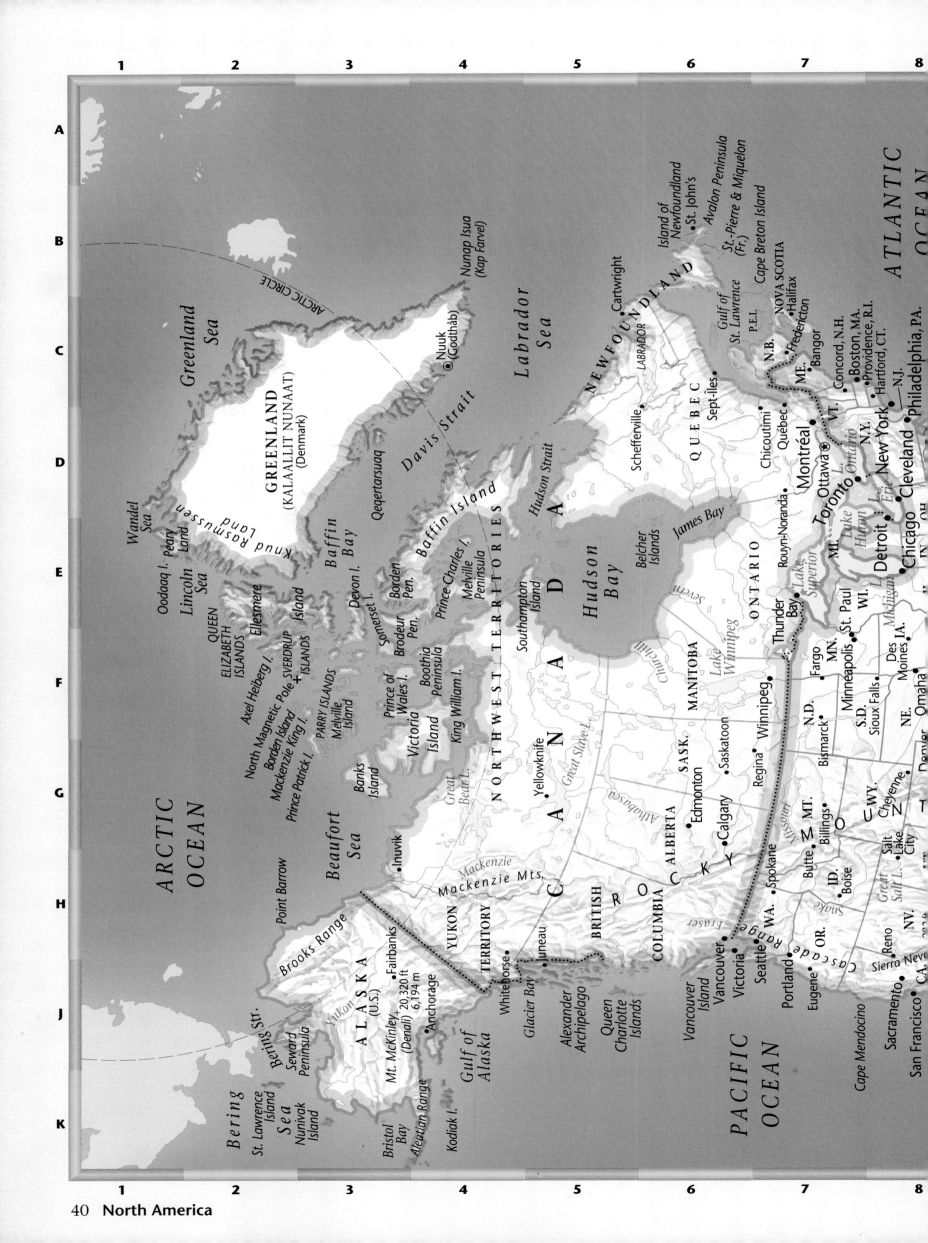

A

B

C

D

E

F

G

H

J

K

BARBADOS

ANTIGUA AND BARBUDA

ST. KITTS & NEVIS

ST. LUCIA

DOMINICA

PUERTO RICO (U.S.)

San Juan

ST. VINCENT AND THE GRENADINES

GRENADA

Port of Spain

TRINIDAD AND TOBAGO

DOMINICAN REPUBLIC

Santo Domingo ⊛

Port-au-Prince ⊛

HAITI

BAHAMAS

Nassau ⊛

⊛ Kingston

JAMAICA

CUBA

CARIBBEAN SEA

Charleston

Jacksonville

GA.

Tampa • FL.

Straits of Florida

Miami

⊛ Havana

(U.K.) Cayman Is.

PANAMA CANAL

⊛ Panama

PANAMA

Gulf of Panama

Gulf of Coiba

I. de Coiba

Isla del Coco (Costa Rica)

EQUATOR

Birmingham

AL.

Jackson

MS.

New Orleans

LA.

Mississippi

Houston

San Antonio

Austin

T.X.

Dallas

Fort Worth

El Paso

Ciudad Juárez

Chihuahua

Sierra Madre Occidental

Monterrey

San Luis Potosí

Sierra Madre Oriental

Guadalajara

México ⊛

M E X I C O

Veracruz

Acapulco

Gulf of Tehuantepec

Gulf of Mexico

Yucatán Pen.

BELIZE

Belmopan ⊛

HONDURAS

Tegucigalpa ⊛

GUATEMALA

San Salvador ⊛

EL SALVADOR

NICARAGUA

Managua ⊛

COSTA RICA

San José ⊛

Rio Grande

Gulf of California

Baja California

Cabo San Lucas

Punta Eugenia

I. Guadalupe (Mexico)

Islas Revillagigedo (Mexico)

TROPIC OF CANCER

600 miles

900 kilometers

Azimuthal Equidistant Projection

North America
A Mix of Rich and Poor

North America includes 23 countries, ranging from little St. Kitts and Nevis, with 40,000 people, to the United States, with 270,200,000. Most of the wealth is concentrated in Canada, Mexico, and the United States. These industrialized economies are linked by the North American Free Trade Agreement (NAFTA). The countries of Central America and the Caribbean are primarily agricultural, although tourism is a major source of income.

The People

Population
470,000,000

Largest country
Canada: 3,849,670 sq mi (9,970,610 sq km)

Largest metropolitan area
México: Pop. 16,908,000

Most densely populated country
Barbados: 1,807 people per sq mi.

Economy
Farming: cattle, grains, cotton, sugar
Industry: machinery, metals, mining

Life expectancy 72 years

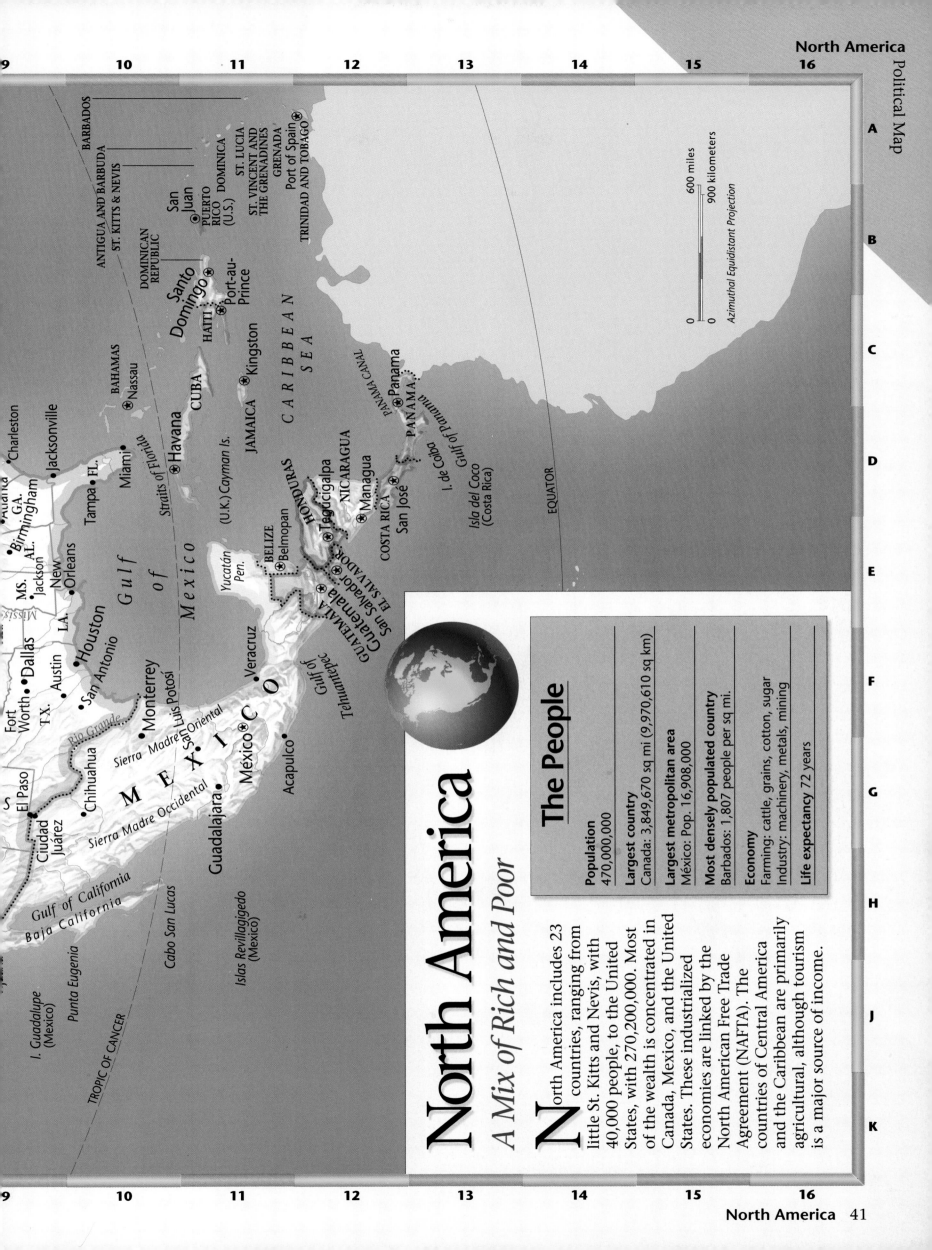

Canada

Largest and least densely populated country in North America, Canada has fewer people than California. Most live within a hundred miles of the United States. Canada is one of the world's leading exporters of minerals, wheat, and timber products.

Canada
Area: 3,849,670 sq mi
(9,970,610 sq km)
Population: 30,600,000
Capital: Ottawa
Languages: English, French

Alberta
Area: 255,290 sq mi
(661,190 sq km)
Population: 2,750,000
Capital: Edmonton

British Columbia
Area: 365,950 sq mi
(947,800 sq km)
Population: 3,712,000
Capital: Victoria

Manitoba
Area: 250,950 sq mi
(649,950 sq km)
Population: 1,127,000
Capital: Winnipeg

New Brunswick
Area: 28,350 sq mi
(73,440 sq km)
Population: 757,000
Capital: Fredericton

Newfoundland
Area: 156,650 sq mi
(405,720 sq km)
Population: 582,000
Capital: St. John's

Northwest Territories
Area: 1,322,910 sq mi
(3,426,320 sq km)
Population: 65,000
Capital: Yellowknife

Nova Scotia
Area: 21,420 sq mi
(55,490 sq km)
Population: 932,000
Capital: Halifax

Ontario
Area: 412,580 sq mi
(1,068,580 sq km)
Population: 11,120,000
Capital: Toronto

Prince Edward Island
Area: 2,180 sq mi
(5,660 sq km)
Population: 133,000
Capital: Charlottetown

Quebec
Area: 594,860 sq mi
(1,540,680 sq km)
Population: 7,346,000
Capital: Québec

Saskatchewan
Area: 251,870 sq mi
(652,330 sq km)
Population: 1,003,000
Capital: Regina

Yukon Territory
Area: 186,660 sq mi
(483,450 sq km)
Population: 34,000
Capital: Whitehorse

St.-Pierre and Miquelon
(France)

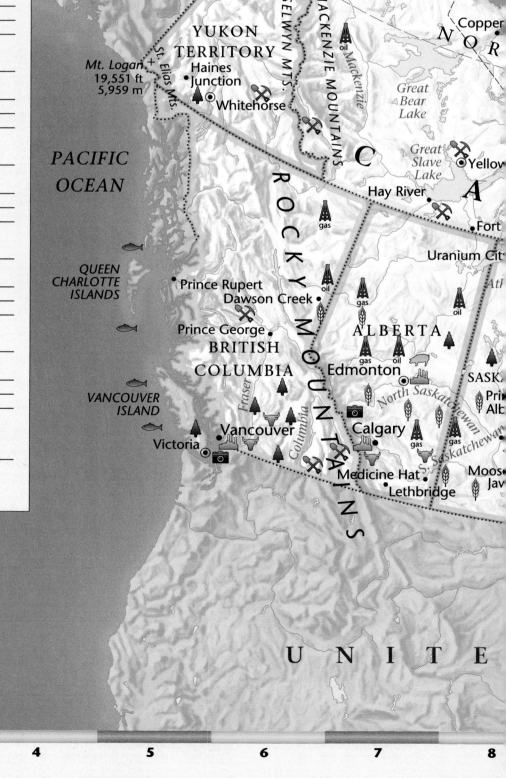

RUSSIA

Bering Str.

ARCTIC

NUNAVUT
On April 1, 1999, Ca
will establish the new
of Nunavut–meaning "e

*BEAUFORT
SEA*

ARCTIC CIRCLE

ALASKA
(U.S.)

Yukon

gas oil
• Tuktoyaktuk
• Inuvik

Amundsen Gulf

Ba
Isla

Copper

N O R

SELWYN MTS

MACKENZIE MOUNTAINS

Mackenzie

*Great
Bear
Lake*

C

*PACIFIC
OCEAN*

Mt. Logan +
19,551 ft
5,959 m

St. Elias Mts.

YUKON
TERRITORY

Haines
• Junction
⊙ Whitehorse

oil

R O C K Y

*Great
Slave
Lake*
• Yello

A

Hay River

Uranium City

gas

Fort

QUEEN
CHARLOTTE
ISLANDS

• Prince Rupert
Dawson Creek •
oil
gas

Ath

oil

Prince George •

M O U N T A I N S

ALBERTA

VANCOUVER
ISLAND

BRITISH
COLUMBIA

Fraser

gas oil

Edmonton ⊙

SASK

Pri
Alb

• Vancouver

Columbia

Calgary
gas gas

North Saskatchewan

Victoria
⊙

Medicine Hat •

Saskatchewan

• Lethbridge

Moose
Jaw

U N I T E

Azimuthal Equidistant Projection

0 ___ 500 miles
0 ___ 500 kilometers

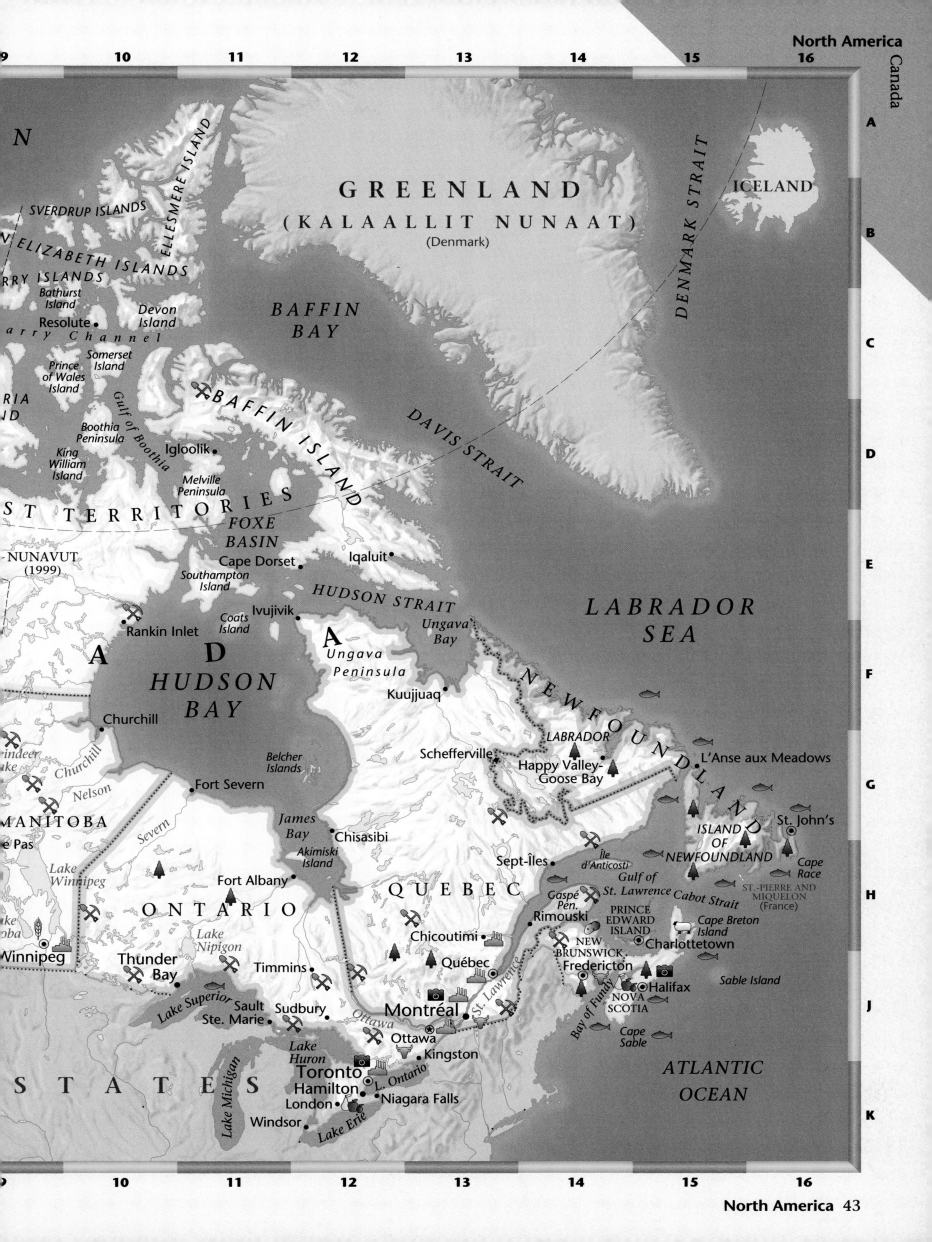

9   **10**   **11**   **12**   **13**   **14**   **15**   **16**

A

B

C

D

E

F

G

H

J

K

SVERDRUP ISLANDS

N

ELIZABETH ISLANDS

RY ISLANDS

Bathurst Island

Resolute

Devon Island

ELLESMERE ISLAND

GREENLAND
(KALAALLIT NUNAAT)
(Denmark)

ICELAND

arry Channel

BAFFIN BAY

Prince of Wales Island

Somerset Island

RIA
D

Gulf of Boothia

Boothia Peninsula

King William Island

Igloolik

BAFFIN ISLAND

Melville Peninsula

ST TERRITORIES

DAVIS STRAIT

DENMARK STRAIT

FOXE BASIN

NUNAVUT
(1999)

Cape Dorset

Southampton Island

Iqaluit

HUDSON STRAIT

LABRADOR SEA

Rankin Inlet

Coats Island

Ivujivik

A

Ungava Bay

Ungava Peninsula

A

HUDSON BAY

Churchill

Belcher Islands

Kuujjuaq

NEWFOUNDLAND

LABRADOR

Schefferville

Happy Valley-
Goose Bay

L'Anse aux Meadows

indeer ake

Churchill

Nelson

Fort Severn

James Bay

St. John's

Severn

Akimiski Island

Chisasibi

MANITOBA
e Pas

Lake Winnipeg

Fort Albany

ONTARIO

QUEBEC

Sept-Îles

Île d'Anticosti

Gulf of St. Lawrence

ISLAND OF NEWFOUNDLAND

Cape Race

ST.-PIERRE AND MIQUELON
(France)

oba

Winnipeg

Lake Nipigon

Chicoutimi

Gaspé Pen.

Rimouski

PRINCE EDWARD ISLAND

Charlottetown

Cape Breton Island

ake

Thunder Bay

Timmins

Québec

NEW BRUNSWICK

Fredericton

Sable Island

Lake Superior

Sault Ste. Marie

Sudbury

Ottawa

Montréal

St. Lawrence

Halifax

NOVA SCOTIA

Cape Sable

Bay of Fundy

STATES

Lake Huron

Lake Michigan

Toronto

Hamilton

London

Windsor

Lake Erie

Ottawa

Kingston

L. Ontario

Niagara Falls

ATLANTIC OCEAN

Cabot Strait

9   **10**   **11**   **12**   **13**   **14**   **15**   **16**

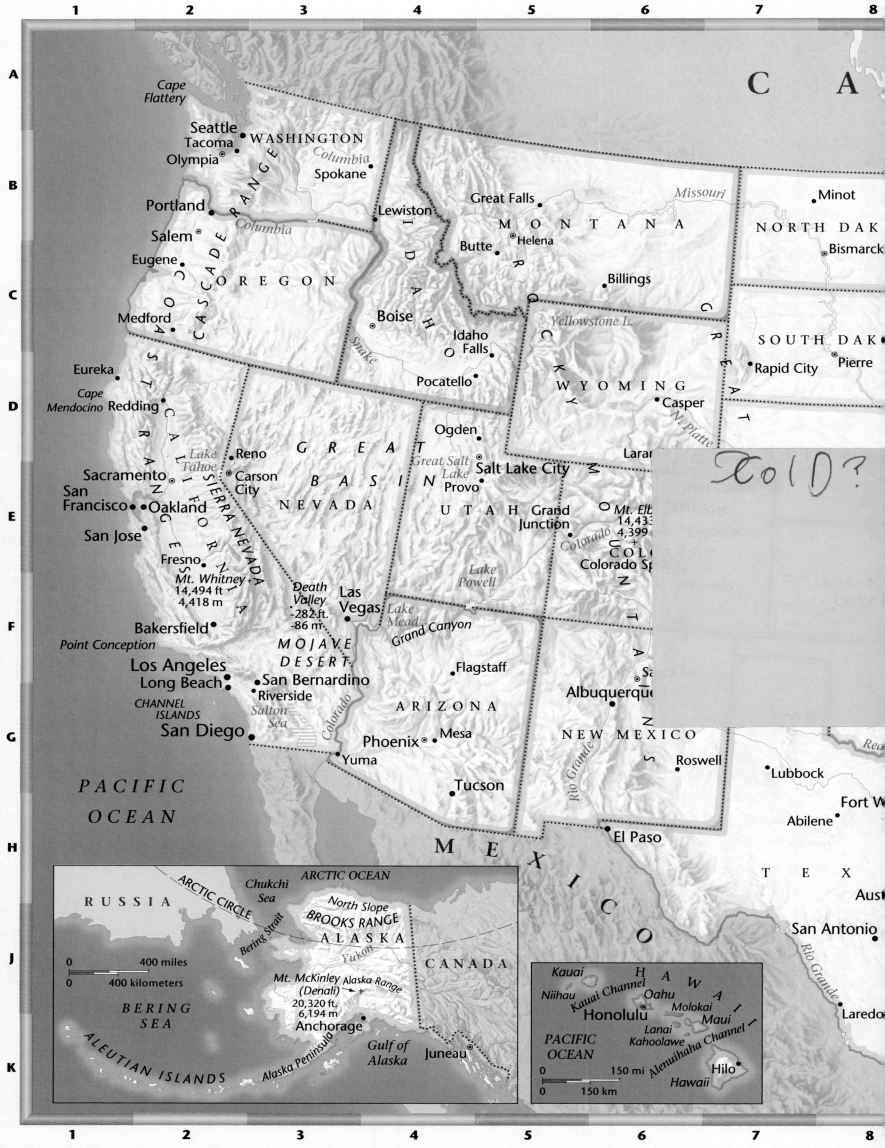

cold?

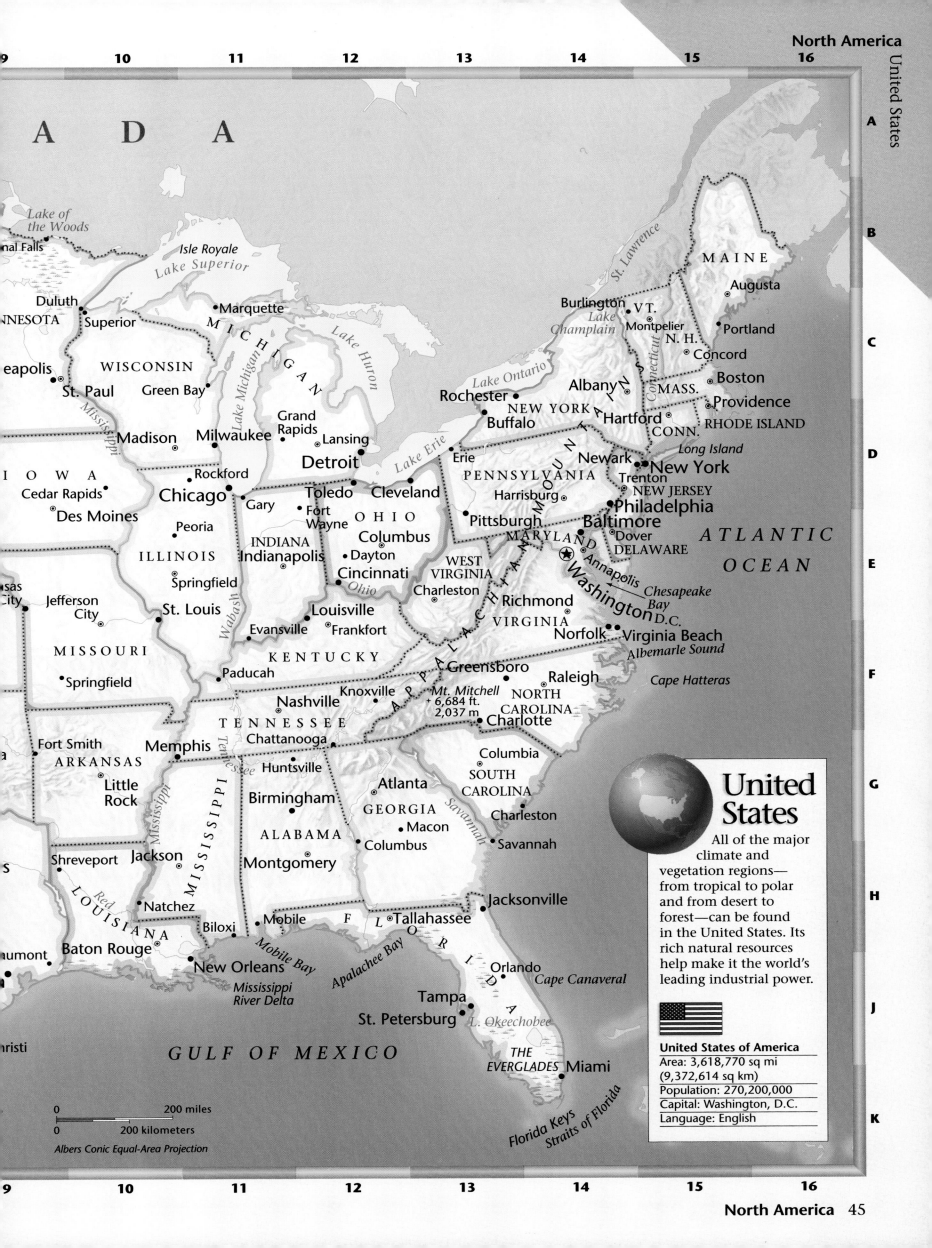

9   10   11   12   13   14   15   16

A
B
C
D
E
F
G
H
J
K

C A N A D A

Lake of the Woods

nal Falls

Isle Royale

Lake Superior

Duluth
•Marquette

NNESOTA   Superior

WISCONSIN

M I C H I G A N

Lake Huron

eapolis

St. Paul   Green Bay•

Madison   Milwaukee   Grand Rapids

Lake Michigan

Detroit   •Lansing

I O W A   Rockford•

Cedar Rapids•   **Chicago**   Gary   **Toledo**   **Cleveland**   *Lake Erie*   Erie

•Des Moines   Peoria•   Fort Wayne   O H I O

ILLINOIS   INDIANA   Columbus

Springfield•   **Indianapolis**   •Dayton

Wabash   Cincinnati•   *Ohio*

Jefferson City   St. Louis   Louisville

nsas City   MISSOURI   Evansville•   •Frankfort

Springfield•   Paducah•   K E N T U C K Y

Fort Smith•   Nashville

Memphis   T E N N E S S E E   Chattanooga

ARKANSAS   Huntsville

Little Rock   Birmingham

Shreveport•   Jackson   M I S S I S S I P P I   Montgomery

L O U I S I A N A   ALABAMA

Natchez•   Biloxi•   Mobile

aumont   Baton Rouge   New Orleans   Mobile Bay   Apalachee Bay

Mississippi River Delta

hristi

G U L F   O F   M E X I C O

Burlington   VT.   •Augusta
Lake Champlain   Montpelier•   •Portland
N. H.   Concord

Rochester•   Albany•   Boston

Lake Ontario   Hartford•   MASS.   •Providence

NEW YORK   Buffalo   CONN.   RHODE ISLAND

Long Island

PENNSYLVANIA   Newark   **New York**

Harrisburg•   Trenton   NEW JERSEY

Pittsburgh•   **Philadelphia**

MARYLAND   **Baltimore**   Dover

WEST VIRGINIA   Washington   DELAWARE   Annapolis

Charleston•   D.C.   Chesapeake Bay

Richmond•   V I R G I N I A   Norfolk•   Virginia Beach

Albemarle Sound

Greensboro•   Raleigh•   Cape Hatteras

Knoxville•   Mt. Mitchell   NORTH CAROLINA

+6,684 ft.   Charlotte•

2,037 m

Columbia•

SOUTH CAROLINA

Atlanta•

G E O R G I A   Charleston•

Macon•   Savannah

Columbus•   Savannah•

Jacksonville•

F L O R I D A   Tallahassee

Orlando•   Cape Canaveral

Tampa•

St. Petersburg   L. Okeechobee

THE EVERGLADES   Miami

Florida Keys   Straits of Florida

A T L A N T I C   O C E A N

St. Lawrence

M A I N E

A P P A L A C H I A N   M O U N T A I N S

Red

Mississippi

Tennessee

Savannah

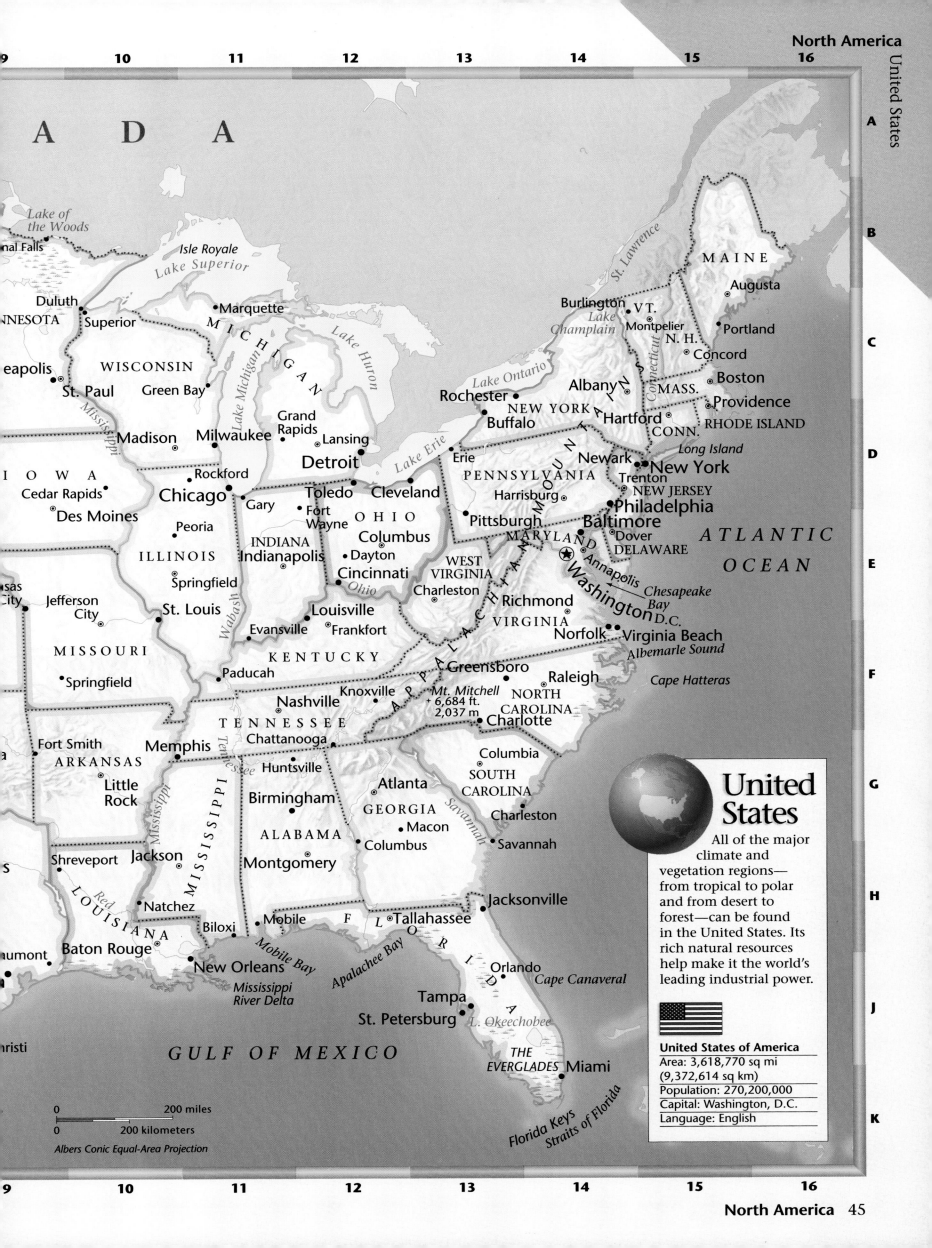

United States

All of the major climate and vegetation regions—from tropical to polar and from desert to forest—can be found in the United States. Its rich natural resources help make it the world's leading industrial power.

United States of America

Area: 3,618,770 sq mi
(9,372,614 sq km)

Population: 270,200,000

Capital: Washington, D.C.

Language: English

---

0 _____ 200 miles

0 _____ 200 kilometers

Albers Conic Equal-Area Projection

Alaska and Hawaii

Alaska is almost a hundred times the size of Hawaii but has only half as many people. Its wealth lies in oil, natural gas, fisheries, and timber, while Hawaii earns most of its income from tourism. Both states have active volcanoes.

Alaska
Area: 591,004 sq mi
(1,530,700 sq km)
Population: 609,000
Capital: Juneau

Hawaii
Area: 6,471 sq mi
(16,750 sq km)
Population: 1,187,000
Capital: Honolulu

ARCTIC CIRCLE

A R C T

C H U K C H I
S E A

Kotzebue Sound

RUSSIA

Bering Str.

SEWA
PENIN

Nome

Norton Soun

St. Lawrence
Island

St. Matthew Island

Nunivak
Island

B E R I N G

S E A

Pribilof
Islands

Br

Attu
Island

Near Islands

A L E U T I A N   I S L A N D S

Unimak I.

AL

Unalaska

Rat Islands

F O X   I S L A N D S

ANDREANOF ISLANDS

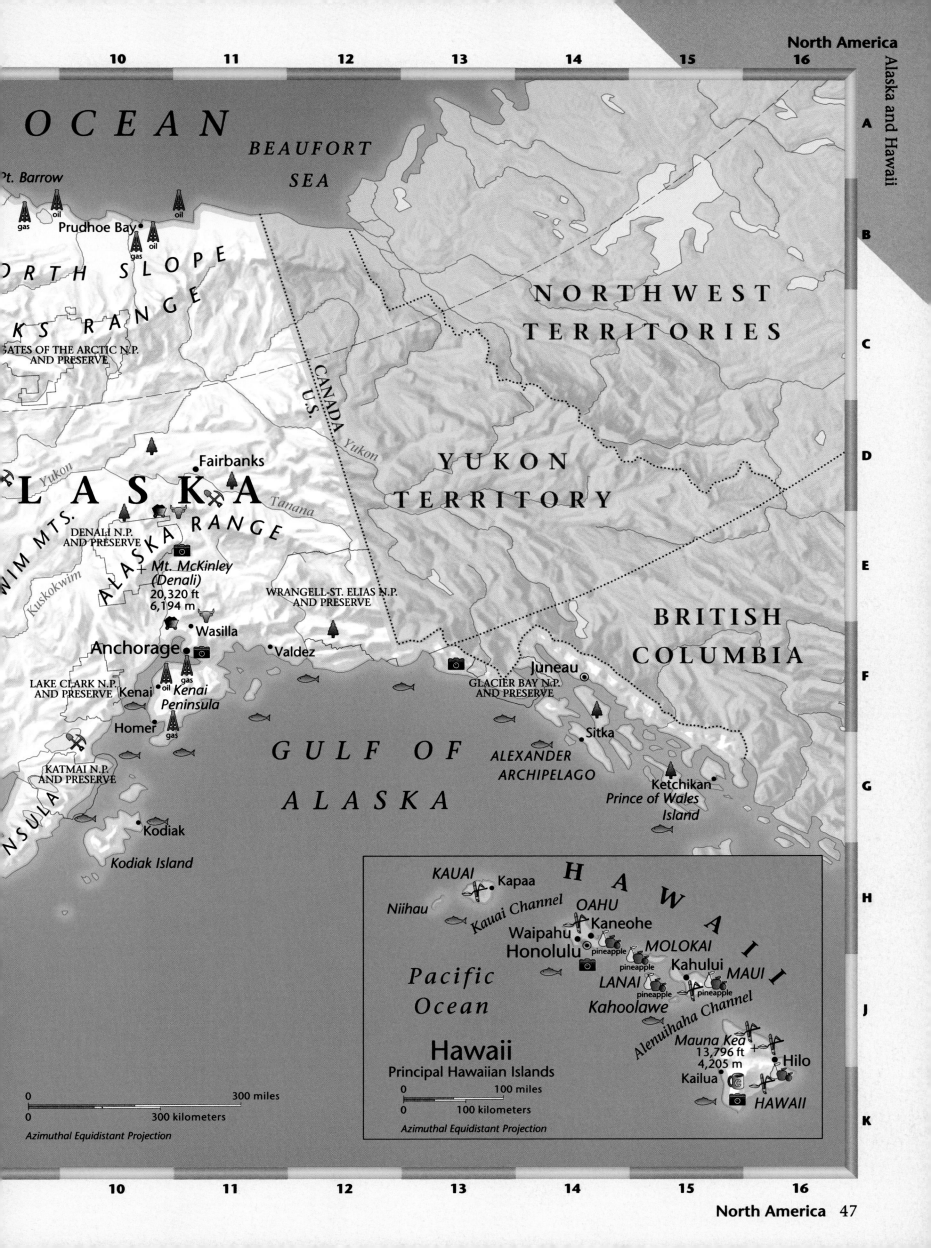

O C E A N

BEAUFORT
SEA

Pt. Barrow

oil
gas
Prudhoe Bay
oil
gas
oil

N O R T H   S L O P E

R O O K S   R A N G E

GATES OF THE ARCTIC N.P.
AND PRESERVE

NORTHWEST
TERRITORIES

CANADA
U.S.

Yukon

Fairbanks

A L A S K A

Yukon

Tanana

YUKON
TERRITORY

BIM MTS.

DENALI N.P.
AND PRESERVE

A L A S K A   R A N G E

Kuskokwim

+ Mt. McKinley
(Denali)
20,320 ft
6,194 m

WRANGELL-ST. ELIAS N.P.
AND PRESERVE

• Wasilla

Anchorage

BRITISH
COLUMBIA

LAKE CLARK N.P.
AND PRESERVE
Kenai
oil
gas
Kenai
Peninsula

Homer
gas

Valdez

Juneau

GLACIER BAY N.P.
AND PRESERVE

E

KATMAI N.P.
AND PRESERVE

PENINSULA

GULF OF
ALASKA

• Sitka

ALEXANDER
ARCHIPELAGO

Ketchikan

Prince of Wales
Island

Kodiak

Kodiak Island

KAUAI   • Kapaa

Niihau

Kauai Channel

H A W A I I

OAHU

Waipahu •
Honolulu
pineapple

Kaneohe

MOLOKAI
pineapple

Kahului

MAUI

Pacific
Ocean

LANAI
pineapple

Kahoolawe

pineapple

Alenuihaha Channel

Mauna Kea
13,796 ft
4,205 m

Hilo

Hawaii

Principal Hawaiian Islands

Kailua

HAWAII

0   300 miles

0   300 kilometers

Azimuthal Equidistant Projection

0   100 miles

0   100 kilometers

Azimuthal Equidistant Projection

A
B
C
D
E
F
G
H
J
K

North America grid labels: 10 11 12 13 14 15 16

A
B
C
D
E
F
G
H
J
K

U T A H

A R I Z O N A

N E V A D A

GREAT BASIN N.P.

Ely

E g a n R a n g e

Rub...

Toiyabe Range

Monitor Range

oil

Hawthorne

Fallon

Carson Sink

Pyramid Lake

Reno

Carson City

Lake Tahoe

S. Lake Tahoe

S I E R R A

N E V A D A

Boundary Peak +13,143 ft 4,006 m

Tonopah

Mono L.

Mojave Desert

Colorado

Gila

Lake Mead

Las Vegas

Boulder City

Death Valley -282 ft -86 m N.P.

DEATH VALLEY

Mt. Whitney +14,494 ft 4,418 m

SEQUOIA N.P.

KINGS CANYON N.P.

YOSEMITE N.P.

Salton Sea

Imperial Valley

JOSHUA TREE N.P.

Indio

Palm Springs

San Bernardino

Riverside

Santa Ana

Los Angeles

Long Beach

oil

Barstow

Ridgecrest

Bakersfield

Lancaster

Santa Barbara

Oxnard

oil

Escondido

El Centro

Calexico

U.S.

MEXICO

Oceanside

San Diego

C A L I F O R N I A

Madera

Fresno

Visalia

Porterville

Tulare

Delano

Hanford

oil

Merced

Turlock

Modesto

Stockton

Lodi

Yuba City

Chico

Sacramento

Sacramento Valley

Sacramento

Napa

Santa Rosa

Ukiah

Vallejo

Oakland

San Francisco

Redwood City

San Jose

Santa Cruz

Monterey

Salinas

San Joaquin Valley

San Joaquin

Atascadero

San Luis Obispo

Santa Maria

Lompoc

oil

Santa Catalina

Santa Cruz

Santa Rosa

CHANNEL IS. N.P.

C H A N N E L I S L A N D S

O C E A N

200 miles

200 kilometers

0

0

Albers Conic Equal-Area Projection

Far Western States

The Sierra Nevada form a barrier between Nevada's desert landscape and California's fertile central valleys. Earthquakes are frequent along the coast and volcanic eruptions are a threat in the Cascade Range.

STATE OF OREGON 1859

Oregon
Area: 97,073 sq mi
(251,419 sq km)
Population: 3,243,000
Capital: Salem

Washington
Area: 68,138 sq mi
(176,477 sq km)
Population: 5,610,000
Capital: Olympia

CALIFORNIA REPUBLIC

California
Area: 158,706 sq mi
(411,049 sq km)
Population: 32,268,000
Capital: Sacramento

Nevada
Area: 110,561 sq mi
(286,352 sq km)
Population: 1,677,000
Capital: Carson City

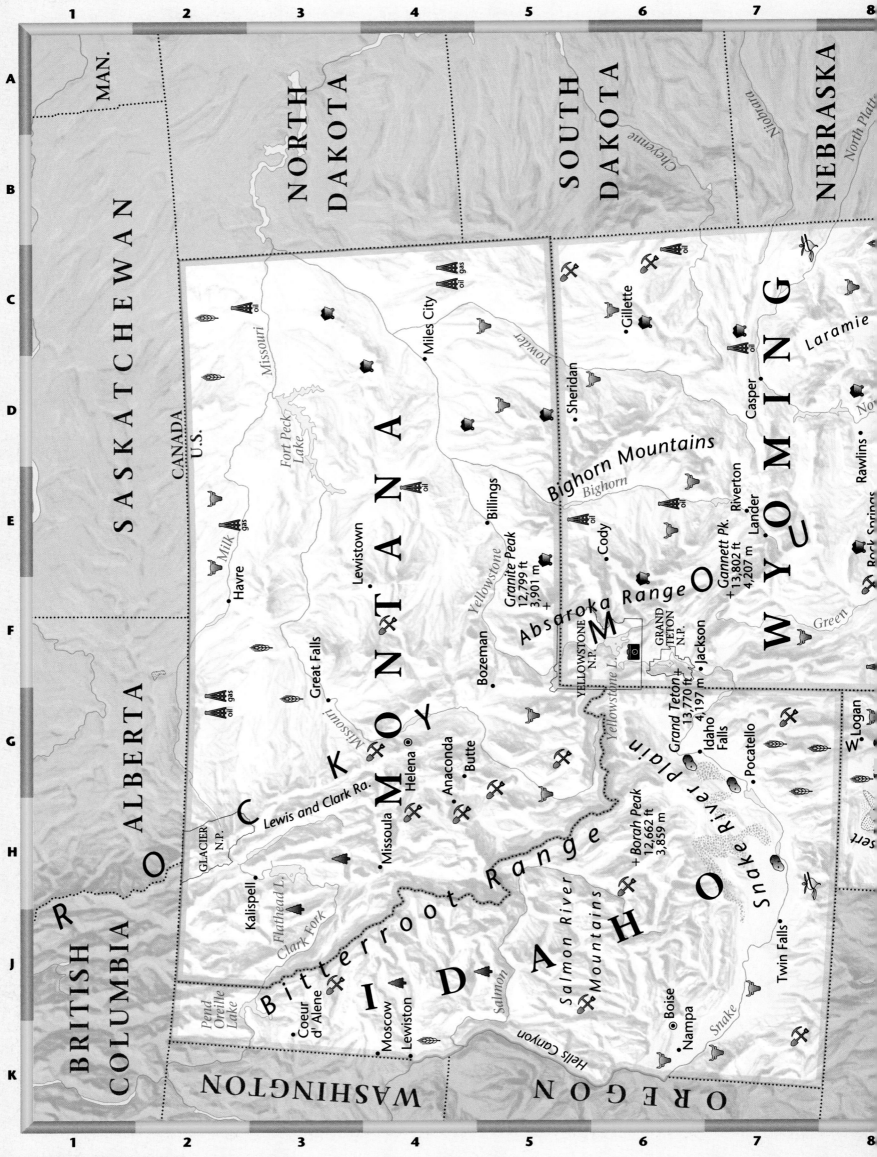

1 **2** **3** **4** **5** **6** **7** **8**

A

MAN.

SASKATCHEWAN

NORTH DAKOTA

SOUTH DAKOTA

NEBRASKA

B

Cheyenne

Niobrara

North Platte

C

BRITISH COLUMBIA

ALBERTA

CANADA

U.S.

Missouri

oil

oil gas

Powder

Gillette

Laramie

oil

oil

D

Fort Peck Lake

Miles City

Sheridan

Bighorn Mountains

Bighorn

Casper

North

Rawlins

E

Milk

gas

Havre

Lewistown

M O N T A N A

oil

Billings

Yellowstone

Granite Peak
12,799 ft
3,901 m

oil

Cody

oil

Riverton
Lander

Gannett Pk.
+ 13,802 ft
4,207 m

W Y O M I N G

Green

Rock Springs

F

Missouri

Great Falls

Bozeman

Absaroka Range

YELLOWSTONE N.P.

Yellowstone L.

GRAND TETON N.P.

Jackson

G

R O C K Y

Helena

Anaconda

Butte

Grand Teton
13,770 ft
4,197 m

Idaho Falls

Pocatello

W. Logan

W.

H

GLACIER N.P.

Lewis and Clark Ra.

Missoula

Range

Salmon River

+ **Borah Peak**
12,662 ft
3,859 m

Snake River Plain

J

Pend Oreille Lake

Kalispell

Flathead L.

Clark Fork

Bitterroot

I D A H O

Coeur d'Alene

Moscow
Lewiston

Mountains

Salmon

Hells Canyon

Boise
Nampa

Snake

Twin Falls

K

WASHINGTON

O R E G O N

1 **2** **3** **4** **5** **6** **7** **8**

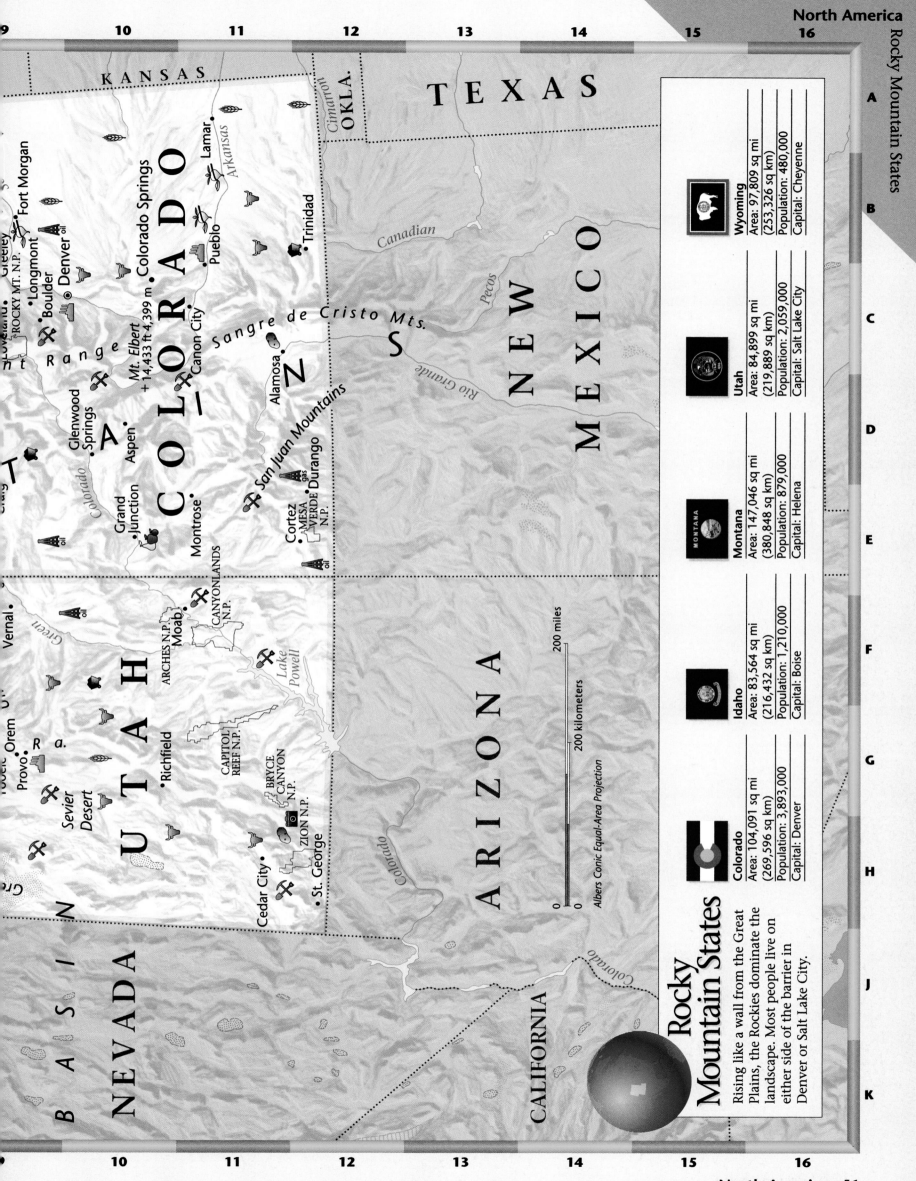

KANSAS

OKLA.

T E X A S

Cimarron

Canadian

Arkansas

Lamar

Colorado Springs

Pueblo

Trinidad

Pecos

N E W

M E X I C O

C O L O R A D O

Denver
oil

Boulder

Longmont

Greeley

Fort Morgan

ROCKY MT. N.P.

Loveland

Range

Glenwood
Springs

Aspen

Mt. Elbert
+14,433 ft 4,399 m

Canon City

Alamosa

Sangre de Cristo Mts.

San Juan Mountains

Durango
gas

Cortez

MESA
VERDE
N.P.

Rio Grande

Grand
Junction

Montrose

Colorado

oil

CANYONLANDS
N.P.

ARCHES N.P.
Moab

*Lake
Powell*

oil

U T A H

Green

Vernal

oil

Orem
Provo

R   a.

Richfield

CAPITOL
REEF N.P.

BRYCE
CANYON
N.P.

ZION N.P.

Cedar City

St. George

*Sevier
Desert*

N E V A D A

B   A   S   I   N

A R I Z O N A

Colorado

CALIFORNIA

Rocky Mountain States

Rising like a wall from the Great Plains, the Rockies dominate the landscape. Most people live on either side of the barrier in Denver or Salt Lake City.

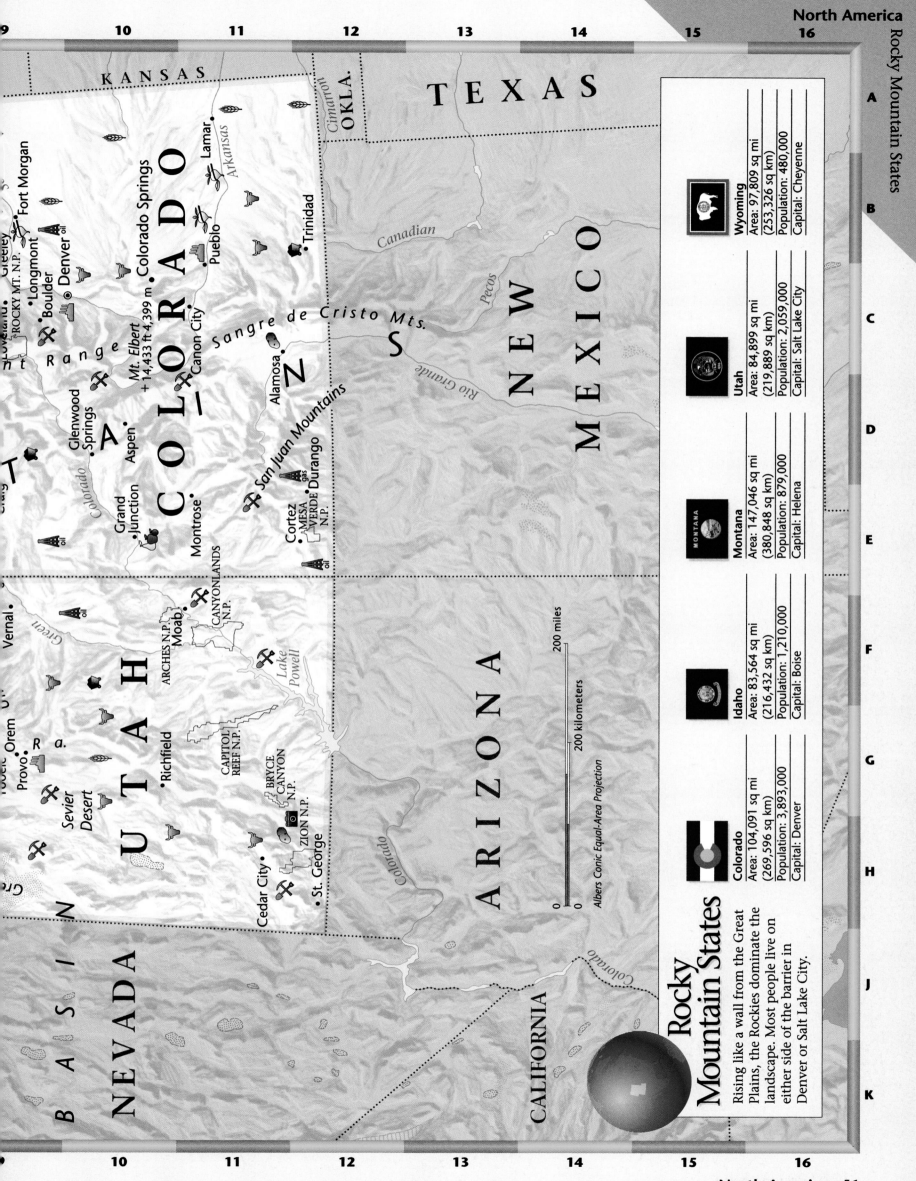

Wyoming
Area: 97,809 sq mi
(253,326 sq km)
Population: 480,000
Capital: Cheyenne

Utah
Area: 84,899 sq mi
(219,889 sq km)
Population: 2,059,000
Capital: Salt Lake City

Montana
Area: 147,046 sq mi
(380,848 sq km)
Population: 879,000
Capital: Helena

Idaho
Area: 83,564 sq mi
(216,432 sq km)
Population: 1,210,000
Capital: Boise

Colorado
Area: 104,091 sq mi
(269,596 sq km)
Population: 3,893,000
Capital: Denver

200 miles

200 kilometers

Albers Conic Equal-Area Projection

Southwestern States

More Native Americans live in this region than in any other. Names like Santa Fe and Rio Grande reflect the area's Spanish heritage. Deserts cover much of Arizona and New Mexico, while grasslands support huge cattle ranches in Texas.

Arizona
Area: 114,000 sq mi
(295,260 sq km)
Population: 4,555,000
Capital: Phoenix

Oklahoma
Area: 69,956 sq mi
(181,186 sq km)
Population: 3,317,000
Capital: Oklahoma City

New Mexico
Area: 121,593 sq mi
(314,925 sq km)
Population: 1,730,000
Capital: Santa Fe

Texas
Area: 266,807 sq mi
(691,030 sq km)
Population: 19,439,000
Capital: Austin

Albers Conic Equal-Area Projection

Map labels

NEVADA

UTAH
Lake Powell

C O L O R

CALIFORNIA

GRAND CANYON N.P.
Grand Canyon
Colorado
Colorado Plateau
Painted Desert

Lake Mead

Kingman

Humphreys Peak
12,633 ft
3,851 m

Tuba City

Shiprock
Farmington
oil
gas
Wheeler 13,161 ft
Taos

Los Alamos

Gallup
Santa Fe
Las

Grants

Albuquerque

Belen

Flagstaff
Winslow
PETRIFIED FOREST N.P.

Lake Havasu City
Prescott
Cottonwood

A R I Z O N A

N E W   M E X I

Socorro

Phoenix
Mesa
Globe

Casa Grande

Truth or Consequences
Rosw

Gila

Yuma

Safford

Gila

Silver City
Alamogordo

SAGUARO N.P.

Tucson
Deming
Las Cruces
CARLSBAD CAVER

Green Valley

Nogales
Sierra Vista
Douglas

GULF OF CALIFORNIA

El Paso
GUADALUPE MTS. N.P.

M E X I

KANSAS

MISSOURI

Miami
Bartlesville
Ponca City
Woodward
Enid
Stillwater
Tulsa
Neosho
White

ARKANSAS

OKLAHOMA
Muskogee
Okmulgee
Oklahoma City
Elk City
Shawnee
Norman
Ouachita Mts.
McAlester
Ada
Lawton
gas oil
Lake Texoma

Black Mesa
4,973 ft
1,516 m
gas
Guymon

gas

Dumas
gas
Pampa
oil

umcari
Amarillo
Canyon
gas

Hereford

Altus
Vernon
Ardmore
oil
Red
Sherman
Paris
Texarkana

vis
Plainview
Wichita Falls
Gainesville
oil
Denton
Greenville

llano
Levelland
Lubbock
Brazos
Mineral Wells
Dallas
Marshall
Longview
Henderson
oil gas
Tyler

acado
Lovington
Snyder
Fort Worth
Waxahachie
Cleburne
Corsicana
Palestine
Nacogdoches
Toledo Bend Reservoir

os
Lamesa
Abilene
Sweetwater
Lufkin

oil oil
Midland
Big Spring
Brownwood
Waco
Trinity

Odessa
San Angelo
Killeen
Temple
Huntsville
Bryan

oil
Pecos
TEXAS
Edwards
Conroe
Beaumont
Port Arthur

Fort Stockton
Plateau
Austin
Houston
Baytown
oil

G BEND N.P.
Kerrville
San Marcos
Galveston

Del Rio
New Braunfels
San Antonio
Bay City

Uvalde
Victoria
Port Lavaca
oil

Eagle Pass
Beeville
oil

Rio Grande
Nueces
Alice
oil gas
Corpus Christi

Kingsville

Laredo

GULF OF

CO
Rio Grande City
oil
McAllen
Harlingen
Brownsville

MEXICO

A
B
C
D
E
F
G
H
J
K

10 11 12 13 14 15 16

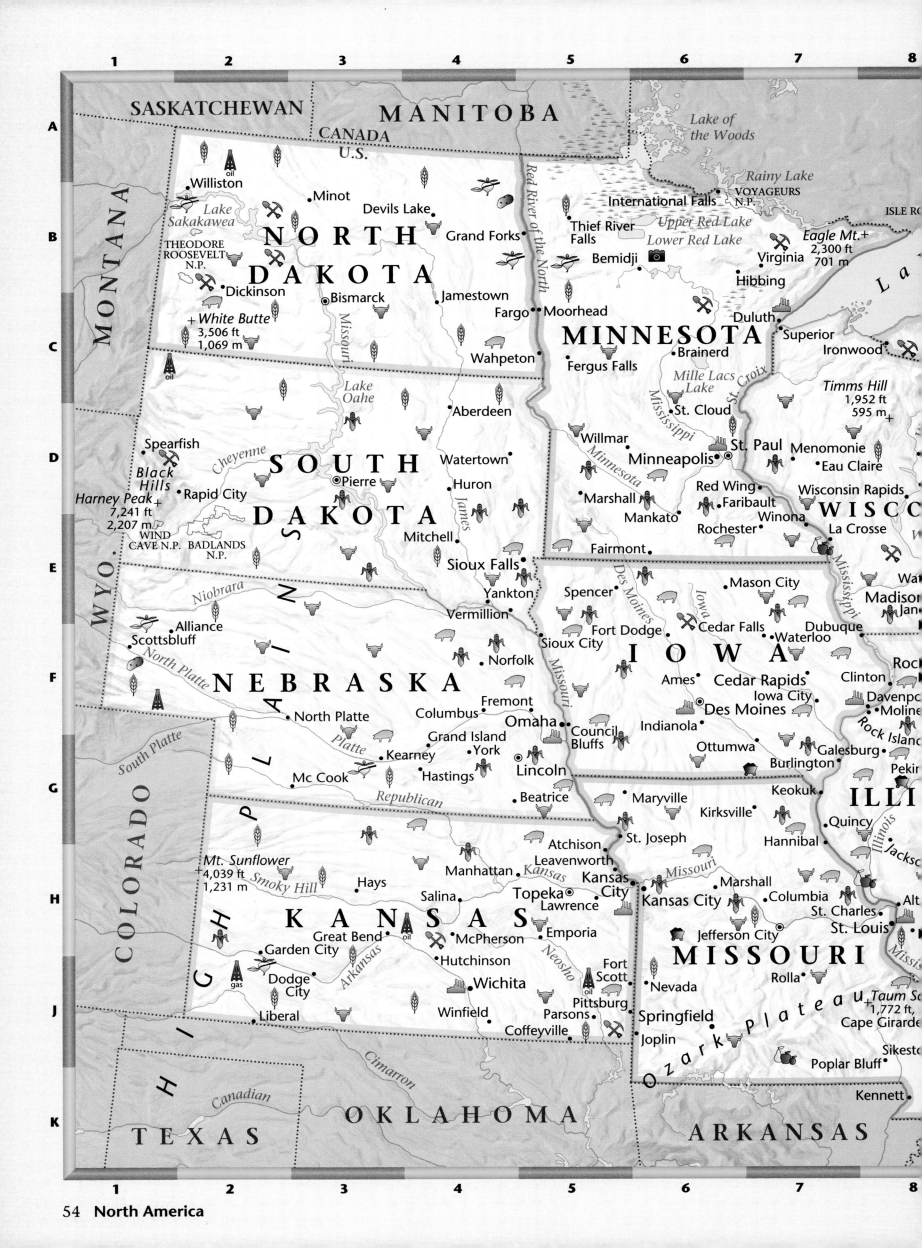

Map grid reference numbers (top and bottom): 1 2 3 4 5 6 7 8

Row letters (left margin): A B C D E F G H J K

SASKATCHEWAN MANITOBA

CANADA
U.S.

Lake of
the Woods

MONTANA

Williston
oil
Minot
Devils Lake

NORTH
DAKOTA

Lake
Sakakawea

THEODORE
ROOSEVELT
N.P.

Grand Forks

International Falls

VOYAGEURS
N.P.

ISLE RO

Thief River
Falls

Upper Red Lake

Rainy Lake

Eagle Mt.+
2,300 ft
701 m

Virginia

Bemidji

Lower Red Lake

Hibbing

Dickinson

Bismarck

Jamestown

Fargo Moorhead

MINNESOTA

Duluth

Superior

Ironwood

+White Butte
3,506 ft
1,069 m

oil

Missouri

Wahpeton

Fergus Falls

Brainerd

La

Mille Lacs
Lake

St. Croix

Timms Hill
1,952 ft
595 m+

Lake
Oahe

Aberdeen

Willmar

St. Cloud

St. Paul

Menomonie

Spearfish

Cheyenne

SOUTH
DAKOTA

Watertown

Huron

Minneapolis

Mississippi

Minnesota

Eau Claire

Red Wing

Wisconsin Rapids

WISCO

Black
Hills

Rapid City

Pierre

Marshall

Faribault

Winona

Mankato

Harney Peak+
7,241 ft
2,207 m
WIND
CAVE N.P. BADLANDS
N.P.

James

Mitchell

Rochester

La Crosse

Fairmont

Sioux Falls

Mason City

Wat

Niobrara

Yankton

Spencer

Des Moines

Madison

Jan

Alliance

Vermillion

Iowa

Cedar Falls

Dubuque

Scottsbluff

North Platte

Fort Dodge

Waterloo

Sioux City

IOWA

North Platte

Norfolk

Ames

Cedar Rapids

Clinton

Roc

NEBRASKA

Columbus

Fremont

Missouri

Iowa City

Davenpo

Moline

North Platte

Grand Island

Omaha

Indianola

Des Moines

Rock Island

Platte

Kearney

York

Council
Bluffs

Ottumwa

Galesburg

Pekir

McCook

Hastings

Lincoln

Burlington

Republican

Beatrice

Maryville

Keokuk

ILLI

Mt. Sunflower
+4,039 ft
1,231 m

Smoky Hill

St. Joseph

Kirksville

Quincy

Illinois

Jacks

Atchison

Leavenworth

Hannibal

KANSAS

Manhattan

Kansas

Kansas
City

Missouri

Marshall

Salina

Topeka

Kansas City

Columbia

St. Charles

Hays

Lawrence

St. Louis

Great Bend

oil

McPherson

Emporia

Jefferson City

MISSOURI

Alt

Garden City

Arkansas

Hutchinson

Neosho

Fort
Scott

Nevada

Rolla

Taum Sa
1,772 ft
Cape Girarde

gas

Dodge
City

Wichita

oil

Pittsburg

Springfield

Ozark Plateau

Liberal

Winfield

Parsons

Joplin

Poplar Bluff

Sikesto

Coffeyville

HIGH PLAINS

Cimarron

Canadian

OKLAHOMA

Kennett

TEXAS

ARKANSAS

COLORADO

WYO.

South Platte

9 10 11 12 13 14 15 16

A
B
C
D
E
F
G
H
J
K

Midwestern States

Vast fields of wheat and corn make this region the nation's breadbasket. Most U.S. hogs and dairy cows are raised here as well. Chicago is the area's most populous city.

Illinois
Area: 56,345 sq mi
(145,934 sq km)
Population: 11,896,000
Capital: Springfield

Missouri
Area: 69,697 sq mi
(180,516 sq km)
Population: 5,402,000
Capital: Jefferson City

Indiana
Area: 36,185 sq mi
(93,720 sq km)
Population: 5,864,000
Capital: Indianapolis

Nebraska
Area: 77,355 sq mi
(200,350 sq km)
Population: 1,657,000
Capital: Lincoln

Iowa
Area: 56,275 sq mi
(145,753 sq km)
Population: 2,852,000
Capital: Des Moines

North Dakota
Area: 70,703 sq mi
(183,121 sq km)
Population: 641,000
Capital: Bismarck

Kansas
Area: 82,277 sq mi
(213,098 sq km)
Population: 2,595,000
Capital: Topeka

Ohio
Area: 41,330 sq mi
(107,044 sq km)
Population: 11,186,000
Capital: Columbus

Michigan
Area: 58,527 sq mi
(151,586 sq km)
Population: 9,774,000
Capital: Lansing

South Dakota
Area: 77,116 sq mi
(199,730 sq km)
Population: 738,000
Capital: Pierre

Minnesota
Area: 84,402 sq mi
(218,601 sq km)
Population: 4,686,000
Capital: St. Paul

Wisconsin
Area: 56,153 sq mi
(145,436 sq km)
Population: 5,170,000
Capital: Madison

ONTARIO

0   200 miles
0   200 kilometers
Albers Conic Equal-Area Projection

Superior

Marquette
Sault Ste. Marie

ft, 603 m

MICHIGAN

Green Bay
Door Pen.

Alpena
Traverse City

Sheboygan
Mt. Pleasant
Bay City
Saginaw
Muskegon
Grand Rapids
Flint
Port Huron

Milwaukee
Grand
Lansing
Detroit
Lake St. Clair

Battle Creek
Kalamazoo
Jackson
Ann Arbor

Lake Erie

Waukegan
Chicago
Toledo
Ashtabula
Lorain
Cleveland

Elkhart
Sandusky
Youngstown
Gary
South Bend
Akron

Fort Wayne
Mansfield
Canton
Kankakee
Lima
Marion
Steubenville

Kokomo
Marion
OHIO
Lafayette
Muncie
Columbus
Zanesville

INDIANA
Springfield
Lancaster

Indianapolis
Dayton
Athens
Terre Haute
Hamilton
Chillicothe

Bloomington
Columbus
Cincinnati
Madison
Portsmouth

Vincennes

Evansville

Lake Michigan

Lake Huron
Saginaw Bay

PENNSYLVANIA

Ohio
Scioto

WEST VIRGINIA
Kanawha

KENTUCKY

VIRGINIA

Cumberland

NORTH CAROLINA

TENNESSEE

Southeastern States

This is the land of cotton—at least in the South. Baltimore and New Orleans are the region's busiest ports.

Alabama
Area: 51,705 sq mi
(133,915 sq km)
Population: 4,319,000
Capital: Montgomery

Arkansas
Area: 53,187 sq mi
(137,754 sq km)
Population: 2,523,000
Capital: Little Rock

Delaware
Area: 2,044 sq mi
(5,294 sq km)
Population: 732,000
Capital: Dover

District of Columbia
Area: 69 sq mi
(178 sq km)
Population: 529,000
Capital: nation's capital

Florida
Area: 58,664 sq mi
(151,939 sq km)
Population: 14,654,000
Capital: Tallahassee

Georgia
Area: 58,910 sq mi
(152,576 sq km)
Population: 7,486,000
Capital: Atlanta

Kentucky
Area: 40,409 sq mi
(104,659 sq km)
Population: 3,908,000
Capital: Frankfort

Louisiana
Area: 47,751 sq mi
(123,675 sq km)
Population: 4,352,000
Capital: Baton Rouge

Maryland
Area: 10,460 sq mi
(27,092 sq km)
Population: 5,094,000
Capital: Annapolis

Mississippi
Area: 47,689 sq mi
(123,515 sq km)
Population: 2,731,000
Capital: Jackson

North Carolina
Area: 52,669 sq mi
(136,413 sq km)
Population: 7,425,000
Capital: Raleigh

South Carolina
Area: 31,113 sq mi
(80,582 sq km)
Population: 3,760,000
Capital: Columbia

Tennessee
Area: 42,144 sq mi
(109,152 sq km)
Population: 5,368,000
Capital: Nashville

Virginia
Area: 40,767 sq mi
(105,586 sq km)
Population: 6,734,000
Capital: Richmond

West Virginia
Area: 24,231 sq mi
(62,758 sq km)
Population: 1,816,000
Capital: Charleston

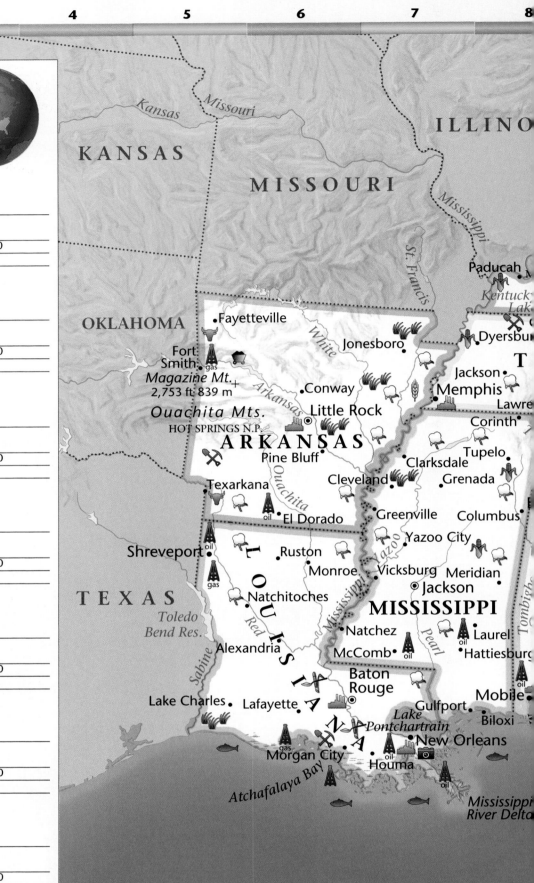

KANSAS

MISSOURI

ILLINOIS

OKLAHOMA

Fayetteville

Fort Smith

Magazine Mt.
2,753 ft 839 m

Ouachita Mts.

HOT SPRINGS N.P.

ARKANSAS

Pine Bluff

Texarkana

El Dorado

Shreveport

TEXAS

Toledo Bend Res.

Alexandria

Lake Charles

Lafayette

LOUISIANA

Morgan City

Atchafalaya Bay

Jonesboro

Conway

Little Rock

Clarksdale

Cleveland

Greenville

Ruston

Monroe

Natchitoches

Natchez

McComb

Baton Rouge

Houma

Paducah

Dyersburg

Jackson

Memphis

Lawre

Corinth

Tupelo

Grenada

Columbus

Yazoo City

Vicksburg

Meridian

Jackson

MISSISSIPPI

Laurel

Hattiesburg

Mobile

Gulfport

Biloxi

New Orleans

Lake Pontchartrain

Mississippi River Delta

White

Arkansas

Ouachita

Red

Sabine

Yazoo

Mississippi

Pearl

Tombigb

Kansas

Missouri

St. Francis

Mississippi

Kentuck Lake

GULF OF ME

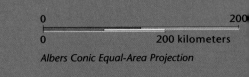

0   200

0   200 kilometers

Albers Conic Equal-Area Projection

9 10 11 12 13 14 15 16

A

PENNSYLVANIA

N.J.

Wheeling Cumberland Hagerstown •Wilmington
Morgantown Frederick **DELAWARE**
OHIO Clarksburg Winchester Baltimore Dover
Parkersburg Washington, D.C.★ Annapolis Delaware Bay
gas oil Cambridge
WEST **SHENANDOAH** Chesapeake Bay Salisbury
Charleston Harrisonburg N.P.
Ashland Huntington **VIRGINIA** Fredericksburg
Frankfort Beckley Charlottesville Potomac
Lexington **VIRGINIA** Richmond
Richmond New James Williamsburg
KENTUCKY Lynchburg Newport News
Somerset Blacksburg Roanoke Petersburg Norfolk Virginia Beach
Bowling Roanoke
Green Kingsport Bristol Greensboro Henderson Elizabeth City
Oak Ridge Durham Albemarle Sound
ESSEE Knoxville Winston-Salem Chapel Hill Raleigh Greenville
Asheville +Mt. Mitchell Cape Hatteras
Chattanooga 6,684 ft 2,037 m **NORTH** Goldsboro Pamlico Sound
GREAT SMOKY **CAROLINA** New
MTS. N.P. Gastonia Fayetteville Bern Cape Lookout
Spartanburg Charlotte Jacksonville
ntsville Dalton Greenville Monroe Lumberton
Rome Rock **SOUTH** Cape Fear
Gainesville Hill Wilmington
Athens Greenwood Columbia Pee Dee Cape Fear
Talladega Atlanta Orangeburg Sumter
Aiken **CAROLINA** Santee Myrtle Beach
Augusta Summerville
GEORGIA Savannah Charleston
Auburn Macon Dublin
Columbus Hilton Head
Tuskegee Americus Vidalia
Eufaula Albany Tifton Savannah
Troy Ozark Douglas
rise Waycross Brunswick
Dothan Thomasville Valdosta
Tallahassee Jacksonville
FLORIDA Lake City
St. Augustine
Gainesville
hama Ocala Daytona Beach
City
Leesburg Titusville
Orlando Cape Canaveral
Kissimmee
Clearwater Lakeland Melbourne
St. Petersburg Tampa Vero Beach
Bradenton Sebring Fort Pierce
Sarasota Port St. Lucie
Lake
Port Charlotte Okeechobee West Palm Beach
Ft. Myers Belle
Glade Fort Lauderdale
Naples
Miami
Everglades N.P. Miami Beach
Key Largo
Florida Bay Florida Keys
Dry Straits of Florida
Tortugas Key West

ATLANTIC OCEAN

BAHAMAS

B

C

D

E

F

G

H

J

K

ONTARIO

QUE

LAKE HURON

Georgian
Bay

St. Lawrence
• Ogdensburg Plattsburgh
Burlingt

*Lake
Champlain*

Adirondack
Mountains Mt. M
+5,344 ft
1,629 n

• Watertown

LAKE ONTARIO

•Oswego

Lockport
Niagara Falls •Rochester Rome
Syracuse Utica Saratoga
Springs

Buffalo *Finger Lakes* Schenectady

LAKE ERIE NEW YORK Albany

Ru

•Ithaca

Erie •Jamestown •Corning •Elmira Binghamton

Poughkeepsie

Meadville Warren Newburgh

Oil City Williamsport Scranton Bridgepo
Wilkes-Barre Stamford

New Castle State College Hazleton Yonke

OHIO PENNSYLVANIA Newark Lon
New York

Pittsburgh Altoona Allentown Bethlehem
Johnstown New Brunswick

•Washington Carlisle Harrisburg •Reading Trenton NEW
JERSEY

Mt. Davis Lancaster York Philadelphia
3,212 ft
+979 m •York Camden

MARYLAND Vineland

WEST •Atlantic City
VIRGINIA VIRGINIA D.C. DEL.

NEW BRUNSWICK

PRINCE EDWARD ISLAND

Caribou

Presque Isle

Mt. Katahdin +
5,269 ft
1,606 m
Moosehead Lake

M A I N E

NOVA SCOTIA

St. John

Kennebec

Penobscot

CANADA
U.S.

maple syrup

ansfield
1,339 m Berlin

maple syrup +
Mt. Washington
6,290 ft
White Mts. 1,917 m
NEW
HAMPSHIRE

tpelier

Claremont

Concord

Keene
Manchester

Nashua

Lowell

CHUSETTS Boston
Worcester
ngfield

ord
CUT

Providence
RHODE Fall River
ISLAND New Bedford

Newport

New London

ound

Bangor

Waterville

Augusta

Lewiston

Brunswick

Portland

Portsmouth

Bar Harbor
ACADIA N.P.

GULF OF MAINE

Provincetown
Cape Cod

cranberries

cranberries

Martha's
Vineyard

Nantucket
Island

A T L A N T I C

O C E A N

0   100 miles
0   100 kilometers

Albers Conic Equal-Area Projection

Northeastern States

This region's most densely populated area extends from Boston to Philadelphia, while a string of industrial cities lies between Buffalo and Albany and in the valley of the Susquehanna River. Glaciers shaped the area's lakes and coastline.

Connecticut
Area: 5,018 sq mi
(12,997 sq km)
Population: 3,270,000
Capital: Hartford

New Hampshire
Area: 9,279 sq mi
(24,032 sq km)
Population: 1,173,000
Capital: Concord

Pennsylvania
Area: 45,308 sq mi
(117,348 sq km)
Population: 12,020,000
Capital: Harrisburg

Maine
Area: 33,265 sq mi
(86,156 sq km)
Population: 1,242,000
Capital: Augusta

New Jersey
Area: 7,787 sq mi
(20,169 sq km)
Population: 8,053,000
Capital: Trenton

Rhode Island
Area: 1,212 sq mi
(3,140 sq km)
Population: 987,000
Capital: Providence

Massachusetts
Area: 8,284 sq mi
(21,456 sq km)
Population: 6,118,000
Capital: Boston

New York
Area: 49,108 sq mi
(127,190 sq km)
Population: 18,137,000
Capital: Albany

Vermont
Area: 9,614 sq mi
(24,900 sq km)
Population: 589,000
Capital: Montpelier

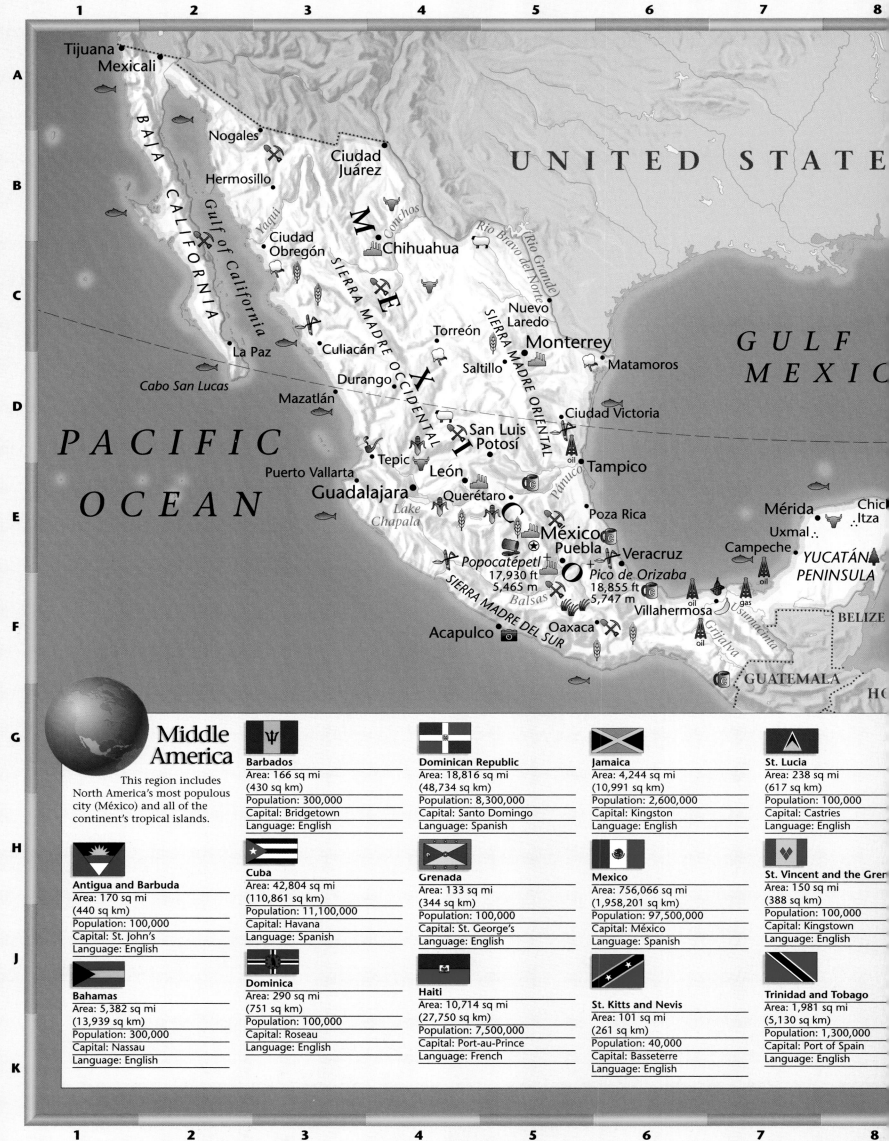

Map labels

Tijuana
Mexicali
Nogales
Hermosillo
Ciudad Juárez
BAJA CALIFORNIA
Gulf of California
Yaqui
Ciudad Obregón
Chihuahua
Conchos
UNITED STATES
Rio Bravo del Norte (Rio Grande)
SIERRA MADRE OCCIDENTAL
Torreón
Nuevo Laredo
Monterrey
SIERRA MADRE ORIENTAL
Matamoros
La Paz
Culiacán
Saltillo
Durango
GULF OF MEXICO
Cabo San Lucas
Mazatlán
Ciudad Victoria
PACIFIC OCEAN
Tepic
San Luis Potosí
oil
Tampico
Puerto Vallarta
León
Pánuco
Guadalajara
Querétaro
Poza Rica
Mérida
Chichén Itzá
Lake Chapala
México
Puebla
Veracruz
Uxmal
Campeche
YUCATÁN PENINSULA
Popocatépetl 17,930 ft 5,465 m
Pico de Orizaba 18,855 ft 5,747 m
oil
Balsas
Villahermosa
oil
gas
Acapulco
SIERRA MADRE DEL SUR
Oaxaca
oil
Usumacinta
Grijalva
BELIZE
GUATEMALA
HO

Middle America

This region includes North America's most populous city (México) and all of the continent's tropical islands.

Barbados
Area: 166 sq mi (430 sq km)
Population: 300,000
Capital: Bridgetown
Language: English

Dominican Republic
Area: 18,816 sq mi (48,734 sq km)
Population: 8,300,000
Capital: Santo Domingo
Language: Spanish

Jamaica
Area: 4,244 sq mi (10,991 sq km)
Population: 2,600,000
Capital: Kingston
Language: English

St. Lucia
Area: 238 sq mi (617 sq km)
Population: 100,000
Capital: Castries
Language: English

Antigua and Barbuda
Area: 170 sq mi (440 sq km)
Population: 100,000
Capital: St. John's
Language: English

Cuba
Area: 42,804 sq mi (110,861 sq km)
Population: 11,100,000
Capital: Havana
Language: Spanish

Grenada
Area: 133 sq mi (344 sq km)
Population: 100,000
Capital: St. George's
Language: English

Mexico
Area: 756,066 sq mi (1,958,201 sq km)
Population: 97,500,000
Capital: México
Language: Spanish

St. Vincent and the Gren
Area: 150 sq mi (388 sq km)
Population: 100,000
Capital: Kingstown
Language: English

Bahamas
Area: 5,382 sq mi (13,939 sq km)
Population: 300,000
Capital: Nassau
Language: English

Dominica
Area: 290 sq mi (751 sq km)
Population: 100,000
Capital: Roseau
Language: English

Haiti
Area: 10,714 sq mi (27,750 sq km)
Population: 7,500,000
Capital: Port-au-Prince
Language: French

St. Kitts and Nevis
Area: 101 sq mi (261 sq km)
Population: 40,000
Capital: Basseterre
Language: English

Trinidad and Tobago
Area: 1,981 sq mi (5,130 sq km)
Population: 1,300,000
Capital: Port of Spain
Language: English

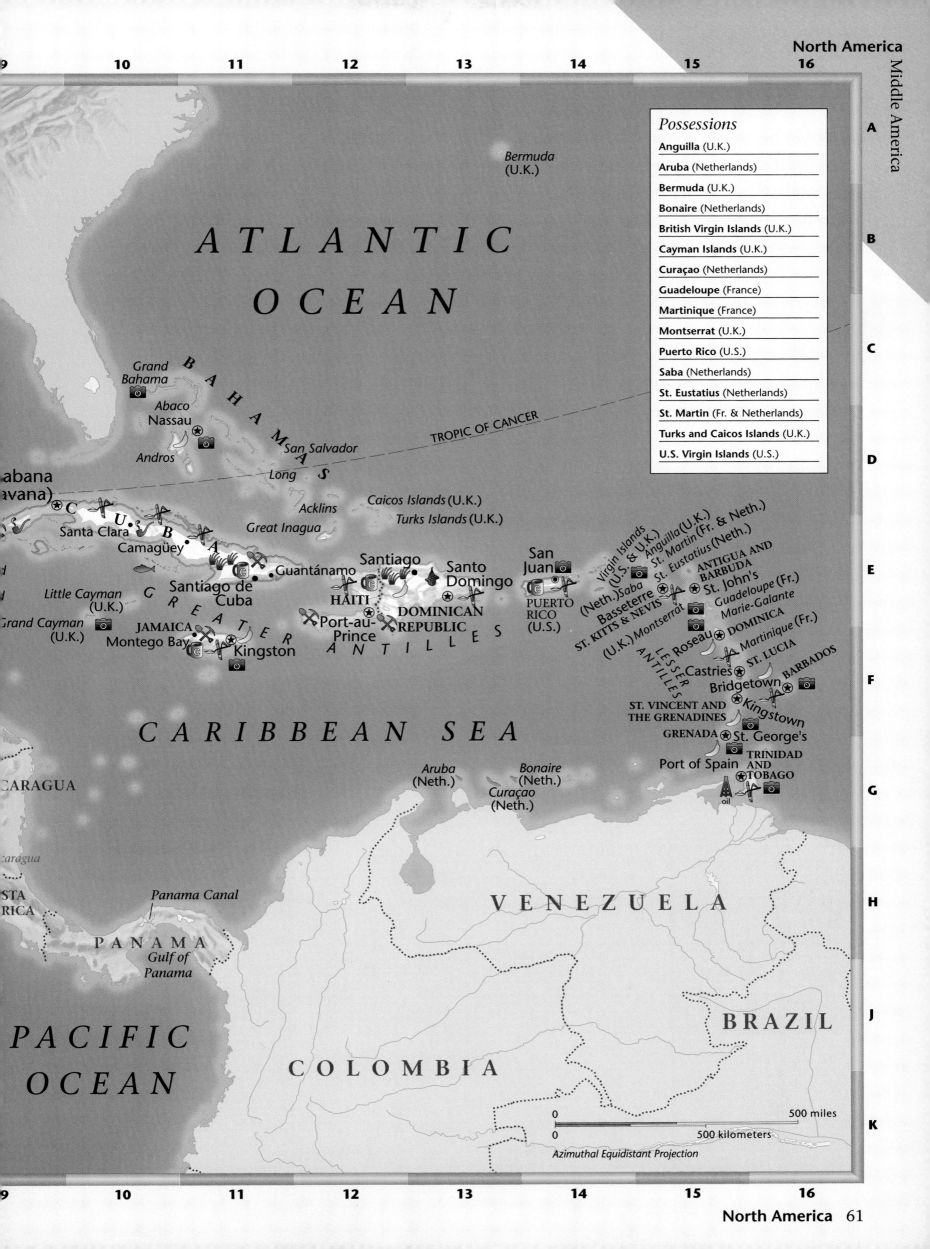

Possessions

Anguilla (U.K.)
Aruba (Netherlands)
Bermuda (U.K.)
Bonaire (Netherlands)
British Virgin Islands (U.K.)
Cayman Islands (U.K.)
Curaçao (Netherlands)
Guadeloupe (France)
Martinique (France)
Montserrat (U.K.)
Puerto Rico (U.S.)
Saba (Netherlands)
St. Eustatius (Netherlands)
St. Martin (Fr. & Netherlands)
Turks and Caicos Islands (U.K.)
U.S. Virgin Islands (U.S.)

ATLANTIC
OCEAN

Bermuda
(U.K.)

*Grand
Bahama*

Abaco
Nassau

Andros

TROPIC OF CANCER

San Salvador

Long

abana
avana)

Santa Clara

Camagüey

CUBA

San Salvador

Acklins

Great Inagua

Caicos Islands (U.K.)
Turks Islands (U.K.)

Santiago

Santo
Domingo

San
Juan

Virgin Islands
(U.S. & U.K.)

Anguilla (U.K.)
St. Martin (Fr. & Neth.)

*Little Cayman
(U.K.)*

Santiago de
Cuba

Guantánamo

HAITI

DOMINICAN
REPUBLIC

PUERTO
RICO
(U.S.)

(Neth.) Saba
Basseterre

St. Eustatius (Neth.)

ANTIGUA AND
BARBUDA

St. John's

*Grand Cayman
(U.K.)*

JAMAICA

Montego Bay

Kingston

Port-au-
Prince

GREATER ANTILLES

ST. KITTS & NEVIS

(U.K.) Montserrat

Guadeloupe (Fr.)

Marie-Galante

Roseau DOMINICA

Martinique (Fr.)

Castries ST. LUCIA

LESSER
ANTILLES

BARBADOS

Bridgetown

CARIBBEAN SEA

ST. VINCENT AND
THE GRENADINES

Kingstown

GRENADA St. George's

*Aruba
(Neth.)*

*Bonaire
(Neth.)*
*Curaçao
(Neth.)*

Port of Spain

TRINIDAD
AND
TOBAGO

oil

CARAGUA

CARA

RICA

STA
RICA

PANAMA

Panama Canal

Gulf of
Panama

VENEZUELA

COLOMBIA

BRAZIL

PACIFIC
OCEAN

0   500 miles
0   500 kilometers

Azimuthal Equidistant Projection

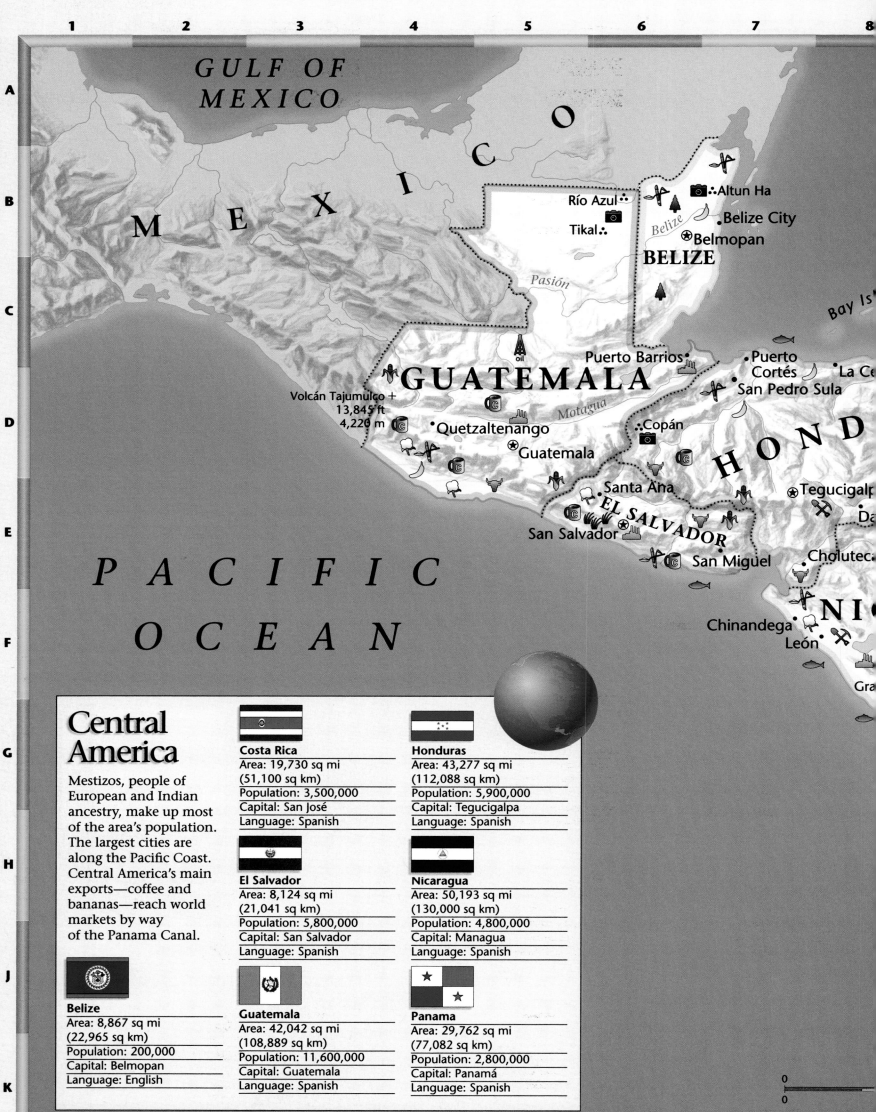

GULF OF MEXICO

M E X I C O

BELIZE

Río Azul

Tikal

Altun Ha

Belize City

Belmopan

Belize

Pasión

Bay Is

oil

GUATEMALA

Volcán Tajumulco +
13,845 ft
4,220 m

Puerto Barrios

Puerto
Cortés

La Ce

San Pedro Sula

Quetzaltenango

Guatemala

Copán

Motagua

H O N D

Santa Ana

Tegucigalp

Da

EL SALVADOR

San Salvador

San Miguel

Choluteca

P A C I F I C

Chinandega

NIC

León

O C E A N

Gra

Central America

Mestizos, people of European and Indian ancestry, make up most of the area's population. The largest cities are along the Pacific Coast. Central America's main exports—coffee and bananas—reach world markets by way of the Panama Canal.

Costa Rica
Area: 19,730 sq mi
(51,100 sq km)
Population: 3,500,000
Capital: San José
Language: Spanish

Honduras
Area: 43,277 sq mi
(112,088 sq km)
Population: 5,900,000
Capital: Tegucigalpa
Language: Spanish

El Salvador
Area: 8,124 sq mi
(21,041 sq km)
Population: 5,800,000
Capital: San Salvador
Language: Spanish

Nicaragua
Area: 50,193 sq mi
(130,000 sq km)
Population: 4,800,000
Capital: Managua
Language: Spanish

Belize
Area: 8,867 sq mi
(22,965 sq km)
Population: 200,000
Capital: Belmopan
Language: English

Guatemala
Area: 42,042 sq mi
(108,889 sq km)
Population: 11,600,000
Capital: Guatemala
Language: Spanish

Panama
Area: 29,762 sq mi
(77,082 sq km)
Population: 2,800,000
Capital: Panamá
Language: Spanish

0

0

Azimuthal Equidista

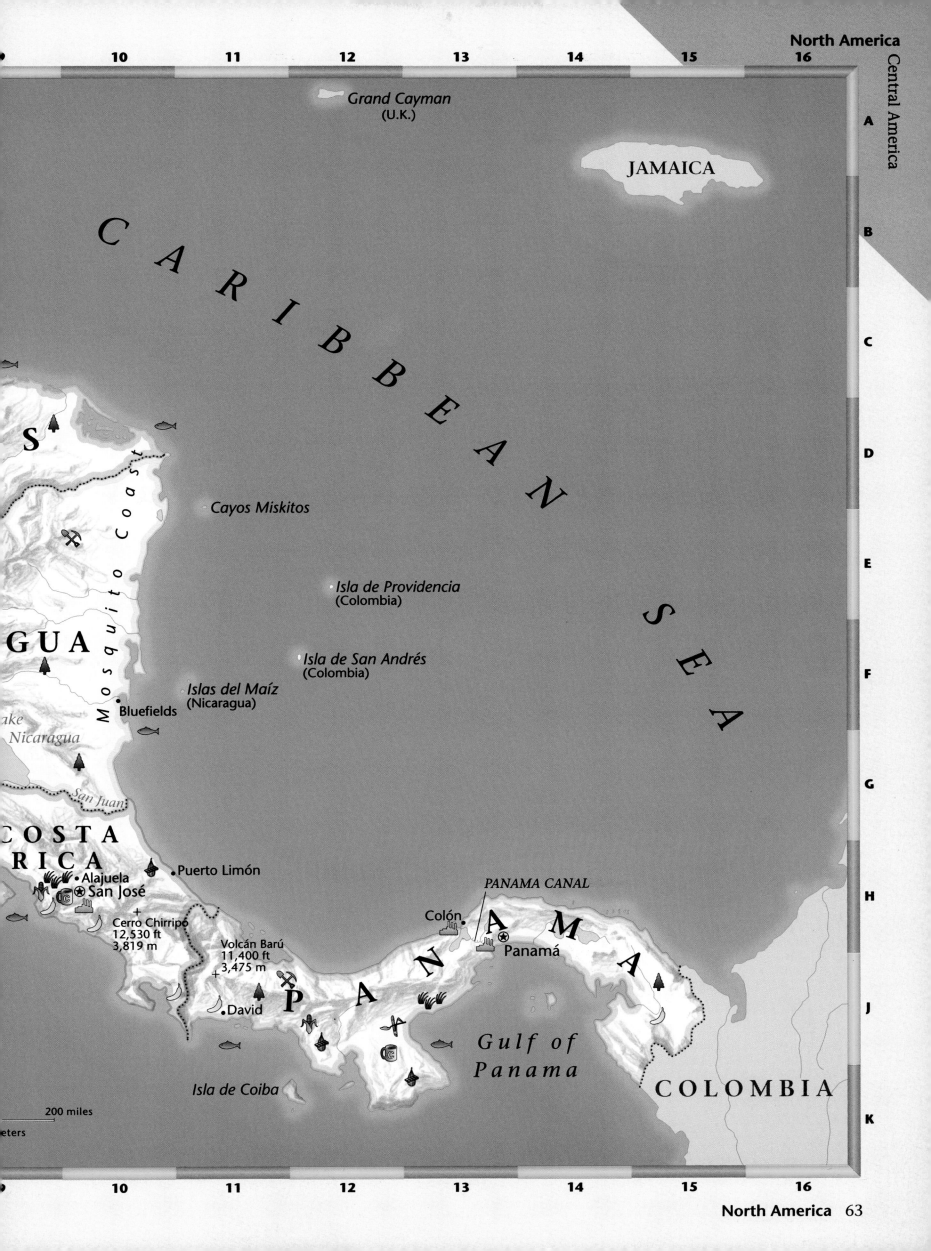

10 11 12 13 14 15 16

Grand Cayman
(U.K.)

JAMAICA

C A R I B B E A N

S E A

S

Mosquito Coast

Cayos Miskitos

Isla de Providencia
(Colombia)

GUA

Isla de San Andrés
(Colombia)

Islas del Maíz
(Nicaragua)

Bluefields

ake
Nicaragua

San Juan

COSTA
RICA

Puerto Limón

Alajuela
San José

Cerro Chirripó
12,530 ft
3,819 m

Volcán Barú
11,400 ft
3,475 m

David

PANAMA CANAL

Colón

Panamá

P A N A M A

Gulf of
Panama

COLOMBIA

Isla de Coiba

200 miles

eters

10 11 12 13 14 15 16

South Am

The coast of South America stretches straight to the horizon in this unusual view showing south at the top and west at the right edge of the page. Flowing along the coast is the cold Peru current, which creates rich fishing grounds. The hammerhead-shaped cape (far right) harbors the Chilean port of Antofagasta. The town exports nitrates and copper mined in the Atacama Desert (far right along the coast). East, under the puffed clouds, lie the Andean mountains, and beyond them the Pampas, the grassy lowlands of Argentina. South America—from the Atacama Desert to the enormous Amazon rain forest—has a vast range of landscapes. Much of the land is still wilderness.

Salt deposits stretch as far as the eye can see in Chile's Atacama Desert, the world's driest place. A cold Pacific current brings fog—but almost no rain—to the desert.

CONNECTION: *You can find the southern tip of South America and the Atacama Desert on the maps on pages 66–67 and 78–79.*

erica

A   1   2   3   4   5   6   7   8

ATLANTIC

OCEAN

São Francisco

B

R

A

Z

I

L

C

Tocantins

Marajó
Island

D

BRAZILIAN

FRENCH
GUIANA

Xingu

SURINAME

E

Amazon

GUYANA

Teles Pires

MATO GROSSO
PLATEAU

HIGHLANDS

Angel Falls
Total drop
3,212 feet, 979 meters

Tapajós

Paraguay

Paraguay

GUIANA HIGHLANDS

B

R

PARAGUAY

F

VENEZUELA

Madeira

A

CHACO

Orinoco

S

LLANOS

A

S

I

BOLIVIA

G

Negro

M

e

N

Salar de Uyuni

A

l

CARIBBEAN SEA

Z

v

Purus

Atacama Dese

Amazon

O

a

Lake
Titicaca

COLOMBIA

N

s

Lake
Maracaibo

H

Ucayali

P

E

R

U

A

N

Marañón

D

J

A

ECUADOR

N

E

S

NORTH
AMERICA

K

Malpelo I.

1   2   3   4   5   6   7   8

South America

Andes and Amazon

South America is a midsize continent that stretches far to the south. It runs from the warm Caribbean Sea, north of the Equator, almost to Antarctica, some 4,700 miles (7,560 kilometers) in all. The Andes, the earth's longest continental mountain chain, run the length of the continent. The Atacama Desert is squeezed between the mountains and the Pacific Ocean. In the north, waters from the eastern slopes of the Andes drain into the mighty Amazon River and its tributaries. Moving south, the Amazon rain forest gives way to grassy plains called the Pampas. Even farther south, the dry plateau region of Patagonia lies in a rain shadow created by the Andes.

The Land

Area
6,880,454 sq mi
(17,819,000 sq km)

Highest mountain
Aconcagua (Argentina):
22,834 ft (6,960 m)

Lowest point
Valdés Peninsula (Argentina):
131 ft (40 m) below
sea level

Longest river
Amazon: 4,000 mi
(6,437 km)

Largest lake
Lake Titicaca (Bolivia-Peru):
3,200 sq mi (8,287 sq km)

Highest waterfall
Angel Falls (Venezuela):
3,212 ft (979 m)

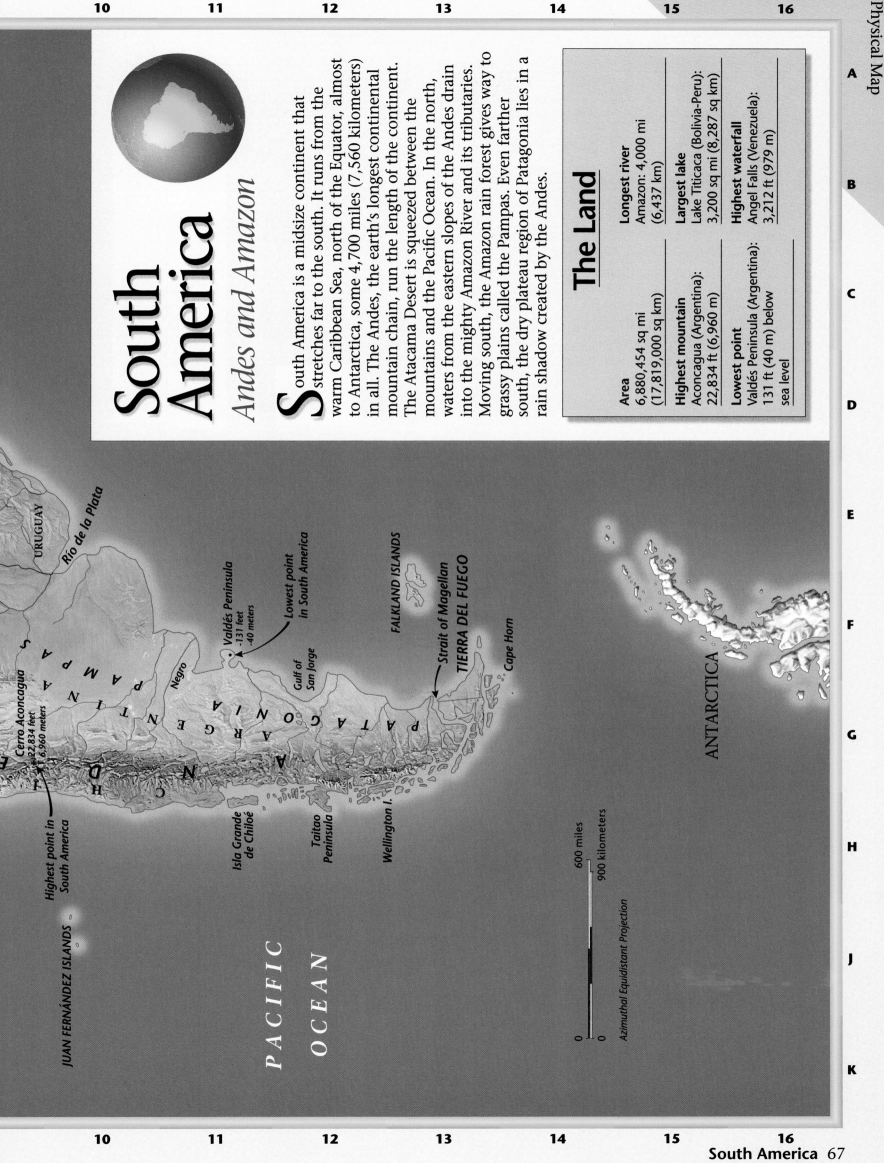

URUGUAY

Río de la Plata

PAMPAS

Cerro Aconcagua
22,834 feet
6,960 meters

*Highest point in
South America*

Negro

ARGENTINA

ANDES

JUAN FERNÁNDEZ ISLANDS

PACIFIC
OCEAN

Isla Grande
de Chiloé

Taitao
Peninsula

Wellington I.

PATAGONIA

Valdés Peninsula
-131 feet
-40 meters

*Lowest point
in South America*

Gulf of
San Jorge

FALKLAND ISLANDS

Strait of Magellan
TIERRA DEL FUEGO

Cape Horn

ANTARCTICA

600 miles

900 kilometers

0

0

Azimuthal Equidistant Projection

South America

A Mix of Old and New Worlds

Spanish conquistadors, searching for gold, arrived in what is now Peru in 1532. Determined to vanquish the native Inca, they found that much of their work had been done for them. Diseases brought from Europe had already killed so many Indians that a handful of Spaniards was able to conquer an entire empire. The ruins of ancient Indian cities today draw tourists from all over the world. Most present-day Indians still live in the Andes, although some seek jobs in the crowded cities.

Spain colonized the land except for Brazil, which was settled by the Portuguese. Most of South America's countries have now been independent for close to 200 years. Colonists brought thousands of enslaved Africans to lands along the Atlantic coast. Today these countries reflect a diverse ethnic mix. Brazil, in particular, shows its African heritage in a rich array of music, dance, religion, and food.

South America is home to the Amazon rain forest, one of the most important ecosystems on earth. Loggers, miners, and ranchers clear huge areas of forest every month. Alarmed governments and citizens worldwide are working to find ways to save this rain forest, its plants and creatures.

▶ **GRACEFUL** *buildings from the early 19th century house modern businesses—including the stock exchange—in Santiago. The city is the capital and economic center of Chile.*

▲ **A BREAKFAST** *drink beloved around the globe will be brewed from this bucketful of Colombian coffee beans. Colombia and Brazil are the world's leading producers of coffee.*

▲ **LOST CITY OF THE INCA** *is the name visitors gave to Machu Picchu, discovered in 1911. These ruins high in the Peruvian Andes may once have been a place of worship.*

▼ **A THREE-TOED SLOTH** *cradles its young. Sloths are found in the forests of Central and South America. In the wet climate, algae grow on their fur, tinting it green.*

▲ **BUNDLES OF TOTORA** *reeds lashed together make a fishing boat on Lake Titicaca, in the Andes. At 12,500 feet (3,810 meters), the lake is the highest in the world that ships can navigate.*

▲ **DESCENDANT OF** *the ancient Inca, a Peruvian Indian carries her child and leads a llama. Llamas are traditional Andean beasts of burden.*

▲ **THE QUICK,** *graceful margay lives in the rain forest of South America. The tree-climbing wild cat, whose dappled fur helps it hide in the leafy shadows, is not much bigger than a small dog. Demand for the margay's handsome coat has helped make it a threatened species.*

▶ **MODERN** *buildings in Bogotá, Colombia, stand tall above the banking district. Northernmost country in the Andes, Colombia borders both the Pacific Ocean and the Caribbean Sea.*

◀ **LAYERS OF GREEN** *make up the lush Amazon rain forest. Different kinds of plants and animals have adapted to life at each layer. Home to nearly half of the earth's plant and animal species, the Amazon is being cleared (above) to make room for people. More than half of the nine million residents of the forest live in booming cities on cleared land.*

▶ **THRILL-SEEKERS** *wearing parachutes dive from the top of Venezuela's Angel Falls, the world's highest waterfall. Ecotourism (visiting a place to see and help conserve its environment) is an important new business in South America.*

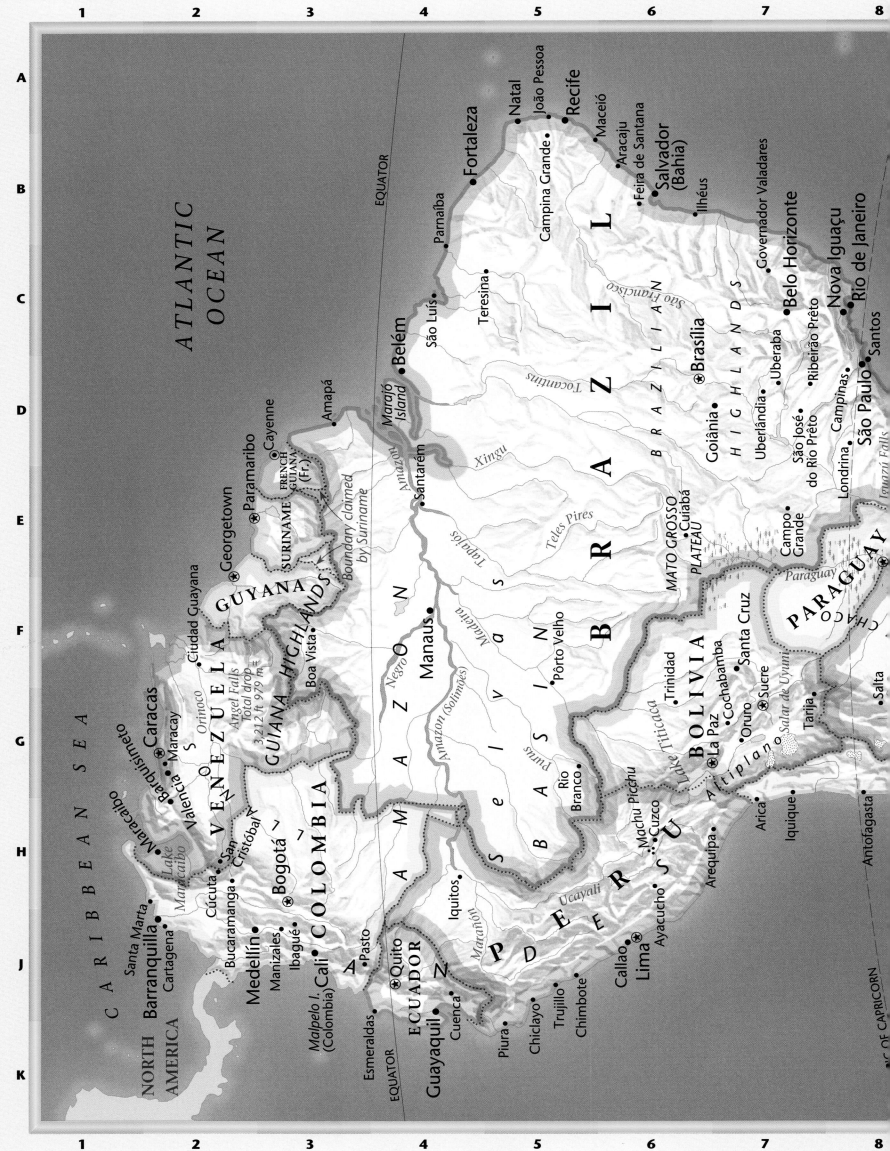

South America

A Colonial Heritage

Just 12 countries—and a French dependency, French Guiana—make up all of South America. Brazil, alone, takes up half the continent and accounts for half its people. Brazil was the only part of South America that was not given to Spain by the Treaty of Tordesillas in 1494. Claimed by Portugal, it is now the world's largest Portuguese-speaking country. Spanish is the dominant language throughout the rest of the continent. After most of South America's countries became independent, many were governed by dictators who controlled national wealth. Development led to huge foreign debts and inflation. Today, democracy is taking hold and economies, particularly Chile's and Argentina's, are improving.

The People

Population
299,900,000

Largest metropolitan areas
São Paulo, Brazil:
Pop. 16,800,000
Buenos Aires, Argentina:
Pop. 11,900,000

Largest country
Brazil: 3,286,488 sq mi
(8,511,347 sq km)

Most densely populated country
Ecuador: 110 people
per sq mi

Economy
Farming: cattle, coffee, fruit
Industry: textiles, mining

Life expectancy
68 years

A
B
C
D
E
F
G
H
J
K

PACIFIC
OCEAN

ANTARCTICA

JUAN FERNÁNDEZ IS.
(Chile)

Coquimbo
Cerro Aconcagua 22,834 ft
6,960 m
Valparaíso
Santiago
Talca
Concepción
Temuco
Puerto Montt
Isla Grande
de Chiloé
Taitao
Peninsula
Wellington I.
Córdoba
Mendoza
Santa
Fe
Rosario
Buenos
Aires
La Plata
URUGUAY
Montevideo
Río de la Plata
Mar del Plata
Bahía Blanca
Viedma
Negro
-131 ft
-40 m
Valdés Peninsula
Comodoro Rivadavia
Golfo
San Jorge
FALKLAND ISLANDS
(ISLAS MALVINAS)
(U.K.)
Stanley
Río Gallegos
Strait of Magellan
TIERRA DEL FUEGO
Ushuaia
Cape Horn
Punta Arenas
CHILE
ARGENTINA
PATAGONIA
Santa María
Uruguay

600 miles
900 kilometers
0
0

Azimuthal Equidistant Projection

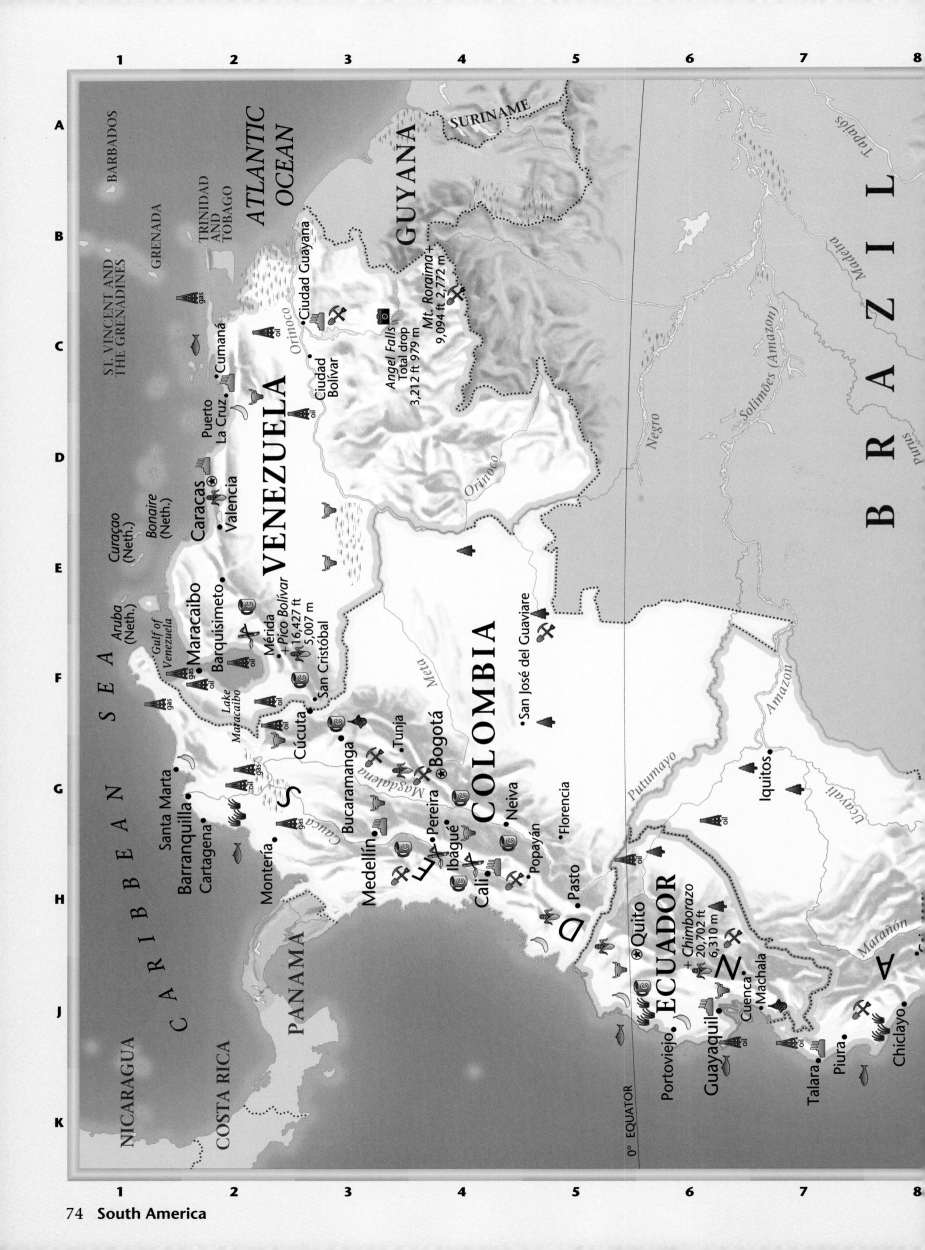

A

B

BARBADOS

ST. VINCENT AND THE GRENADINES

GRENADA

TRINIDAD AND TOBAGO

ATLANTIC OCEAN

SURINAME

GUYANA

B R A Z I L

Tapajós

Madeira

C

Cumaná•

Puerto La Cruz•

Ciudad Guayana•

Orinoco

Ciudad Bolívar•

Mt. Roraima+ 9,094 ft 2,772 m

Angel Falls Total drop 3,212 ft 979 m

Negro

Solimões (Amazon)

Purus

D

Caracas⊛

Valencia•

VENEZUELA

Orinoco

B R A Z I L

E

Curaçao (Neth.)

Bonaire (Neth.)

Maracaibo•

Barquisimeto•

Mérida•

+Pico Bolívar 16,427 ft 5,007 m

Meta

F

Aruba (Neth.)

Gulf of Venezuela

Lake Maracaibo

San Cristóbal•

Cúcuta•

San José del Guaviare•

Amazon

Ucayali

C A R I B B E A N   S E A

G

Santa Marta•

Barranquilla•

Cartagena•

Montería•

Bucaramanga•

•Tunja

Bogotá⊛

COLOMBIA

Neiva•

Florencia•

Putumayo

Iquitos•

Magdalena

Cauca

H

PANAMA

Medellín•

Pereira•

Ibagué•

Cali•

Popayán•

Pasto•

Quito⊛

+Chimborazo 20,702 ft 6,310 m

Marañón

J

NICARAGUA

COSTA RICA

Portoviejo•

Guayaquil•

ECUADOR

Cuenca•

Machala•

Talara•

Piura•

Chiclayo•

K

0° EQUATOR

A
B
C
D
E
F
G
H
J
K

PARAGUAY

Paraguay

BRAZIL

URU.

Uruguay

Paraná

Paraná

ARGENTINA

CHILE

Guaporé

BOLIVIA

•Trinidad

Mamoré

•Santa Cruz

oil

oil

•Cochabamba

✦Sucre

Potosí

•Tarija

•Oruro

La Paz

Nevado Sajama
21,463 ft
6,542 m

A N D E S

Madre de Dios

Madre de Dios

Juruena

•Machu Picchu

•Cuzco

Lake
Titicaca

•Arequipa

PERU

•Huancayo

Apurímac

•Ica

•Lima

Callao•

PACIFIC
OCEAN

TROPIC OF CAPRICORN

400 miles

400 kilometers

0
0

Azimuthal Equidistant Projection

Northwestern South America

This region, except for oil-rich Venezuela, is dominated by the Andes. Andean mines produce most of the world's emeralds. Much of the world's coffee grows on Andean slopes.

Ecuador
Area: 109,484 sq mi
(283,561 sq km)
Population: 12,000,000
Capital: Quito
Language: Spanish

Peru
Area: 496,225 sq mi
(1,285,220 sq km)
Population: 24,400,000
Capital: Lima
Languages: Quechua,Spanish

Venezuela
Area: 352,144 sq mi
(912,050 sq km)
Population: 22,600,000
Capital: Caracas
Language: Spanish

Bolivia
Area: 424,164 sq mi
(1,098,581 sq km)
Population: 7,800,000
Capitals: La Paz, Sucre
Languages: Aymara,
Quechua, Spanish

Colombia
Area: 439,737 sq mi
(1,138,914 sq km)
Population: 38,600,000
Capital: Bogotá
Language: Spanish

orgetown
Paramaribo
Cayenne
URINAME
FRENCH
GUIANA
(France)

undary claimed
by Suriname
Macapá

Amazon
Marajó
Island
Belém

Santarém
São Luís
Parnaíba

Imperatriz
Teresina
Fortaleza

Natal

João Pessoa

Recife
Juàzeiro
Maceió

B R A Z I L
Aracaju

Feira de Santana

Salvador (Bahia)

Vitória da Conquista

Cuiabá
Brasília

Goiânia

Governador Valadares
Uberlândia

Belo Horizonte
Vitória
Campo
Grande
Ribeirão Prêto

Juiz de Fora
Londrina
Rio de Janeiro
São Paulo
São José dos Campos
Iguazú
Falls
Santos

Curitiba

Joinvile

Uruguay

Santa Maria
Pôrto Alegre
Patos
Lagoon
Pelotas
RUGUAY

Xingu
Tocantins
Araguaia
São Francisco
Teles Pires
Tapajós

Northeastern South America

This region has both the world's largest rain forest and its largest river by volume, the Amazon. Rich mines bring wealth but threaten local cultures and the environment.

Brazil
Area: 3,286,488 sq mi
(8,511,347 sq km)
Population: 160,300,000
Capital: Brasília
Language: Portuguese

Guyana
Area: 83,000 sq mi
(214,969 sq km)
Population: 800,000
Capital: Georgetown
Language: English

Suriname
Area: 63,037 sq mi
(163,265 sq km)
Population: 400,000
Capital: Paramaribo
Language: Dutch

French Guiana (France)

A T L A N T I C

O C E A N

1 2 3 4 5 6 7 8

BRAZIL

OCEAN

Patos Lagoon

Iguazú Falls

Concepción

Ciudad del Este

Posadas

URUGUAY

Montevideo

PARAGUAY

Asunción

Villarrica

Corrientes

Salto

Paraguay

Formosa

Resistencia

Paraná

Santa Fe

Paraná

Río de

La Plata

Buenos Aires

La Plata

BOLIVIA

Mamoré

Rosario

A

San Miguel
de Tucumán

Santiago
del Estero

N

Córdoba

T

I

M

Salta

oil

San Juan

Cerro Aconcagua
22,834 ft 6,960 m

Mendoza

gas

oil

Lake
Titicaca

A N D E S

ATACAMA DESERT

PERU

Arica

Iquique

Antofagasta

La Serena

Valparaíso

Santiago

A
T

TROPIC OF CAPRICORN

OCEAN

1 2 3 4 5 6 7 8

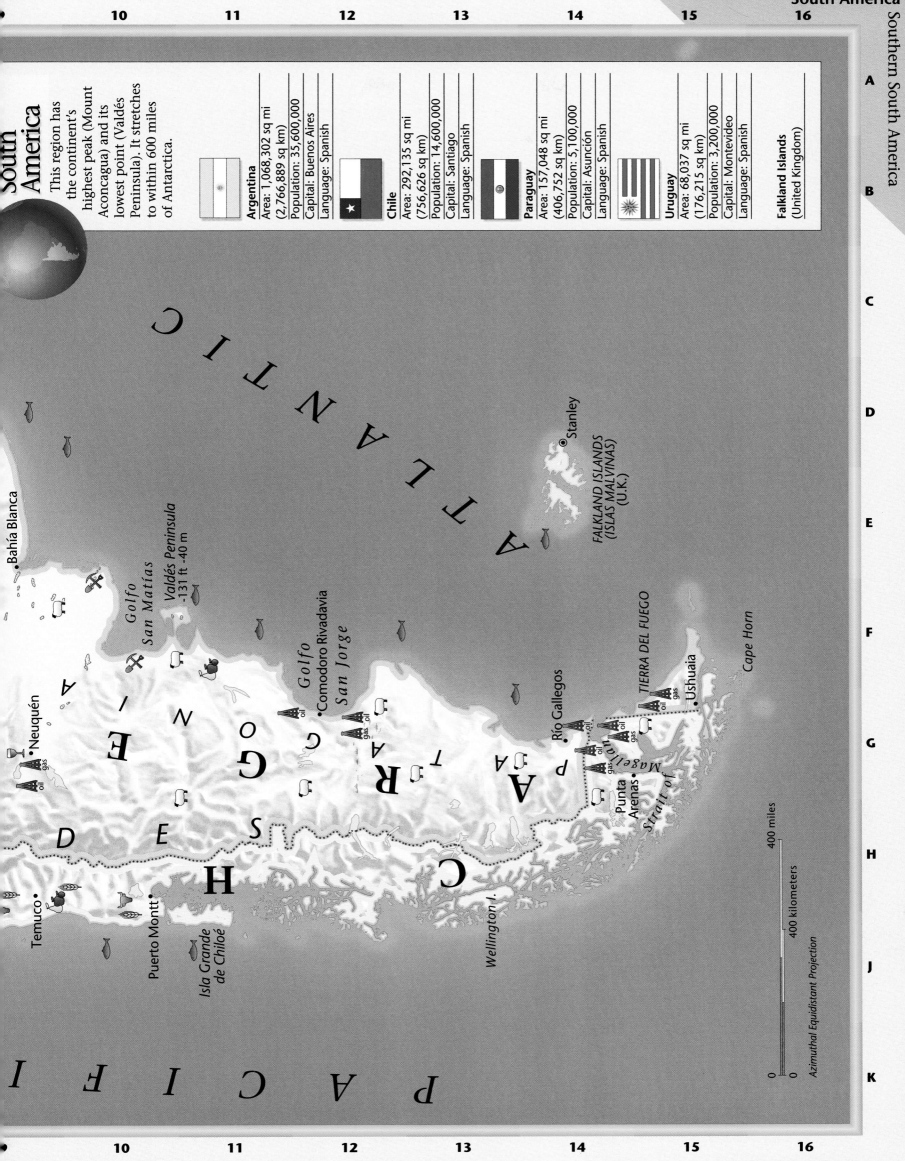

South America

This region has the continent's highest peak (Mount Aconcagua) and its lowest point (Valdés Peninsula). It stretches to within 600 miles of Antarctica.

Argentina
Area: 1,068,302 sq mi
(2,766,889 sq km)
Population: 35,600,000
Capital: Buenos Aires
Language: Spanish

Chile
Area: 292,135 sq mi
(756,626 sq km)
Population: 14,600,000
Capital: Santiago
Language: Spanish

Paraguay
Area: 157,048 sq mi
(406,752 sq km)
Population: 5,100,000
Capital: Asunción
Language: Spanish

Uruguay
Area: 68,037 sq mi
(176,215 sq km)
Population: 3,200,000
Capital: Montevideo
Language: Spanish

Falkland Islands
(United Kingdom)

ATLANTIC

PACIFIC

Bahía Blanca

Golfo San Matías

Valdés Peninsula
-131 ft -40 m

Neuquén
oil
gas

ANDES

Golfo San Jorge
Comodoro Rivadavia
oil
gas
oil

Temuco

Puerto Montt

Isla Grande de Chiloé

Wellington I.

PATAGONIA

Stanley

FALKLAND ISLANDS
(ISLAS MALVINAS)
(U.K.)

TIERRA DEL FUEGO

Cape Horn

Río Gallegos
oil

Ushuaia
oil
gas

Punta Arenas

Strait of Magellan
gas

400 miles

400 kilometers

Azimuthal Equidistant Projection

Europe

The island of Sicily dwarfs the toe of the boot-shaped peninsula of Italy, which juts into the blue waters of the Mediterranean Sea. The Strait of Messina separates island from mainland. Just west of the strait on Sicily, a white plume of smoke reveals the location of the volcano Mount Etna. Long before geologists understood plate tectonics, Greek storytellers explained Etna's rumblings as roars from a monster, Typhon, imprisoned in the volcano by the god Zeus.

Although it is a relatively small continent, Europe has had an enormous influence on the rest of the globe, culturally and politically. Because most countries border the sea along Europe's many peninsulas, these nations have ready access to the outside world.

Snow-covered Mount Etna lets off steam behind the elegant buildings of Taormina, in eastern Sicily. Etna is the highest active volcano in Europe.

CONNECTION: *You can find Sicily and the "boot" of Italy on the maps on pages 82–83 and 92–93.*

Europe
Land of Long Coasts

Europe is a small continent—only Australia is smaller—with a great range of landscapes. Its most marked feature is its irregular coastline, cut with inlets, bays, and peninsulas, great and small. Rocky highlands, scrubbed by glaciers, cover Europe's northwestern edge. The Alps form a chain across southern Europe, blocking cold northern winds from the mild Mediterranean region. In the east, the Ural Mountains separate Europe and Asia. The continent has a number of great navigable rivers, including the Danube, Rhine, Volga, and Rhône.

The Land

Area
4,066,241 sq mi
(10,530,750 sq km)

Highest mountain
El'brus (Russia): 18,510 ft
(5,642 m)

Lowest point
Caspian Sea: 92 ft (28 m)
below sea level

Longest river
Volga (Russia): 2,290 mi
(3,685 km)

Largest lake
Ladoga (Russia): 6,853 sq mi
(17,703 sq km)

Largest island
Great Britain: 84,215 sq mi
(218,100 sq km)

0 ____ 600 miles
0 ____ 900 kilometers
Azimuthal Equidistant Projection

Jan Mayen

ICELAND
Vatnajökull

NORWEGIAN

Faroe Islands

Shetland Islands

Outer Hebrides

Orkney Islands

BRITISH ISLES

Highlands

NORTH SEA

ATLANTIC OCEAN

UNITED

IRELAND   IRISH SEA   Great Britain

KINGDOM

NETH.

English Channel   BELGIUM   GER.

LUX.

Brittany   Rhine

Seine

Loire   FRANCE   Danu

Bay of Biscay   Mont Blanc
15,771 feet
4,807 meters   SWITZ. LIECH.

Massif Central   Rhône   A L

Cantabrian Mountains   Pyrenees   MONACO   Riviera   SAN M

Douro   ANDORRA

Tagus   IBERIAN   Ebro

PORTUGAL   SPAIN   Corsica

PENINSULA   VATIC

Baetic Mountains   Balearic Islands   Sardinia

Strait of Gibraltar   M   TYRR

E

D   Sic

I

T

AFRICA

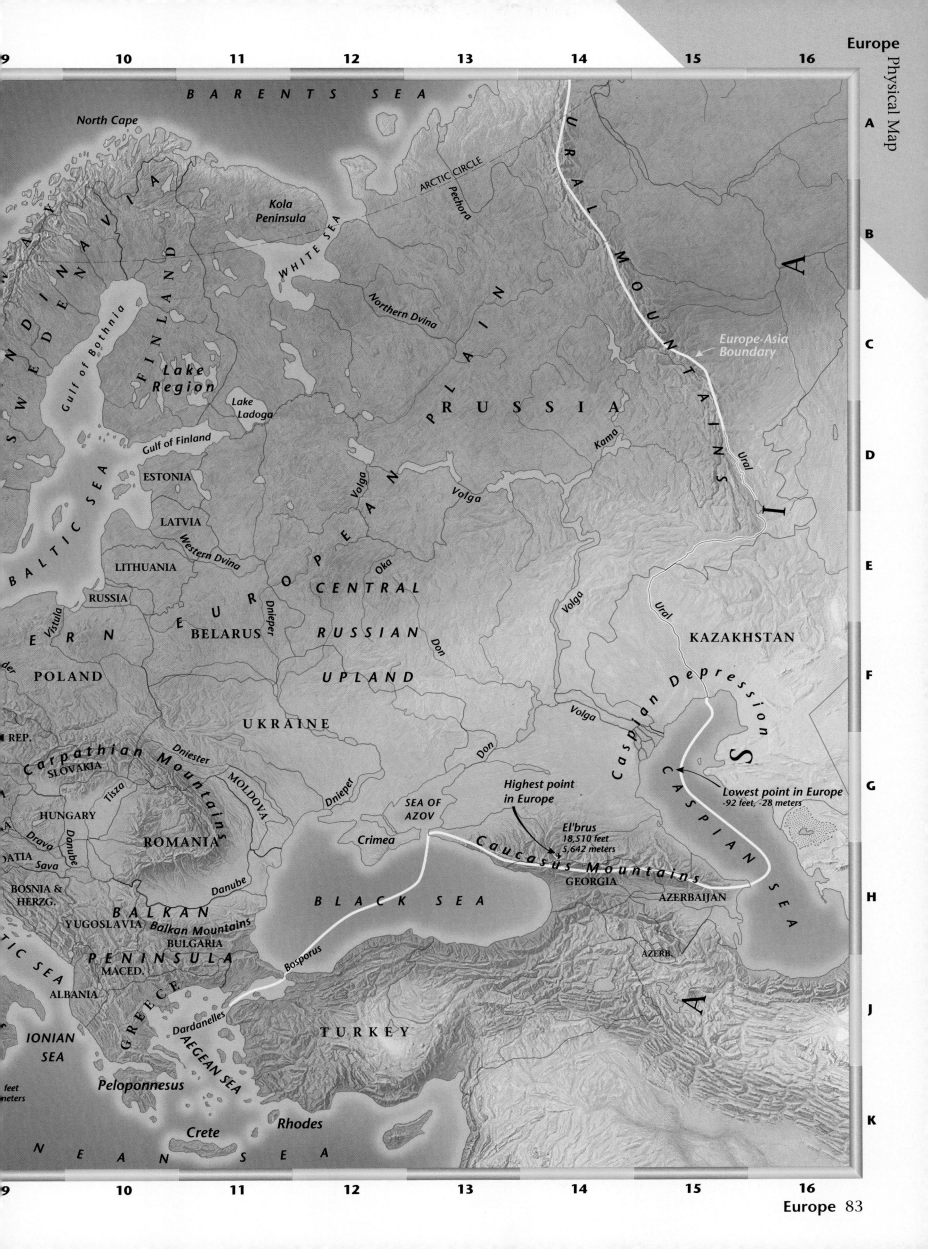

BARENTS SEA

North Cape

Kola
Peninsula

ARCTIC CIRCLE

Pechora

URAL MOUNTAINS

*Europe-Asia
Boundary*

WHITE SEA

Northern Dvina

SCANDINAVIA

SWEDEN

FINLAND

Gulf of
Bothnia

Lake
Region

Lake
Ladoga

EUROPEAN PLAIN

RUSSIA

Kama

Ural

Gulf of Finland

BALTIC SEA

ESTONIA

Volga

Volga

LATVIA

Western Dvina

Dnieper

LITHUANIA

RUSSIA

Oka

CENTRAL

Volga

Ural

KAZAKHSTAN

Vistula

EUROPEAN

BELARUS

RUSSIAN

Don

POLAND

UPLAND

der

UKRAINE

Volga

Caspian Depression

REP.

Carpathian Mountains

Dniester

Don

SLOVAKIA

MOLDOVA

Tisza

Dnieper

CASPIAN SEA

HUNGARY

ROMANIA

SEA OF
AZOV

**Highest point
in Europe**

Lowest point in Europe
-92 feet, -28 meters

Drava

Danube

Crimea

El'brus
18,510 feet
5,642 meters

S

Sava

Danube

Caucasus Mountains

BOSNIA &
HERZG.

BLACK SEA

GEORGIA

AZERBAIJAN

BALKAN

YUGOSLAVIA

Balkan Mountains

AZERB.

BULGARIA

PENINSULA

MACED.

ALBANIA

Bosporus

TIC SEA

GREECE

Dardanelles

TURKEY

IONIAN
SEA

AEGEAN SEA

Peloponnesus

N

Crete

Rhodes

EAN SEA

feet
meters

Europe
Cultural Colossus

Twenty-five hundred years ago in a tiny European city-state no bigger than Buffalo, New York, is today, an extraordinary flowering of the arts and sciences occurred. The place was Athens, in ancient Greece. The arts and sciences developed there—and along with later Roman additions—have had a deep influence on Western civilization as we know it today. Europe enjoyed a second period of enlightenment during the Renaissance. In that era, from the 14th to the 17th century, ideas from the ancient Greeks were revived, and arts and sciences had a rebirth.

Present-day Europe benefits from this cultural heritage. Many areas are like living museums. Beautiful old buildings bustle with people who live and work there, often in high-tech industries. Setting aside historic rivalries, many European nations are becoming a united economic force by joining the European Union, first established in 1987. These countries face the challenge of making the former communist countries of Eastern Europe part of the industrialized West.

▼ **FOOTBALL EUROPEAN** *style is what's known as soccer in the United States and Canada.*

◀ **THE FAIRY-TALE CASTLE**
*of Neuschwanstein, built for
"Mad" King Ludwig, rises above
the Bavarian Alps, in southern
Germany. Castles, once the
homes and fortresses of kings
and nobles, can
be found
throughout
Europe.*

▼ **GIRLS AT A WEDDING**
*in Bavaria, Germany's largest
state, wear traditional dresses
and flowering wreaths.*

▲ **BUILT FOR SPEED,** *a Eurostar train waits in a Paris
train station for its next trip to London. Eurostar trains
travel between France and England via a tunnel—
known as the Chunnel—under the English Channel.
The high-speed trains can reach 100 miles per hour
(160 kilometers per hour) during the three-hour journey.*

▲ **HOW MANY RUBLES FOR A HAMBURGER?** *Moscow,
the Russian capital, shows signs of foreign influence. In
the early 1990s, after the breakup of the Soviet Union,
Russia began to open up to outside businesses.*

▲ **THE JAGGED PEAK** of the Matterhorn towers above the town of Zermatt, in the Swiss Alps. Not conquered until 1865, the mountain has sent many climbers to their deaths. The Alps owe their sharp angles to glacial erosion and their geologic youth.

◄ **EUROPE'S** largest Christian church, St. Peter's Basilica, forms the heart of the world's smallest independent nation—Vatican City— which is completely surrounded by Rome.

▲ **FLOWERS BLOOM** on a barge in Amsterdam, capital of the Netherlands. Canals throughout the country provide watery highways and drain the land, most of which is at or below sea level.

◀ **TREASURES OF THE ART WORLD** *grace the Uffizi Museum in Florence, the Italian city that is known as the birthplace of the Renaissance. Artists such as Michelangelo and Raphael created their masterpieces and inspired others during this period.*

▲ **TURRETS, TOWERS,** *and domes rise above Prague, the historic capital of the Czech Republic. Eastern European countries such as this one are changing and modernizing after years of communist rule.*

▶ **DRESSED FOR A FESTIVE** *occasion, this Greek boy wears his country's national costume. Day-to-day, most Europeans wear modern clothes.*

▲ **A BOUNTIFUL HARVEST** *of grapes fills a wagon in a vineyard in Tuscany, one of the 20 self-governing regions that make up Italy. Fertile soil and mild winters make parts of Italy and other Mediterranean countries ideal for farming.*

▲ **WEARING** *tall hats known as toques, a small army of chefs works furiously in a restaurant in Roanne, France. The French are known around the world for their fine cooking.*

▼ **A MYSTERIOUS STONE CIRCLE** *built in ancient times, Stonehenge is one of the most famous sites in England. Stonehenge may have been constructed as an early astronomical observatory.*

Europe
East Meets West Today

Europe is home to the world's third largest population: 728 million people live in 43 countries. The continent is commonly divided into eastern and western regions. Eastern Europe, which includes countries that were once part of or controlled by the former Soviet Union, extends roughly from Poland to Greece and east to the Caspian Sea and Ural Mountains. Western Europe, which includes the wealthy nations of the European Union and their neighbors, stretches to the Atlantic Ocean. No longer divided by political systems, the two regions can work together to solve common problems.

The People

Population
728,000,000

Largest metropolitan areas
Paris, France: Pop. 9,600,000
Moscow, Russia: Pop. 9,300,000
London, England: Pop. 7,600,000

Largest country
Ukraine: 233,206 sq mi
(604,000 sq km)

Most densely populated country
Monaco: 31,719 people
in 0.6 sq mi

Economy
Farming: vegetables, fruit, grains
Industry: chemicals, machinery

Life expectancy
73 years

9 10 11 12 13 14 15 16

North Cape
Hammerfest
Tromsø
Vadsø
Kirkenes
Pechenga
Barents Sea
Tobseda
Surgut
A
Narvik
Ivalo
D
Murmansk
ARCTIC CIRCLE
Pechora
Khanty Mansiysk
Kiruna
Kirovsk
Kola Peninsula
Ob
White Sea
Luleå
Kemi
Umba
Severodvinsk
Arkhangel'sk
Serov
B
Namsos
Oulu
Kem'
Syktyvkar
Nizhniy Tagil
ndheim
Umeå
Vaasa
Kuopio
Lake Onega
RUSSIA
Perm'
C
Åre
Pori
Tampere
Lake Ladoga
Yekaterinburg
Chelyabinsk
Sundsvall
Turku
Helsinki
St. Petersburg
Kirov
EUROPE-ASIA BOUNDARY
Stockholm
Uppsala
Tallinn
Novgorod
Yaroslavl'
Kazan'
Ufa
D
teborg
ESTONIA
Tver'
Nizhniy Novgorod
Gotland
Riga
LATVIA
Moscow
Orenburg
enhagen
Daugavpils
Samara
E
Malmö
Baltic Sea
LITHUANIA
Vitsyebsk
Smolensk
Ryazan'
Penza
Oral
Gdansk
RUSSIA
Vilnius
Saratov
Volga
KAZAKHSTAN
Berlin
Kaunas
Minsk
Bryansk
Ural
Bydgoszcz
BELARUS
Kursk
Volgograd
Atyrau
F
claw
Warsaw
Homyel'
Astrakhan'
POLAND
Chernihiy
Łódź
L'viv
Sumy
Kharkiv
CASPIAN
Prague
Kraków
Kiev
UKRAINE
Poltava
Donets'k
Rostov
CH REP.
Carpathian Mts.
Vinnytsya
Dnipropetrovs'k
nna
Dniester
SLOVAKIA
MOLDOVA
Stavropol'
G
Bratislava
Chisinau
Sea of Azov
SEA
Budapest
Odesa
Kerch
El'brus 18,510 ft 5,642 m
Groznyy
-92 ft -28 m
HUNGARY
Crimea
Caucasus Mountains
SLOVENIA
ROMANIA
Simferopol'
Zagreb
Belgrade
Bucharest
Yalta
GEORGIA
T'bilisi
AZERBAIJAN
Baku
H
CROATIA
Sevastopol'
BOSN. & HERZG.
YUG.
Danube
Constanta
BLACK SEA
Bat'umi
Gäncä
Sarajevo
Balkan Mts.
Varna
AZERB.
Sofia
BULGARIA
Trabzon
Tirana
Skopje
Istanbul
Bosporus
Samsun
Erzurum
Ionian Sea
MACED.
Thessaloníki
Zonguldak
Sivas
Bitlis
ALBANIA
Bursa
Ankara
ples
Dardanelles
Eskisehir
Kayseri
J
Messina
GREECE
Aegean Sea
Izmir
Konya
TURKEY
Mardin
atania
Pátrai
Adana
ALTA
Peloponnesus
Athens
Antioch
Kalámai
Antalya
Sea of Crete
Rhodes
Crete
Irákleion
0 600 miles
0 900 kilometers
K
Azimuthal Equidistant Projection

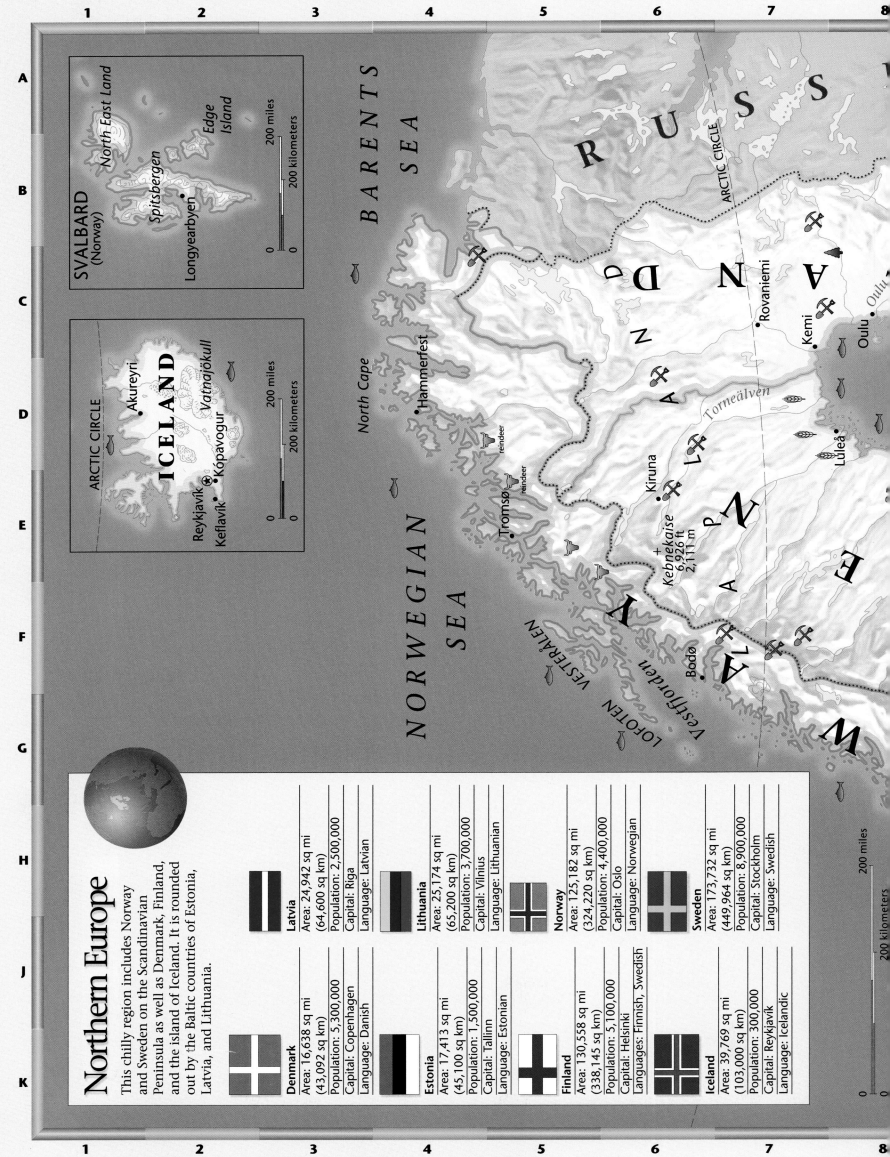

SVALBARD
(Norway)

North-East Land

Edge Island

Spitsbergen

Longyearbyen

200 miles

200 kilometers

0

0

ICELAND

ARCTIC CIRCLE

Akureyri

Vatnajökull

Reykjavík

Kópavogur

Keflavík

200 miles

200 kilometers

0

0

B A R E N T S   S E A

R U S S

F I N L A N D

ARCTIC CIRCLE

Rovaniemi

Kemi

Oulu

Oulu

North Cape

Hammerfest

Torneälven

reindeer

reindeer

Tromsø

Kiruna

Kebnekaise
6,926 ft
2,111 m

Luleå

N O R W E G I A N   S E A

L A P P L A N D

S W E

VESTERÅLEN

LOFOTEN

Vestfjorden

Bodø

N O R W A Y

Northern Europe

This chilly region includes Norway and Sweden on the Scandinavian Peninsula as well as Denmark, Finland, and the island of Iceland. It is rounded out by the Baltic countries of Estonia, Latvia, and Lithuania.

Latvia
Area: 24,942 sq mi
(64,600 sq km)
Population: 2,500,000
Capital: Riga
Language: Latvian

Lithuania
Area: 25,174 sq mi
(65,200 sq km)
Population: 3,700,000
Capital: Vilnius
Language: Lithuanian

Norway
Area: 125,182 sq mi
(324,220 sq km)
Population: 4,400,000
Capital: Oslo
Language: Norwegian

Sweden
Area: 173,732 sq mi
(449,964 sq km)
Population: 8,900,000
Capital: Stockholm
Language: Swedish

Denmark
Area: 16,638 sq mi
(43,092 sq km)
Population: 5,300,000
Capital: Copenhagen
Language: Danish

Estonia
Area: 17,413 sq mi
(45,100 sq km)
Population: 1,500,000
Capital: Tallinn
Language: Estonian

Finland
Area: 130,558 sq mi
(338,145 sq km)
Population: 5,100,000
Capital: Helsinki
Languages: Finnish, Swedish

Iceland
Area: 39,769 sq mi
(103,000 sq km)
Population: 300,000
Capital: Reykjavik
Language: Icelandic

200 miles

200 kilometers

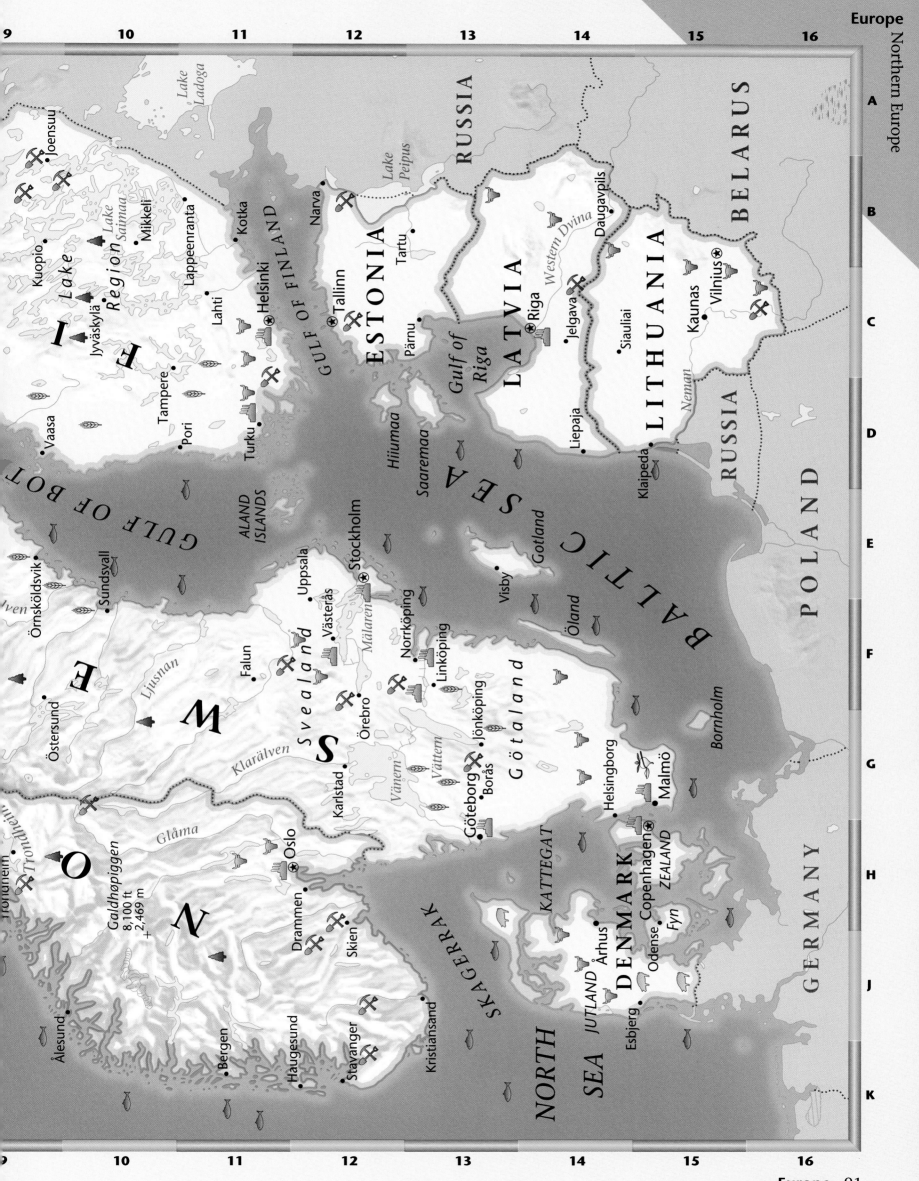

A
B
C
D
E
F
G
H
J
K

9 10 11 12 13 14 15 16

Lake Ladoga

Joensuu

Kuopio

Mikkeli

Lappeenranta

Jyväskylä

Lake Saimaa

Lake Region

F I N L A N D

Lahti

Kotka

Lake Peipus

Narva

RUSSIA

Tampere

Pori

Vaasa

Turku

Helsinki

GULF OF FINLAND

Tallinn

Tartu

ESTONIA

Pärnu

Hiiumaa

Saaremaa

BELARUS

Daugavpils

Western Dvina

Riga

Jelgava

LATVIA

Gulf of Riga

Siauliai

Vilnius

Kaunas

LITHUANIA

Neman

Liepaja

Klaipeda

RUSSIA

POLAND

GULF OF BOT

Örnsköldsvik

Sundsvall

Ljusnan

* Åland ISLANDS*

Stockholm

Uppsala

Västerås

Mälaren

Norrköping

Linköping

Visby

Gotland

Öland

BALTIC SEA

Bornholm

Östersund

Falun

S

Klarälven

Svealand

Örebro

Karlstad

Vänern

Vättern

Jönköping

Göteborg

Borås

Götaland

Helsingborg

Malmö

GERMANY

Trondheim

Galdhøpiggen
8,100 ft
+2,469 m

N

O

Glåma

Drammen

Oslo

Skien

SKAGERRAK

KATTEGAT

Helsingborg

Copenhagen

ZEALAND

Fyn

Odense

DENMARK

JUTLAND

Århus

Esbjerg

Ålesund

Bergen

Haugesund

Stavanger

Kristiansand

NORTH SEA

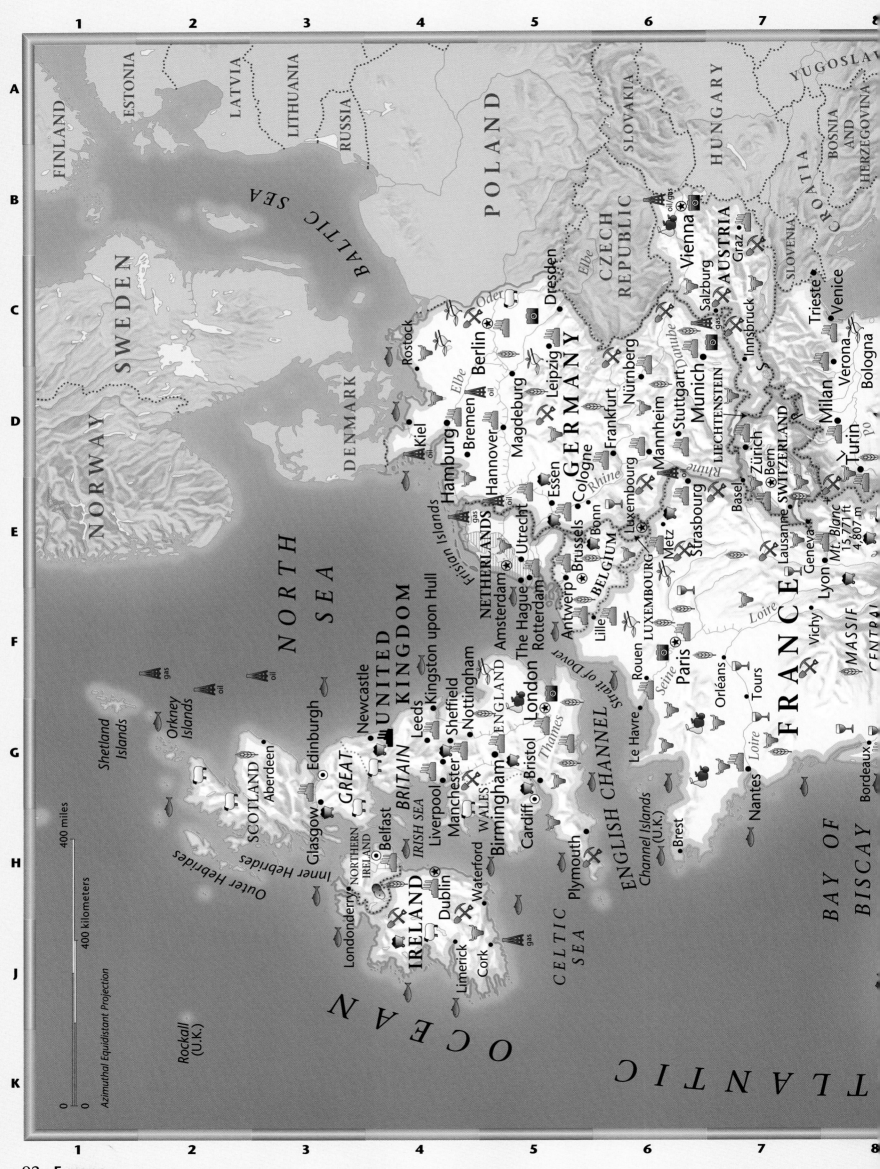

A B C D E F G H J K

1 2 3 4 5 6 7 8

FINLAND
ESTONIA
LATVIA
LITHUANIA
RUSSIA
POLAND
CZECH REPUBLIC
SLOVAKIA
HUNGARY
YUGOSLAV
CROATIA
BOSNIA AND HERZEGOVINA
SLOVENIA

NORWAY
SWEDEN
BALTIC SEA
DENMARK

Rostock
Kiel
Hamburg
Bremen
Hannover
Magdeburg
Berlin
Dresden
Leipzig
GERMANY
Frankfurt
Nürnberg
Essen
Cologne
Bonn
Mannheim
Stuttgart
Munich
Oder
Elbe
Elbe
Rhine
Rhine
Danube
Salzburg
Innsbruck
LIECHTENSTEIN
Vienna
AUSTRIA
Graz
Trieste
Venice
Verona
Milan
Bologna
Turin
Po

Frisian Islands
NETHERLANDS
Utrecht
Amsterdam
The Hague
Rotterdam
Antwerp
BELGIUM
Brussels
Lille
LUXEMBOURG
Luxembourg
Metz
Strasbourg
Basel
Zürich
Bern
SWITZERLAND
Lausanne
Geneva
Lyon
Mt. Blanc
15,771 ft
4,807 m
MASSIF
CENTRAL
Vichy

NORTH SEA

Shetland Islands
Orkney Islands
oil
gas
oil
gas

SCOTLAND
Aberdeen
Edinburgh
Glasgow
GREAT
BRITAIN
Newcastle
UNITED KINGDOM
Kingston upon Hull
Leeds
Sheffield
Nottingham
ENGLAND
London
Thames
Birmingham
WALES
Cardiff
Bristol
Manchester
Liverpool
Belfast
NORTHERN IRELAND
IRISH SEA
Outer Hebrides
Inner Hebrides
Londonderry
Dublin
IRELAND
Limerick
Cork
Waterford
gas
CELTIC SEA
Plymouth
Brest
Channel Islands (U.K.)
ENGLISH CHANNEL
Strait of Dover
Le Havre
Rouen
Paris
Seine
Orléans
Tours
Nantes
FRANCE
Loire
Loire
Bordeaux
BAY OF BISCAY

Rockall (U.K.)

ATLANTIC OCEAN

400 miles
400 kilometers
Azimuthal Equidistant Projection

oil/gas
oil
oil
oil
oil
oil
gas
gas

A
B
C
D
E
F
G
H
J
K

IONIAN SEA

Bari

Gulf of Taranto

Mt. Vesuvius
4,203 ft
1,281 m

Catania
Syracuse

Valletta

Naples

Messina

Rome

VATICAN CITY

SICILY

Palermo

MALTA

TYRRHENIAN SEA

MEDITERRANEAN SEA

CORSICA (France)

Ajaccio

SARDINIA (Italy)

Cagliari

TUNISIA

ALGERIA

MOR.

Barcelona

Minorca

Majorca
Palma

BALEARIC ISLANDS (Spain)

BALEARIC SEA

ANDORRA

Valencia

Cartagena

SPAIN

Valladolid

Zaragoza

Duero

Salamanca

Madrid

Toledo

SIERRA MORENA

Cordoba

Málaga

GIBRALTAR (U.K.)

Ceuta (Sp.)

Seville

Cádiz

Strait of Gibraltar

Tagus

Guadiana

Oporto

Duero

PORTUGAL

Coimbra

Lisbon

Western Europe

Crowded with countries large and small, western Europe contains most of the continent's wealthy, industrialized nations. Since the late 1980s, 15 countries have joined to form the European Union (EU). Its goal is to promote freer trade and economic unity throughout Europe.

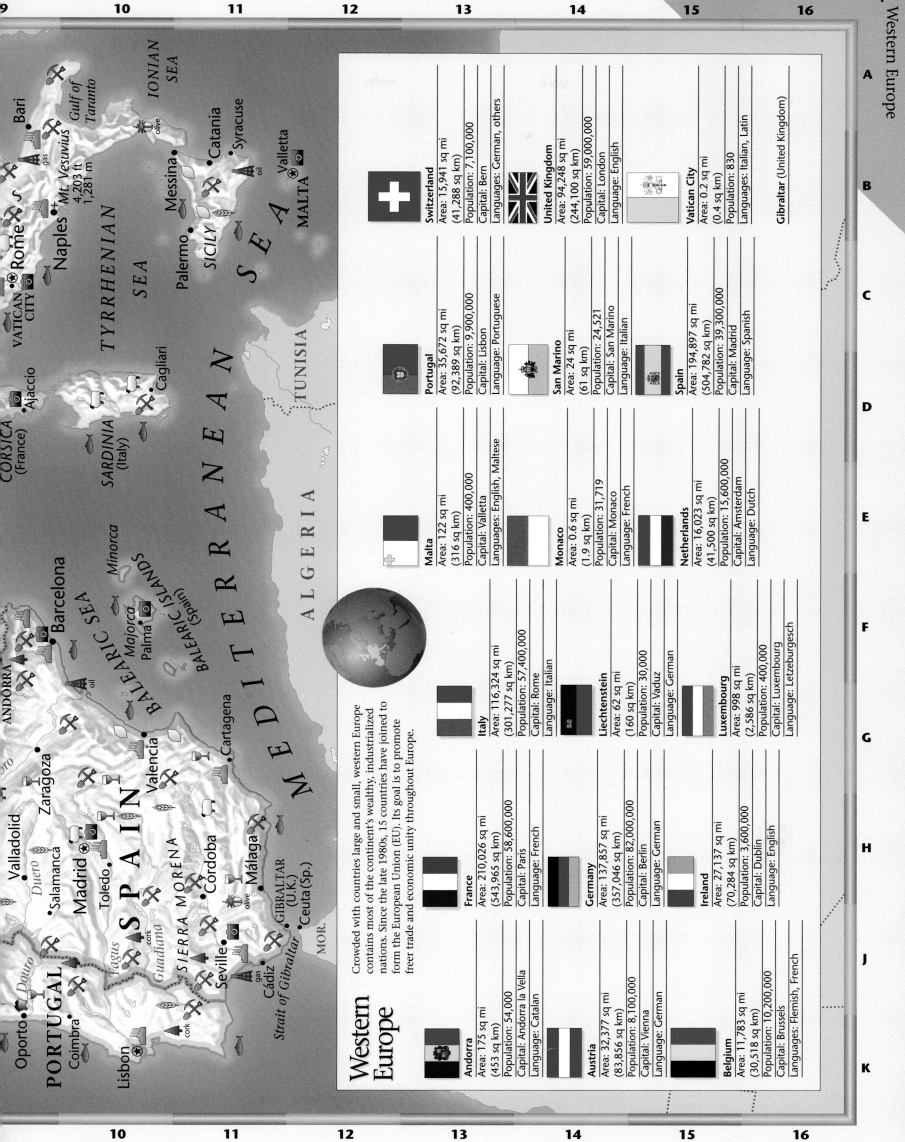

Switzerland
Area: 15,941 sq mi
(41,288 sq km)
Population: 7,100,000
Capital: Bern
Languages: German, others

United Kingdom
Area: 94,248 sq mi
(244,100 sq km)
Population: 59,000,000
Capital: London
Language: English

Vatican City
Area: 0.2 sq mi
(0.4 sq km)
Population: 830
Languages: Italian, Latin

Gibraltar (United Kingdom)

Portugal
Area: 35,672 sq mi
(92,389 sq km)
Population: 9,900,000
Capital: Lisbon
Language: Portuguese

San Marino
Area: 24 sq mi
(61 sq km)
Population: 24,521
Capital: San Marino
Language: Italian

Spain
Area: 194,897 sq mi
(504,782 sq km)
Population: 39,300,000
Capital: Madrid
Language: Spanish

Malta
Area: 122 sq mi
(316 sq km)
Population: 400,000
Capital: Valletta
Languages: English, Maltese

Monaco
Area: 0.6 sq mi
(1.9 sq km)
Population: 31,719
Capital: Monaco
Language: French

Netherlands
Area: 16,023 sq mi
(41,500 sq km)
Population: 15,600,000
Capital: Amsterdam
Language: Dutch

Italy
Area: 116,324 sq mi
(301,277 sq km)
Population: 57,400,000
Capital: Rome
Language: Italian

Liechtenstein
Area: 62 sq mi
(160 sq km)
Population: 30,000
Capital: Vaduz
Language: German

Luxembourg
Area: 998 sq mi
(2,586 sq km)
Population: 400,000
Capital: Luxembourg
Language: Letzeburgesch

France
Area: 210,026 sq mi
(543,965 sq km)
Population: 58,600,000
Capital: Paris
Language: French

Germany
Area: 137,857 sq mi
(357,046 sq km)
Population: 82,000,000
Capital: Berlin
Language: German

Ireland
Area: 27,137 sq mi
(70,284 sq km)
Population: 3,600,000
Capital: Dublin
Language: English

Andorra
Area: 175 sq mi
(453 sq km)
Population: 54,000
Capital: Andorra la Vella
Language: Catalan

Austria
Area: 32,377 sq mi
(83,856 sq km)
Population: 8,100,000
Capital: Vienna
Language: German

Belgium
Area: 11,783 sq mi
(30,518 sq km)
Population: 10,200,000
Capital: Brussels
Languages: Flemish, French

A1 SWEDEN
A1 DENMARK
A6 LATVIA

B6 LITHUANIA
B5 *fish*

BALTIC SEA

C4 Gdynia
C4 *Gulf of Gdansk*
C6 Kaliningrad
C6 RUSSIA
C4 Gdansk
C2 Koszalin
C1 Szczecin
C6 *fish*

D5 Olsztyn
D6 Hrodna
B6 **BE**
D6 Bialystok
D3 Poznan
D1 GERMANY
D3 *Odra*
D4 *Vistula*
D4 Warsaw
D7 Brest
D7 *Pinsk*

E3 Kalisz
E4 Łódz
E4 POLAND
E2 Legnica
E2 Liberec
E2 Wrocław
E2 Walbrzych
E3 Opole
E1 Prague
E2 Plzen
E5 Kielce
E5 Lublin
E4 Czestochowa
E7 Luts'k
E7 R

F2 CZECH REPUBLIC
F4 Bytom
F4 Katowice
F4 Kraków
F3 Ostrava
F4 Bielsko-Biata
F2 Brno
F6 Rzeszów
F6 *gas*
F6 *oil*
F7 L'viv
F7 **U**

G2 *Danube*
G2 Bratislava
G4 SLOVAKIA
G2 *oil*
G5 Kosice
G6 Uzhhorod
G6 CARPATHIAN
G7 Kam'yanets'-Podil's'kyy
G7 Chernivisti
G7 Khmel'nyts'
F6 *oil*
F6 *gas*

H1 ITALY
H2 AUSTRIA
H2 SLOVENIA
H3 Gyor
H4 Miskolc
H4 Budapest
H4 Székesffehérvár
H4 HUNGARY
H3 *gas*
H5 *Tisza*
H5 *gas*

J3 Pécs
J4 Szeged
J3 *Drava*
J4 *Danube*
J2 CROATIA
J7 ROMANI

K1 ADRIATIC SEA
K3 BOSNIA AND HERZEGOVINA
K4 YUGOSLAVIA
K6 *Danube*

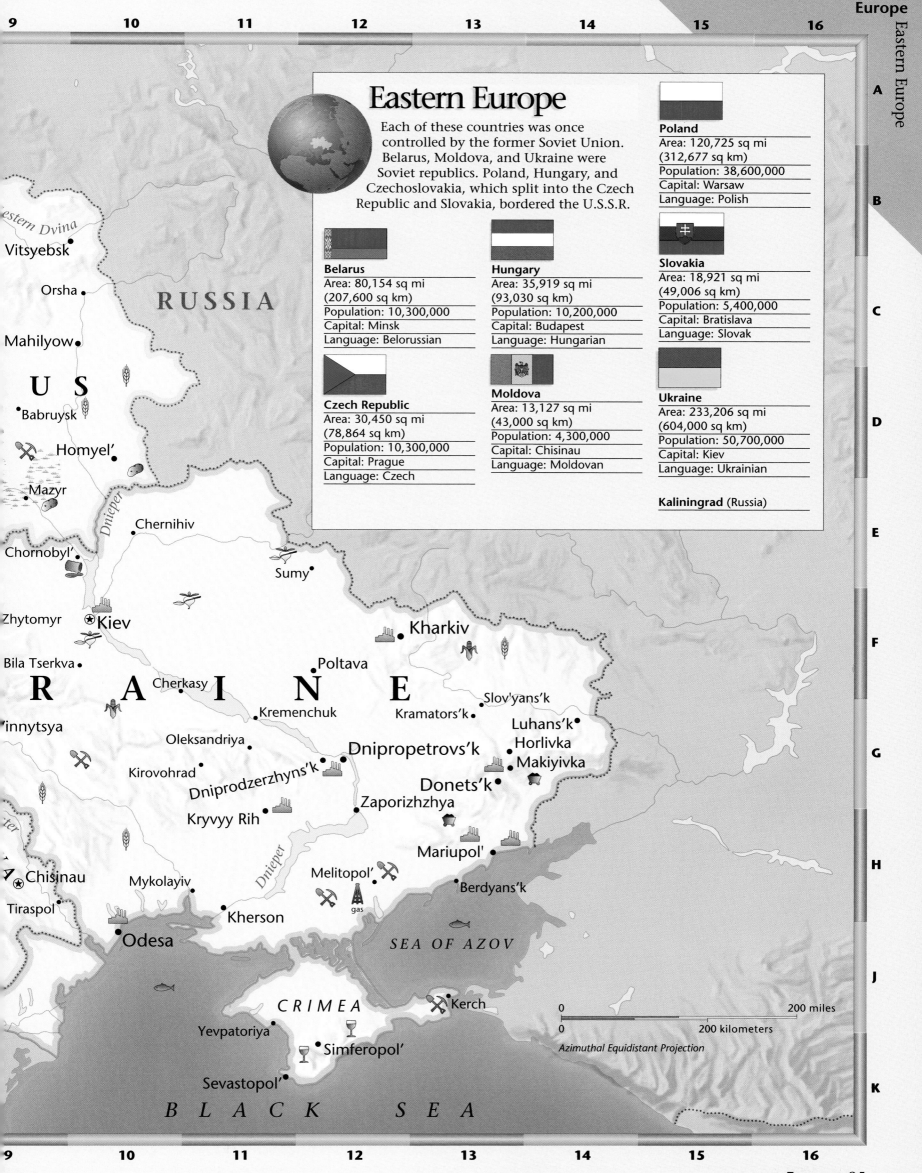

Eastern Europe

Each of these countries was once controlled by the former Soviet Union. Belarus, Moldova, and Ukraine were Soviet republics. Poland, Hungary, and Czechoslovakia, which split into the Czech Republic and Slovakia, bordered the U.S.S.R.

Poland
Area: 120,725 sq mi (312,677 sq km)
Population: 38,600,000
Capital: Warsaw
Language: Polish

Belarus
Area: 80,154 sq mi (207,600 sq km)
Population: 10,300,000
Capital: Minsk
Language: Belorussian

Hungary
Area: 35,919 sq mi (93,030 sq km)
Population: 10,200,000
Capital: Budapest
Language: Hungarian

Slovakia
Area: 18,921 sq mi (49,006 sq km)
Population: 5,400,000
Capital: Bratislava
Language: Slovak

Czech Republic
Area: 30,450 sq mi (78,864 sq km)
Population: 10,300,000
Capital: Prague
Language: Czech

Moldova
Area: 13,127 sq mi (43,000 sq km)
Population: 4,300,000
Capital: Chisinau
Language: Moldovan

Ukraine
Area: 233,206 sq mi (604,000 sq km)
Population: 50,700,000
Capital: Kiev
Language: Ukrainian

Kaliningrad (Russia)

Vitsyebsk

Orsha

Mahilyow

RUSSIA

U S

Babruysk

Homyel'

Mazyr

Chornobyl'

Zhytomyr

Chernihiv

Sumy

Kiev

Bila Tserkva

Kharkiv

R A I N E

Poltava

innytsya

Cherkasy

Kremenchuk

Slov'yans'k

Kramators'k

Luhans'k

Oleksandriya

Dnipropetrovs'k

Horlivka

Makiyivka

Kirovohrad

Dniprodzerzhyns'k

Donets'k

Kryvyy Rih

Zaporizhzhya

Mariupol'

Dnieper

Melitopol'

Berdyans'k

gas

Chisinau

Mykolayiv

Tiraspol

Kherson

Odesa

SEA OF AZOV

CRIMEA

Kerch

Yevpatoriya

0   200 miles
0   200 kilometers

Azimuthal Equidistant Projection

Simferopol'

Sevastopol'

BLACK   SEA

Western Dvina

Dnieper

GERMANY

SLOVAKIA

SWITZERLAND

LIECHTENSTEIN

AUSTRIA

Danube

HUNGARY

Tisza

Baia

TRANS

Oradea

Cluj-Na

Drava

Arad

R

Maribor

SLOVENIA

Subotica

Timisoara

Ljubljana

oil

Zagreb

Resita

Gulf of Venice

Rijeka

CROATIA

Osijek

Novi Sad

T

Sava

Tisa

Banja Luka

BOSNIA AND

Sava

gas

Iro

SAN MARINO

Zadar

BOSNIA AND

Belgrade

Dar

HERZEGOVINA

Zenica

ITALY

Split

Sarajevo

Kragujevac

YUGOSLAVIA

CORSICA
(France)

Mostar

Ni

ADRIATIC SEA

Dubrovnik

Pec

Pristina

Podgorica

Sof

Shkodër

B

A

Tetovo

Skopje

Tirana

MACEDONIA

SARDINIA
(Italy)

Durrës

oil

P

N

TYRRHENIAN
SEA

Elbasan

Bitola

Thessaloníki

ALBANIA

Vlorë

Olympus
9,570 ft
2,917 m

Lárisa

Strait of Otranto

Corfu

GREECE

IONIAN
SEA

IONIAN ISLANDS

SICILY

Pátrai

Corinth

Olympia

PELOPONNE

Sparta

0   200 miles

0   200 kilometers

Azimuthal Equidistant Projection

Gulf of Messinia

olive

TUNISIA

MEDITERRANEAN

UKRAINE

MOLDOVA

Botosani

Iasi

Dniester

Prut

ARPATHIAN MOUNTAINS

oil

gu Mures

NIA

Brasov

NIAN ALPS

Ploiesti

oil

charest

oil

Galati

Braila

Tulcea

Constanta

BLACK
SEA

Ruse

even

N M T S.

Varna

oil

GARIA

Sliven

Burgas

Stara Zagora

lovdiv

S.

ULA

la   Thrace

Bosporus

TURKEY

Sea of
Marmara

Dardanelles

Chios

AN SEA

SPORADES

ades

Rhodes

Rhodes

CRETE

Iráklion
(Candia)

TE

olive

SEA

CYPRUS

SYRIA

LEBANON

The Balkans

Named for the mountain range that runs from Yugoslavia to the Black Sea, this area includes some of the continent's oldest and newest countries. Four of its members—Bosnia and Herzegovina, Croatia, Macedonia, and Slovenia—were part of Yugoslavia until the early 1990s.

Greece
Area: 50,962 sq mi
(131,990 sq km)
Population: 10,500,000
Capital: Athens
Language: Greek

Macedonia
Area: 9,928 sq mi
(25,713 sq km)
Population: 2,100,000
Capital: Skopje
Language: Macedonian

Albania
Area: 11,100 sq mi
(28,748 sq km)
Population: 3,400,000
Capital: Tirana
Language: Albanian

Romania
Area: 91,699 sq mi
(237,500 sq km)
Population: 22,500,000
Capital: Bucharest
Language: Romanian

Bosnia and Herzegovina
Area: 19,741 sq mi
(51,129 sq km)
Population: 3,600,000
Capital: Sarajevo
Language: Serbo-Croat

Slovenia
Area: 7,719 sq mi
(20,251 sq km)
Population: 2,000,000
Capital: Ljubljana
Language: Slovenian

Bulgaria
Area: 42,823 sq mi
(110,912 sq km)
Population: 8,300,000
Capital: Sofia
Language: Bulgarian

Yugoslavia
Area: 39,450 sq mi
(102,173 sq km)
Population: 10,600,000
Capital: Belgrade
Language: Serbian

Croatia
Area: 21,829 sq mi
(56,538 sq km)
Population: 4,800,000
Capital: Zagreb
Language: Croatian

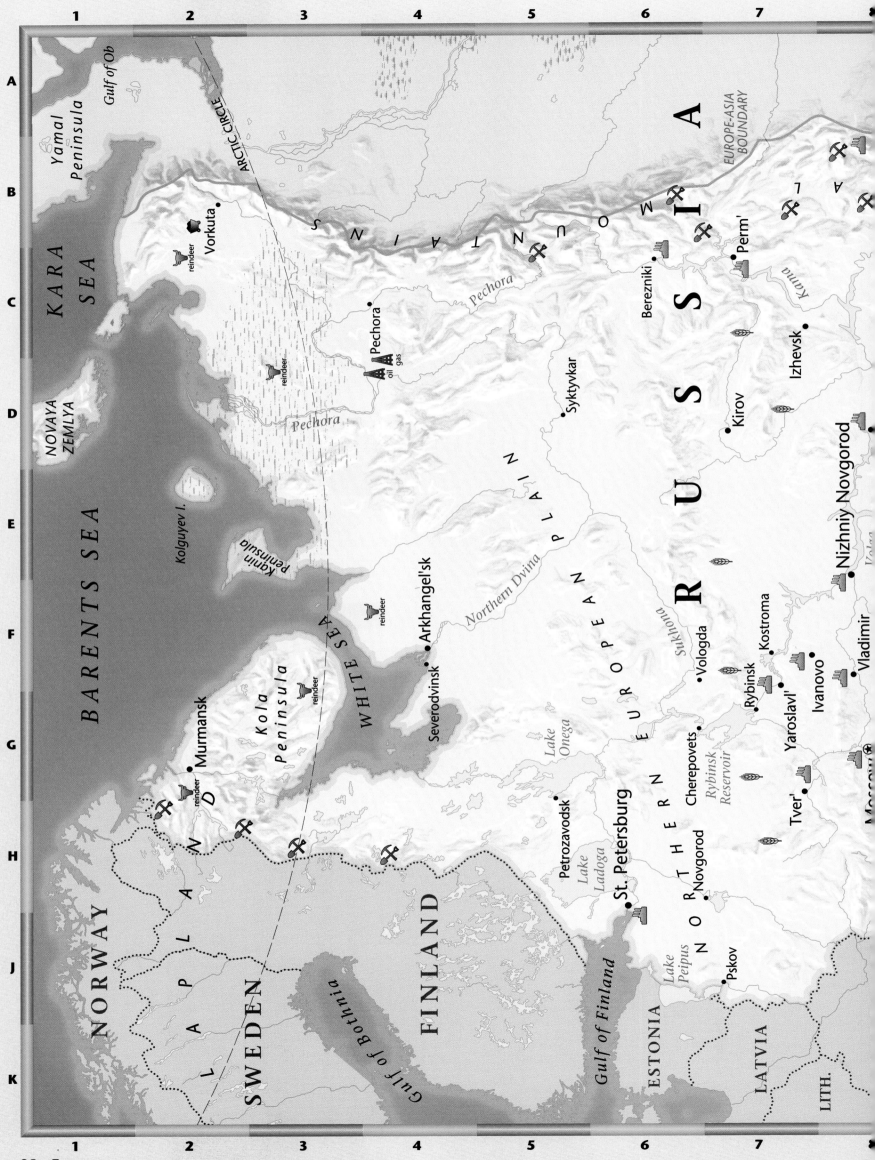

A
B
C
D
E
F
G
H
J
K

1 2 3 4 5 6 7 8

Gulf of Ob

Yamal Peninsula

ARCTIC CIRCLE

KARA SEA

Vorkuta
reindeer

Pechora

MOUNTAINS

EUROPE-ASIA BOUNDARY

Perm'

Berezniki

Izhevsk

NOVAYA ZEMLYA

reindeer

Pechora
oil gas

Syktyvkar

Kirov

Kama

BARENTS SEA

Kolguyev I.

Kanin Peninsula

Pechora

Northern Dvina

EUROPEAN PLAIN

RUSSIA

Nizhniy Novgorod

reindeer
Arkhangel'sk

Sukhona

Vologda

Kostroma

Vladimir

Volga

Severodvinsk

WHITE SEA

Kola Peninsula

reindeer
Murmansk

L A P L A N D

reindeer

Rybinsk
Reservoir

Cherepovets

Rybinsk

Yaroslavl'

Ivanovo

Lake Onega

SOUTHERN

Petrozavodsk

Lake Ladoga

Novgorod

St. Petersburg

Tver'

NORWAY

SWEDEN

Gulf of Bothnia

FINLAND

Gulf of Finland

Lake Peipus

Pskov

ESTONIA

LATVIA

LITH.

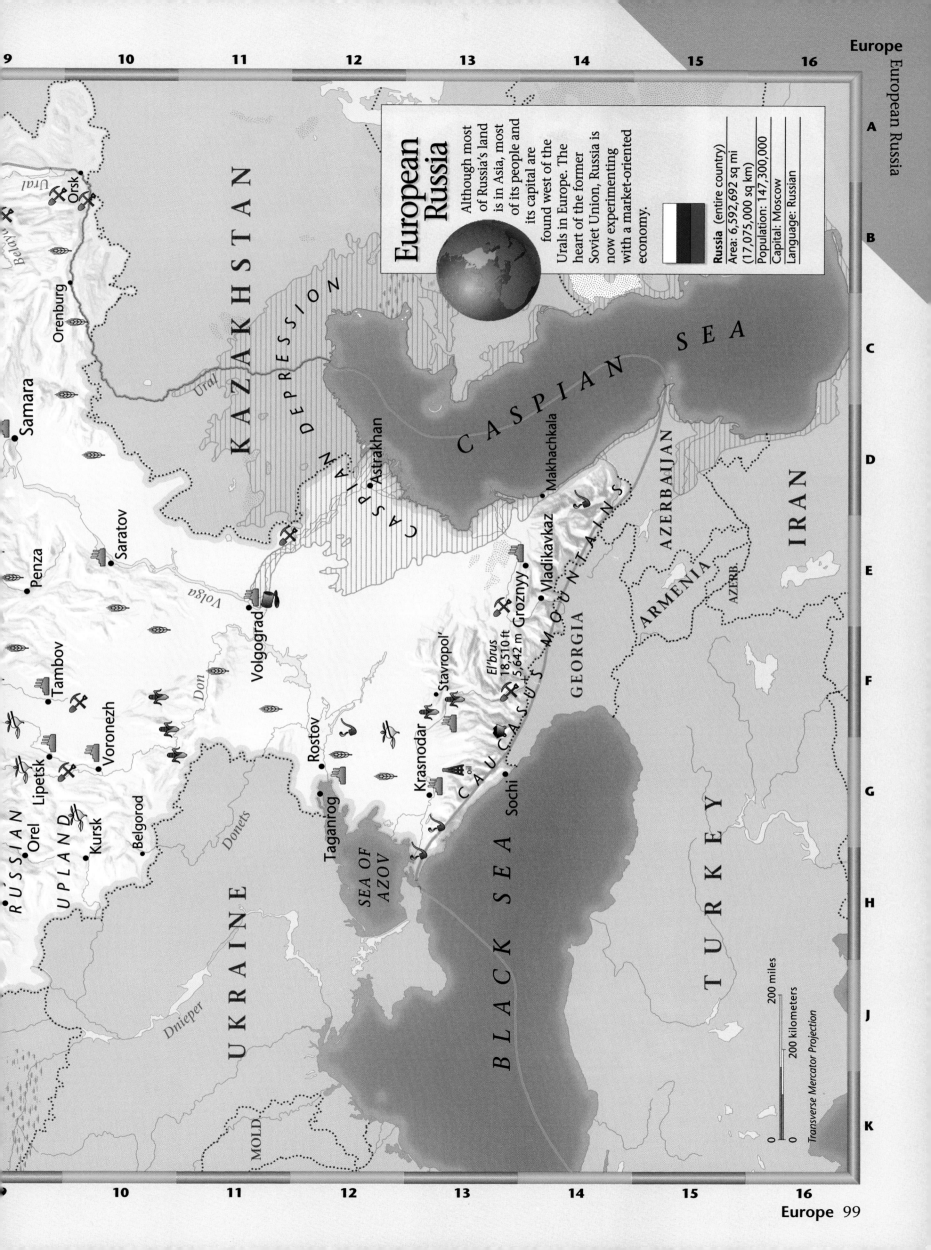

European Russia

Although most of Russia's land is in Asia, most of its people and its capital are found west of the Urals in Europe. The heart of the former Soviet Union, Russia is now experimenting with a market-oriented economy.

Russia (entire country)
Area: 6,592,692 sq mi
(17,075,000 sq km)
Population: 147,300,000
Capital: Moscow
Language: Russian

KAZAKHSTAN

Ural

Orsk

Orenburg

Beloya

Samara

Saratov

Penza

Tambov

Voronezh

Lipetsk

Orel

Kursk

Belgorod

RUSSIAN

UPLAND

Don

Donets

Dnieper

UKRAINE

MOLD.

Volgograd

Volga

DEPRESSION

CASPIAN

Astrakhan

CASPIAN SEA

Makhachkala

Vladikavkaz

Grozny'

Stavropol'

El'brus
18,510 ft
5,642 m

CAUCASUS MOUNTAINS

Krasnodar

Rostov

Taganrog

oil

Sochi

**SEA OF
AZOV**

BLACK SEA

GEORGIA

ARMENIA

AZERBAIJAN

AZERB.

IRAN

TURKEY

200 miles

200 kilometers

Transverse Mercator Projection

Africa

The salty waters of the Red Sea (right) and the Gulf of Aden (far right) fill the gap formed as geologic forces tear the Arabian Peninsula away from Africa. The rumpled-looking area at center is the Great Rift Valley, which rends East Africa like a pair of hatchet cuts. In about 50 million years, say geologists, a huge chunk of East Africa from Eritrea to Mozambique will break away from the rest of the continent, just as Madagascar broke away from what is now Mozambique millions of years ago.

Africa's position on the globe—straddling the Equator and lying almost entirely within the tropics—gives it the warmest average annual temperature of all the continents.

Radiant with color, schools of lyre-tailed goldfish swim among coral in the Red Sea. Although it is shallow along its shores, the sea plunges to a central trough more than 7,000 feet (2,134 meters) deep.

CONNECTION: *You can find East Africa and the Red Sea on the maps on pages 102–103 and 112–113.*

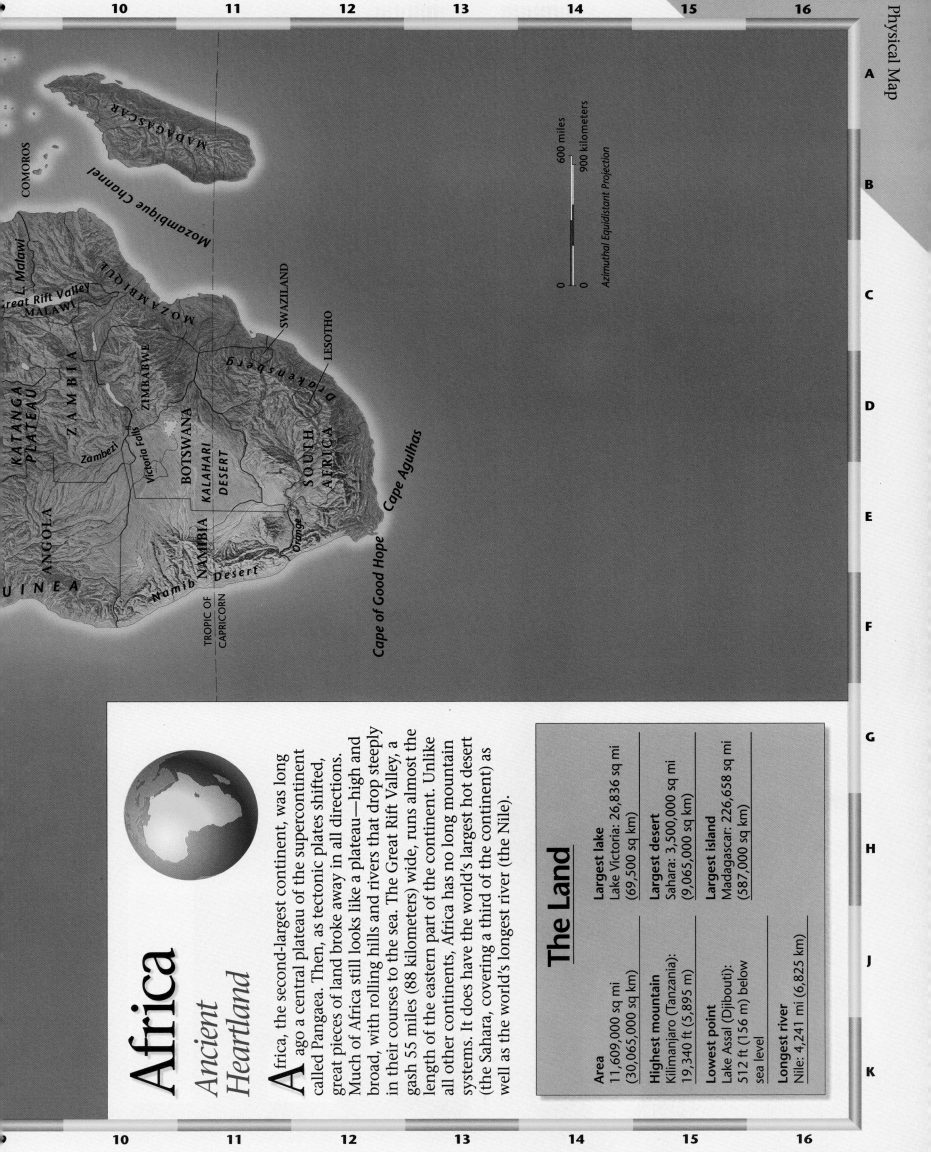

Africa

Ancient Heartland

Africa, the second-largest continent, was long ago a central plateau of the supercontinent called Pangaea. Then, as tectonic plates shifted, great pieces of land broke away in all directions. Much of Africa still looks like a plateau—high and broad, with rolling hills and rivers that drop steeply in their courses to the sea. The Great Rift Valley, a gash 55 miles (88 kilometers) wide, runs almost the length of the eastern part of the continent. Unlike all other continents, Africa has no long mountain systems. It does have the world's largest hot desert (the Sahara, covering a third of the continent) as well as the world's longest river (the Nile).

The Land

Area
11,609,000 sq mi
(30,065,000 sq km)

Highest mountain
Kilimanjaro (Tanzania):
19,340 ft (5,895 m)

Lowest point
Lake Assal (Djibouti):
512 ft (156 m) below
sea level

Longest river
Nile: 4,241 mi (6,825 km)

Largest lake
Lake Victoria: 26,836 sq mi
(69,500 sq km)

Largest desert
Sahara: 3,500,000 sq mi
(9,065,000 sq km)

Largest island
Madagascar: 226,658 sq mi
(587,000 sq km)

600 miles
900 kilometers
Azimuthal Equidistant Projection

Africa
Changing Continent

The roar of a lion. A river of wildebeests migrating across the plain. These images conjure up the traditional picture of Africa. It is a continent perhaps best known for its extraordinary natural heritage—abundant wildlife, grasslands, rain forests, and sculpted desert sands. It is here, on African soil, that early humans evolved.

Today, in the densely populated countries of central and East Africa, people desperately need land for farms and livestock. In many places, wildlife is squeezed onto shrinking habitat. Some countries hope to safeguard the future by setting aside huge national parks that would attract tourists. This could bring money into a continent where few nations are industrialized.

Africa has seen more change in this century than any other continent. Just 50 years ago, almost every country belonged to a European power. Today, all but three have won independence. However, Africa's problems are far from over. Freedom brings the challenges of self-government, and ethnic and religious rivalries cause ongoing civil wars.

▼ **THE ELEPHANT'S NEED** for habitat conflicts more and more with the human demand for land.

▲ **THE WINDS OF CHANGE** blow over Cape Town, one of South Africa's three capital cities. Until 1993, racist laws kept the country's black Africans in poverty. A new constitution promises a better future.

▼ **A MINER MOVES MOUNTAINS** for metal—gold ore—deep in an African mine. Mining is a major industry in several African countries. The continent is the source of much of the world's gold and diamonds.

◄ **BOLD** *patterns and brilliant colors give a festive air to a crowded marketplace in southern Africa. At open-air markets such as this one, different ethnic groups meet to trade.*

◄**SERENELY SURVEYING** *the savanna, a giraffe trio towers above the landscape. Africa's wildlife draws visitors from around the world.*

▲ **AS FAST AS A SPEEDING** *car, the cheetah can run at up to 70 miles per hour (113 kilometers per hour). Already extinct in India, this cat is becoming rare in Africa as well.*

▶ **A TUAREG** *nomad skirts the crest of a dune in the Sahara. The Sahara is the world's largest hot desert, covering an area about the size of the lower 48 U.S. states. Drought and overgrazing in the Sahel, a semiarid region bordering the Sahara, are expanding the desert.*

▲ **IMAGINATION CAN'T COMPARE** *with the terrifying reality children face in wartime. Here, young refugees in Mozambique use art as therapy to express their fears. Since 1950, almost every African nation has experienced war.*

▶ **NINGA TRIBAL DRUMMERS** *inspire a leaping dancer in Burundi. Hundreds of tribes speaking hundreds of languages live in Africa south of the Sahara.*

▶ **CRADLING THE WORDS** *of the Prophet Muhammad, a young Bedouin studies a lesson from the Koran, the sacred book of Islam. Bedouin are Arab nomads who traditionally roamed across North Africa on camels. Today, many Bedouin live a more settled existence.*

▲ **SLEEK AND MODERN,** *high-rise buildings catch the sun in the Kenyan capital of Nairobi. The city is the commercial center of East Africa. It is home to universities, museums, and international organizations.*

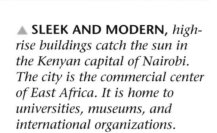

▲ **EGYPT'S** *ancient sands yield their secrets reluctantly. In 1922 archaeologists uncovered four treasure-filled rooms of the tomb of the teenage King Tutankhamun— also known as King Tut. Countless ancient tombs remain unexcavated beneath shifting desert sands.*

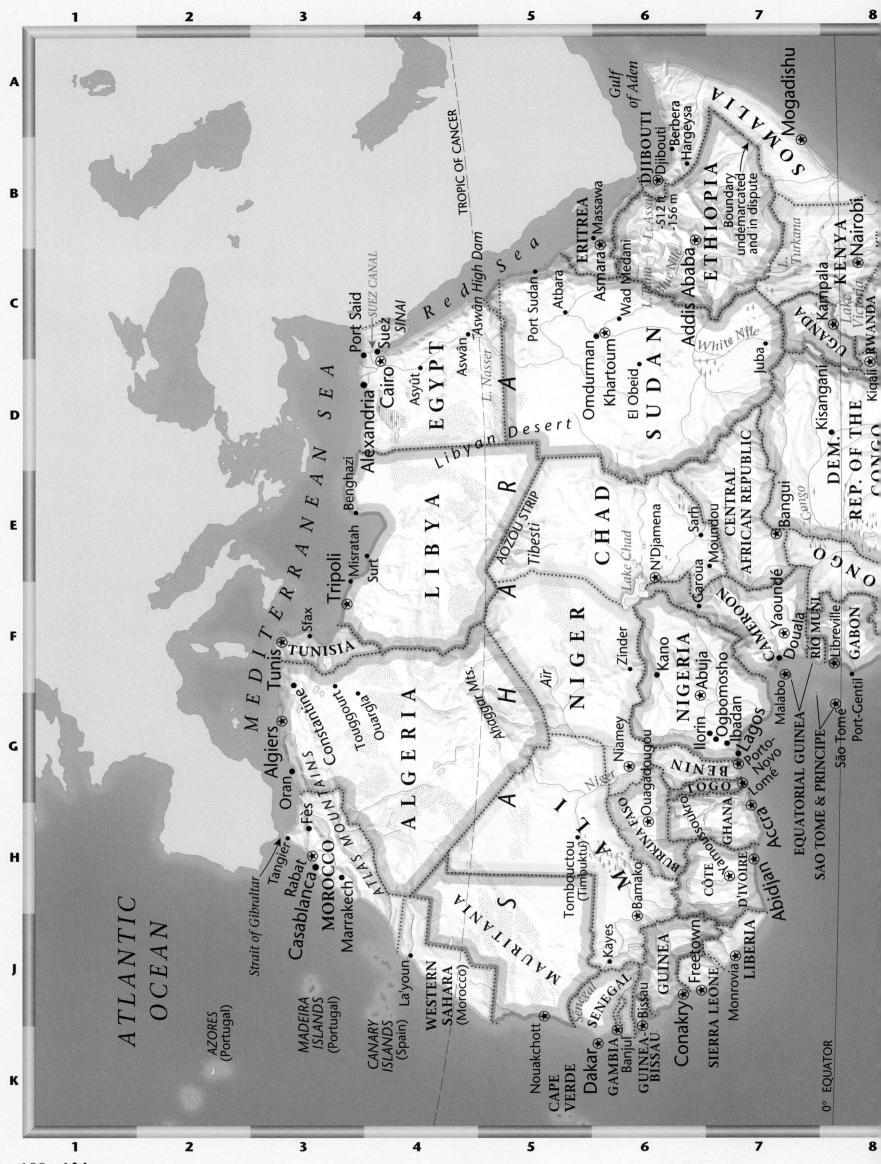

ATLANTIC
OCEAN

AZORES
(Portugal)

MADEIRA
ISLANDS
(Portugal)

CANARY
ISLANDS
(Spain)

WESTERN
SAHARA
(Morocco)

La'youn

Strait of Gibraltar

Tangier
Rabat
Casablanca
Fès
Marrakech

MOROCCO

ATLAS MOUNTAINS

M E D I T E R R A N E A N   S E A

Oran
Algiers
Constantine
Tunis
TUNISIA
Sfax

Tripoli
Misratah
Surt
Benghazi

L I B Y A

Alexandria
Port Said
Suez
Cairo
SINAI
SUEZ CANAL

TROPIC OF CANCER

E G Y P T

Asyût
Aswân
Aswân High Dam
L. Nasser

Libyan Desert

Red Sea

Port Sudan
Atbara
Omdurman
Khartoum
El Obeid

S U D A N

White Nile
Blue Nile

ERITREA
Massawa
Asmara
Wad Medani

Gulf
of Aden

DJIBOUTI
Djibouti
Berbera
Hargeysa

L. Assal
-512 ft.
-156 m

ETHIOPIA

Addis Ababa

Boundary
undemarcated
and in dispute

S O M A L I A

Mogadishu

Juba

L. Turkana
L. Tana

UGANDA
Kampala

KENYA
Nairobi

Lake
Victoria
RWANDA
Kigali

A L G E R I A

Touggourt
Ouargla

Ahaggar Mts.

Tibesti

Aozou Strip

Aïr

N I G E R

Zinder

C H A D

Lake Chad
N'Djamena
Sarh
Moundou
Garoua

CENTRAL
AFRICAN REPUBLIC

Bangui
Kisangani

DEM.
REP. OF THE
CONGO

CONGO

Congo

S A H A R A

M A L I

Tombouctou
(Timbuktu)

Niger

Niamey
Ouagadougou
BURKINA FASO

Bamako

Kano
Kayes

NIGERIA

Abuja
Ilorin
Ibadan
Ogbomosho
Lagos
Porto-Novo
BENIN
TOGO
Lomé
Accra
GHANA

CAMEROON

Yaoundé
Douala
Malabo
RIO MUNI
Libreville
Port-Gentil
GABON

EQUATORIAL GUINEA

São Tomé
SAO TOME & PRINCIPE

M A U R I T A N I A

Nouakchott

CAPE
VERDE

Dakar
SENEGAL
GAMBIA
Banjul
GUINEA-
BISSAU
Bissau
GUINEA

Senegal

Conakry
Freetown
SIERRA LEONE
Monrovia
LIBERIA

Yamoussoukro
CÔTE
D'IVOIRE
Abidjan

0° EQUATOR

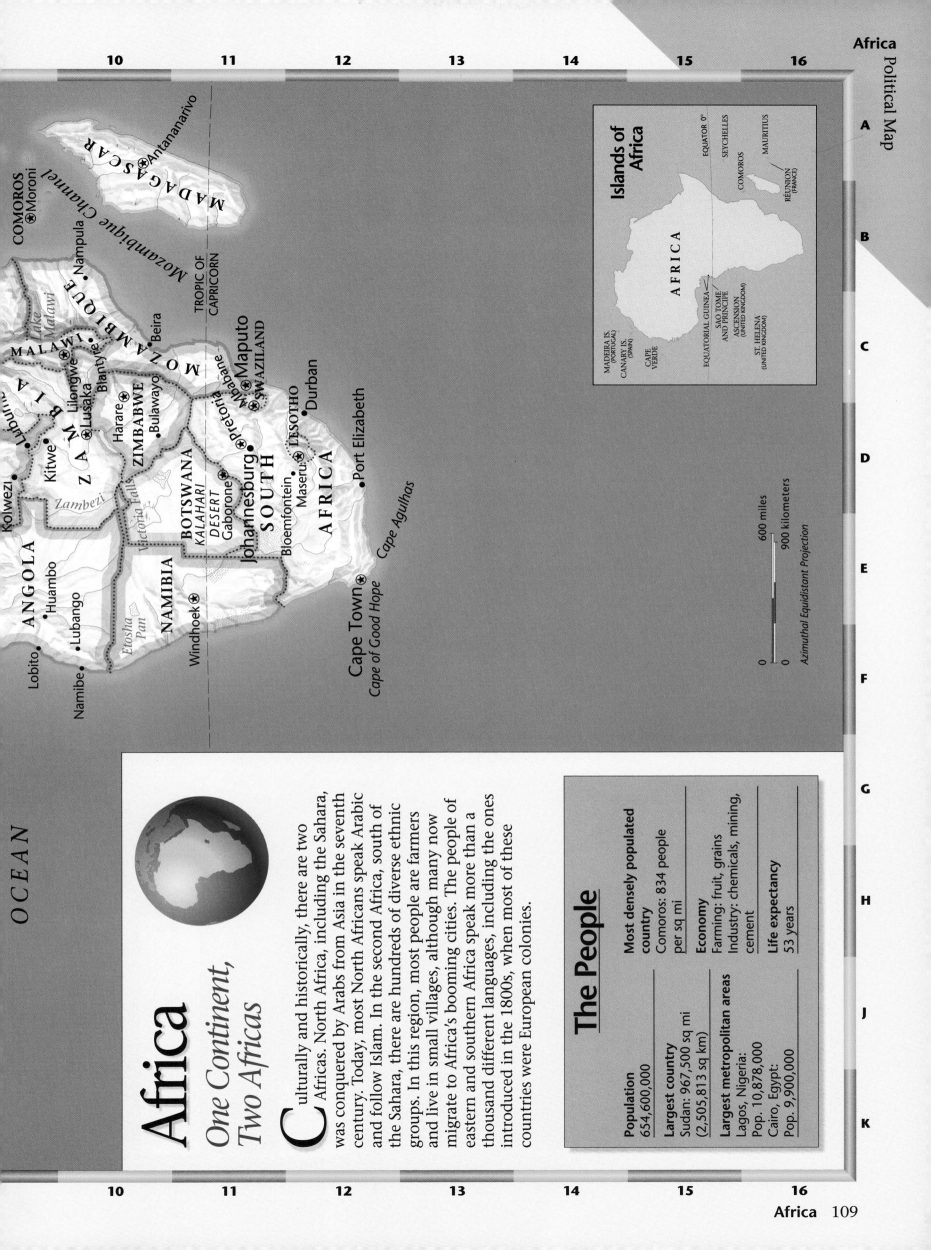

A B C D E F G H J K

10 11 12 13 14 15 16

Islands of Africa

EQUATOR 0°

SEYCHELLES

MAURITIUS

COMOROS

RÉUNION (FRANCE)

A F R I C A

MADEIRA IS. (PORTUGAL)

CANARY IS. (SPAIN)

CAPE VERDE

EQUATORIAL GUINEA

SAO TOME AND PRINCIPE

ASCENSION (UNITED KINGDOM)

ST. HELENA (UNITED KINGDOM)

COMOROS
⊛Moroni

MADAGASCAR

⊛Antananarivo

Nampula

Mozambique Channel

TROPIC OF CAPRICORN

Lake Malawi

MALAWI

⊛Lilongwe

Blantyre

Beira

MOZAMBIQUE

Lusaka⊛

Harare⊛

ZIMBABWE

Bulawayo

Mbabane⊛

Maputo⊛

SWAZILAND

Durban

LESOTHO

Maseru⊛

Pretoria⊛

Johannesburg

Gaborone⊛

BOTSWANA

KALAHARI DESERT

Bloemfontein

SOUTH

AFRICA

Port Elizabeth

Cape Agulhas

ZAMBIA

Lusaka⊛

Kitwe

Kolwezi

Victoria Falls

Zambezi

Etosha Pan

ANGOLA

Huambo

Lubango

Lobito

Namibe

NAMIBIA

Windhoek⊛

Cape Town⊛

Cape of Good Hope

OCEAN

600 miles

900 kilometers

0

0

Azimuthal Equidistant Projection

Africa

One Continent, Two Africas

Culturally and historically, there are two Africas. North Africa, including the Sahara, was conquered by Arabs from Asia in the seventh century. Today, most North Africans speak Arabic and follow Islam. In the second Africa, south of the Sahara, there are hundreds of diverse ethnic groups. In this region, most people are farmers and live in small villages, although many now migrate to Africa's booming cities. The people of eastern and southern Africa speak more than a thousand different languages, including the ones introduced in the 1800s, when most of these countries were European colonies.

The People

Population
654,600,000

Largest country
Sudan: 967,500 sq mi
(2,505,813 sq km)

Largest metropolitan areas
Lagos, Nigeria:
Pop. 10,878,000
Cairo, Egypt:
Pop. 9,900,000

Most densely populated country
Comoros: 834 people per sq mi

Economy
Farming: fruit, grains
Industry: chemicals, mining, cement

Life expectancy
53 years

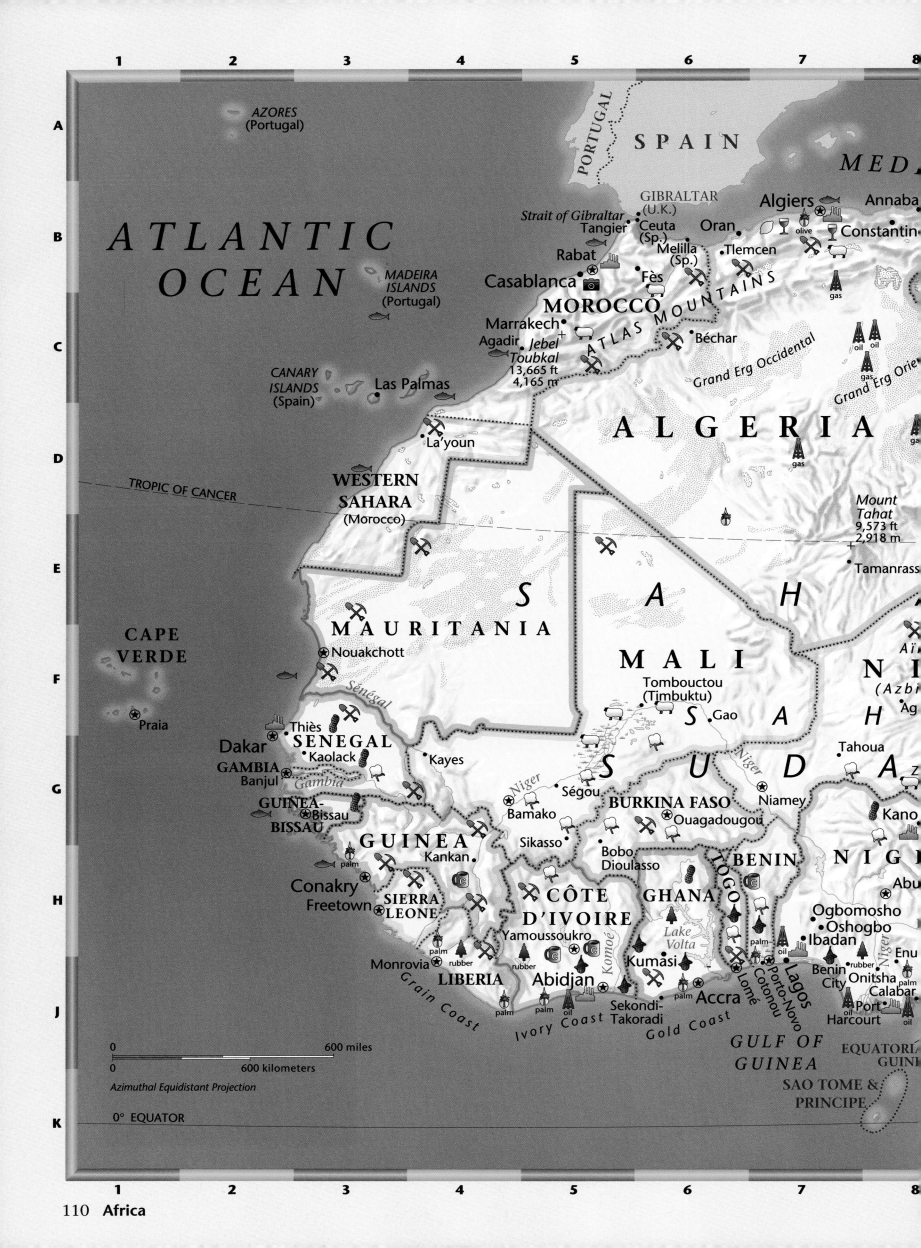

ATLANTIC
OCEAN

AZORES
(Portugal)

*MADEIRA
ISLANDS*
(Portugal)

PORTUGAL

SPAIN

MED

GIBRALTAR
(U.K.)
Strait of Gibraltar
Tangier • Ceuta
(Sp.)
Rabat • Melilla
(Sp.)
Casablanca • Fès

Algiers • • Annaba
olive • Constantin
Oran
• Tlemcen
gas

MOROCCO

ATLAS MOUNTAINS

Marrakech
Agadir • *Jebel
Toubkal*
13,665 ft
4,165 m

• Béchar

Grand Erg Occidental

oil • oil
gas • *Grand Erg Orien*

*CANARY
ISLANDS*
(Spain) • Las Palmas

ALGERIA

gas

• La'youn

gas

TROPIC OF CANCER

WESTERN
SAHARA
(Morocco)

*Mount
Tahat*
9,573 ft
2,918 m

• Tamanrass

CAPE
VERDE

MAURITANIA

⭑ Nouakchott

S   A   H

M A L I

N I
(*Azbi*

• Aï

• Ag

Sénégal

Tombouctou
(Timbuktu)
• Gao

S

A

H

• Praia

Thiès
SENEGAL
Dakar • • Kaolack

GAMBIA
Banjul • *Gambia*

GUINEA-
⭑ Bissau
BISSAU

• Kayes

U

D

Az
• Tahoua

A

Niger

GUINEA
Kankan •

• Ségou
BURKINA FASO
⭑ Bamako
• Sikasso

Niger

• Niamey

Kano •

NIG

palm

Conakry
Freetown
SIERRA
LEONE

CÔTE
D'IVOIRE

Bobo
Dioulasso

⭑ Ouagadougou

BENIN

TOGO

Abu

Ogbomosho
• Oshogbo

Yamoussoukro

GHANA

*Lake
Volta*

Ibadan

Monrovia
rubber
LIBERIA

Kumasi •
rubber

Abidjan

palm

oil
Porto-Novo
Cotonou

Benin
City

rubber
• Onitsha

palm
Calabar

Komoé

Accra

Lagos
Lomé

Enu

palm
Port
Harcourt

oil

0   600 miles
0   600 kilometers

Azimuthal Equidistant Projection

Sekondi-
Takoradi

Grain Coast

Ivory Coast

Gold Coast

*GULF OF
GUINEA*

EQUATORIA
GUIN

SAO TOME &
PRINCIPE

0° EQUATOR

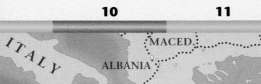

ITALY
ALBANIA
MACED.
GREECE
MALTA

NEAN SEA

...poli
Misratah
Gulf of Sidra
Benghazi
Tubruq

OLITANIA

gas
oil
oil
oil
Sabha

L I B Y A

CYRENAICA

ZAN

R

A

R

L

CHAD

Lake
Chad

CENTRAL AFRICAN
REPUBLIC

OON

DEMOCRATIC
REPUBLIC
OF THE
CONGO

CONGO

Congo

UGANDA

KENYA

RWANDA

Lake
Victoria

Northwestern Africa

This area stretches from the Atlas Mountains along the coast of the Mediterranean Sea to the Gulf of Guinea. The region includes several of Africa's leading oil-producing countries—Algeria, Libya, and Nigeria.

Algeria
Area: 919,595 sq mi
(2,381,741 sq km)
Population: 29,800,000
Capital: Algiers
Language: Arabic

Benin
Area: 43,484 sq mi
(112,622 sq km)
Population: 5,900,000
Capital: Porto-Novo
Language: French

Burkina Faso
Area: 105,869 sq mi
(274,200 sq km)
Population: 10,900,000
Capital: Ouagadougou
Language: French

Cape Verde
Area: 1,557 sq mi
(4,033 sq km)
Population: 400,000
Capital: Praia
Language: Portuguese

Côte D'Ivoire
Area: 124,504 sq mi
(322,463 sq km)
Population: 15,000,000
Capital: Yamoussoukro
Language: French

Gambia
Area: 4,361 sq mi
(11,295 sq km)
Population: 1,200,000
Capital: Banjul
Language: English

Ghana
Area: 92,100 sq mi
(238,537 sq km)
Population: 18,100,000
Capital: Accra
Language: English

Guinea
Area: 94,926 sq mi
(245,857 sq km)
Population: 7,500,000
Capital: Conakry
Language: French

Guinea-Bissau
Area: 13,948 sq mi
(36,125 sq km)
Population: 1,100,000
Capital: Bissau
Language: Portuguese

Liberia
Area: 43,000 sq mi
(111,369 sq km)
Population: 2,300,000
Capital: Monrovia
Language: English

Libya
Area: 679,362 sq mi
(1,759,540 sq km)
Population: 5,600,000
Capital: Tripoli
Language: Arabic

Mali
Area: 478,841 sq mi
(1,240,192 sq km)
Population: 9,900,000
Capital: Bamako
Language: French

Mauritania
Area: 397,955 sq mi
(1,030,700 sq km)
Population: 2,400,000
Capital: Nouakchott
Language: Arabic

Morocco
Area: 275,117 sq mi
(712,550 sq km)
Population: 28,200,000
Capital: Rabat
Language: Arabic

Niger
Area: 489,191 sq mi
(1,267,000 sq km)
Population: 9,800,000
Capital: Niamey
Language: French

Nigeria
Area: 365,669 sq mi
(923,768 sq km)
Population: 107,100,000
Capital: Abuja
Language: English

Senegal
Area: 75,955 sq mi
(196,722 sq km)
Population: 8,800,000
Capital: Dakar
Language: French

Sierra Leone
Area: 27,699 sq mi
(71,740 sq km)
Population: 4,400,000
Capital: Freetown
Language: English

Togo
Area: 21,925 sq mi
(56,785 sq km)
Population: 4,700,000
Capital: Lomé
Language: French

Tunisia
Area: 63,170 sq mi
(163,610 sq km)
Population: 9,300,000
Capital: Tunis
Language: Arabic

Western Sahara
Administered by Morocco, Western Sahara is a disputed area. Some residents are fighting for independence, but it has not yet gained international recognition as a separate country.

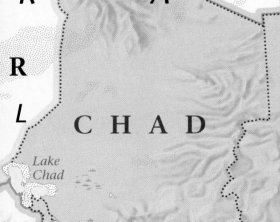

Northeastern Africa

This region is home to Africa's largest country, Sudan, as well as one of the world's oldest nations, Egypt. It also contains Africa's longest river (Nile), its largest lake (Victoria), and its highest peak (Kilimanjaro).

Somalia
Area: 246,201 sq mi (637,657 sq km)
Population: 10,200,000
Capital: Mogadishu
Language: Somali

Sudan
Area: 967,500 sq mi (2,505,813 sq km)
Population: 27,900,000
Capital: Khartoum
Language: Arabic

Tanzania
Area: 364,900 sq mi (945,087 sq km)
Population: 29,500,000
Capital: Dar es Salaam
Languages: English, Swahili

Uganda
Area: 91,134 sq mi (236,036 sq km)
Population: 20,600,000
Capital: Kampala
Language: English

Eritrea
Area: 46,842 sq mi (121,320 sq km)
Population: 3,600,000
Capital: Asmara
Language: Tigrinya

Ethiopia
Area: 424,934 sq mi (1,100,580 sq km)
Population: 58,700,000
Capital: Addis Ababa
Language: Amharic

Kenya
Area: 224,961 sq mi (582,646 sq km)
Population: 28,800,000
Capital: Nairobi
Languages: English, Swahili

Rwanda
Area: 10,169 sq mi (26,338 sq km)
Population: 7,700,000
Capital: Kigali
Languages: French, Kinyarwanda, others

Burundi
Area: 10,747 sq mi (27,834 sq km)
Population: 6,100,000
Capital: Bujumbura
Languages: French, Kirundi

Djibouti
Area: 8,958 sq mi (23,200 sq km)
Population: 600,000
Capital: Djibouti
Languages: Arabic, French

Egypt
Area: 386,662 sq mi (1,001,449 sq km)
Population: 64,800,000
Capital: Cairo
Language: Arabic

OMAN

SAUDI ARABIA

RUSSIA

ROMANIA

YUG.

BULGARIA

MACED.

GREECE

TURKEY

BLACK SEA

SYRIA

IRAQ

LEBANON

CYPRUS

ISRAEL

JORDAN

MEDITERRANEAN SEA

RED SEA

Gulf of Aqaba

Suez Canal

Sinai

Gulf of Suez

oil

oil

oil

Port Said

Cairo

Suez

Alexandria

Tanta

El Gîza

El Faiyûm

El Minya

Asyût

dates

dates

EGYPT

EASTERN DESERT

WESTERN DESERT

Nile

Thebes

Luxor

Aswân

1st Cataract

Aswân High Dam

Lake Nasser

NUBIAN DESERT

Port Sudan

Treaty Boundary

3rd Cataract

4th Cataract

5th

LIBYA

LIBYAN DESERT

Qattâra Depression

-436 ft
-133 m

DESERT

TROPIC OF CANCER

YEMEN

Socotra
(Yemen)

GULF OF ADEN

DJIBOUTI
⊛ Djibouti

• Hargeysa

• Harer

Dire
Dawa

Gonder •

Bahir Dar •

• Dese

Lake
Tana

Blue Nile

Addis Ababa ⊛

ETHIOPIAN

HIGHLANDS

E T H I O P I A

Jima •

Boundary
undemarcated
and in dispute

S O M A L I A

Webi Shabeelle

Mogadishu
⊛

Merca •

Chisimayu •

EQUATOR 0°

I N D I A N   O C E A N

S E Y C H E L L E S

COMOROS

400 miles

400 kilometers

Azimuthal Equidistant Projection

0

0

S U D A N

El Obeid •

Wad Medani •

White Nile

Malakal •

Bahr el Arab

Wau •

Sue

White Nile

Juba •

El Fasher •

Nyala •

CENTRAL
AFRICAN
REPUBLIC

Lake Turkana
(Lake Rudolph)

K E N Y A

Kisumu •

Nakuru •
Nairobi •

+ *Mt. Kenya*
17,058 ft
5,199 m

Mombasa •

sisal

Zanzibar •

Dar es Salaam ⊛

sisal

sisal

T A N Z A N I A

Dodoma •

Mbeya •

L. Malawi

MALAWI

L. Malawi

Rift Valley

Eastern

+ *Kilimanjaro*
19,340 ft
5,895 m

U G A N D A

Jinja •
Kampala •

Victoria Nile

Lake
Victoria

Mwanza •

Tabora •

Western   *Rift Valley*

RWANDA

Kigali ⊛

BURUNDI

Bujumbura ⊛

Lake Tanganyika

ZAMBIA

Albert Nile

Lake
Albert

Lake
Edward

Lake
Kivu

DEMOCRATIC

REPUBLIC

OF THE

CONGO

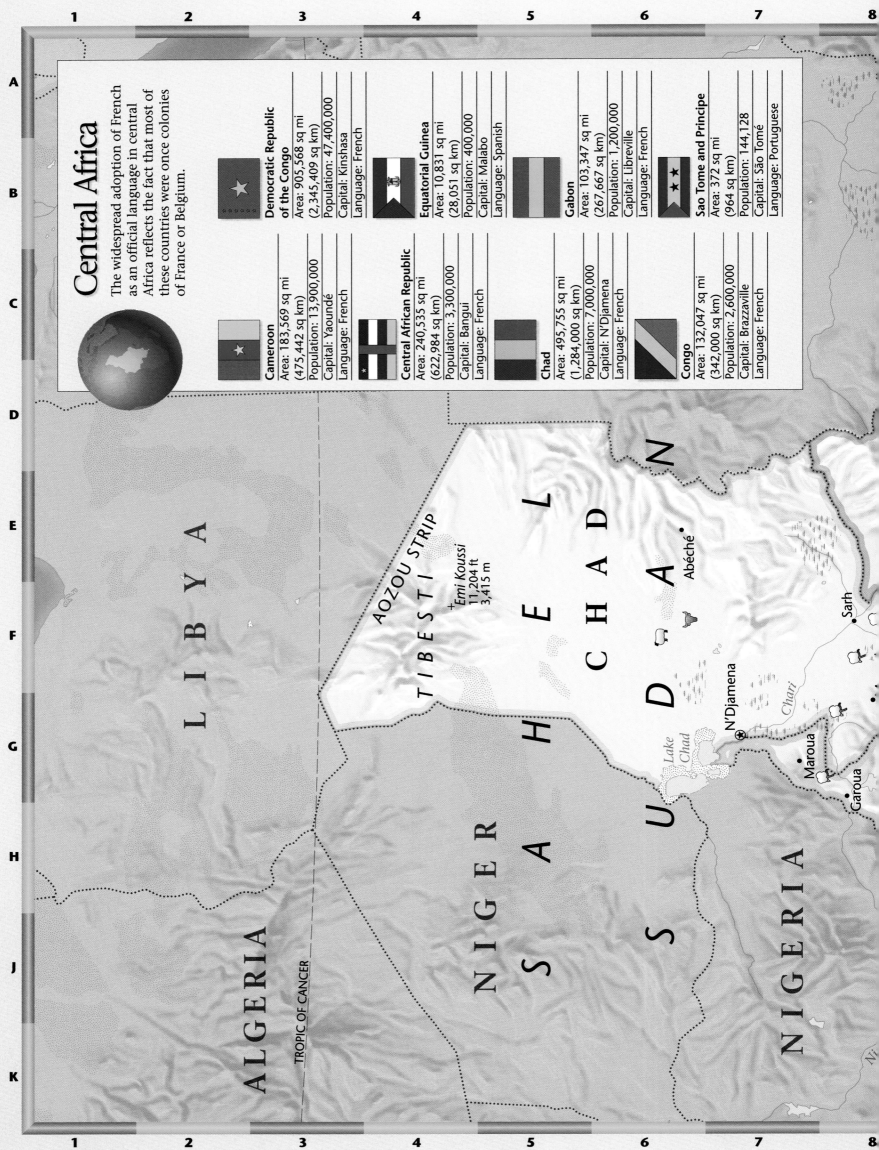

Central Africa

The widespread adoption of French as an official language in central Africa reflects the fact that most of these countries were once colonies of France or Belgium.

Democratic Republic of the Congo
Area: 905,568 sq mi
(2,345,409 sq km)
Population: 47,400,000
Capital: Kinshasa
Language: French

Equatorial Guinea
Area: 10,831 sq mi
(28,051 sq km)
Population: 400,000
Capital: Malabo
Language: Spanish

Gabon
Area: 103,347 sq mi
(267,667 sq km)
Population: 1,200,000
Capital: Libreville
Language: French

Sao Tome and Principe
Area: 372 sq mi
(964 sq km)
Population: 144,128
Capital: São Tomé
Language: Portuguese

Cameroon
Area: 183,569 sq mi
(475,442 sq km)
Population: 13,900,000
Capital: Yaoundé
Language: French

Central African Republic
Area: 240,535 sq mi
(622,984 sq km)
Population: 3,300,000
Capital: Bangui
Language: French

Chad
Area: 495,755 sq mi
(1,284,000 sq km)
Population: 7,000,000
Capital: N'Djamena
Language: French

Congo
Area: 132,047 sq mi
(342,000 sq km)
Population: 2,600,000
Capital: Brazzaville
Language: French

LIBYA

ALGERIA

TROPIC OF CANCER

AOZOU STRIP

TIBESTI

+ Emi Koussi
11,204 ft
3,415 m

SAHEL

CHAD

Abéché

Sarh

Chari

N'Djamena

Lake Chad

SUDAN

NIGER

NIGERIA

Maroua

Garoua

Map labels

UGANDA

Lake Victoria

Lake Albert

EQUATOR

RWANDA

BURUNDI

TANZANIA

Lake Tanganyika

Lake Edward

Lake Kivu

MALAWI

Lake Malawi

MOZAMBIQUE

Lake Mweru

Rift Valley

Isiro

Butembo

Bukavu

Kalemie

Lubumbashi

Likasi

ZAMBIA

Mitumba Mountains

Kolwezi

Boyoma Falls (Stanley Falls)

Lualaba

(Congo)

Kindu

Kisangani

rubber

Lomami

Bumba

Congo

rubber

DEMOCRATIC

REPUBLIC

OF THE

CONGO

Mbuji-Mayi

Mwene-Ditu

Kamina

Bambari

Gemena

Lisala

rubber

rubber

rubber

rubber

palm

Mbandaka

Kananga

palm

Kasai

Bangui

Ubangi

Ilebo

Kikwit

Tshikapa

palm

Bandundu

Kasai

ANGOLA

CAMEROON

Nkongsamba

Douala

Yaoundé

Ebolowa

palm

rubber

CONGO

Mossaka

palm

Kwango

Kinshasa

Congo

Brazzaville

Matadi

Boma

oil

CABINDA (Angola)

Pointe-Noire

oil

Malabo

EQUATORIAL GUINEA

Bata

RÍO MUNI

palm

GABON

Libreville

Lambaréné

palm

Port-Gentil

oil

oil

Príncipe

SÃO TOMÉ & PRINCIPE

São Tomé

São Tomé

ATLANTIC

OCEAN

400 miles

400 kilometers

Azimuthal Equidistant Projection

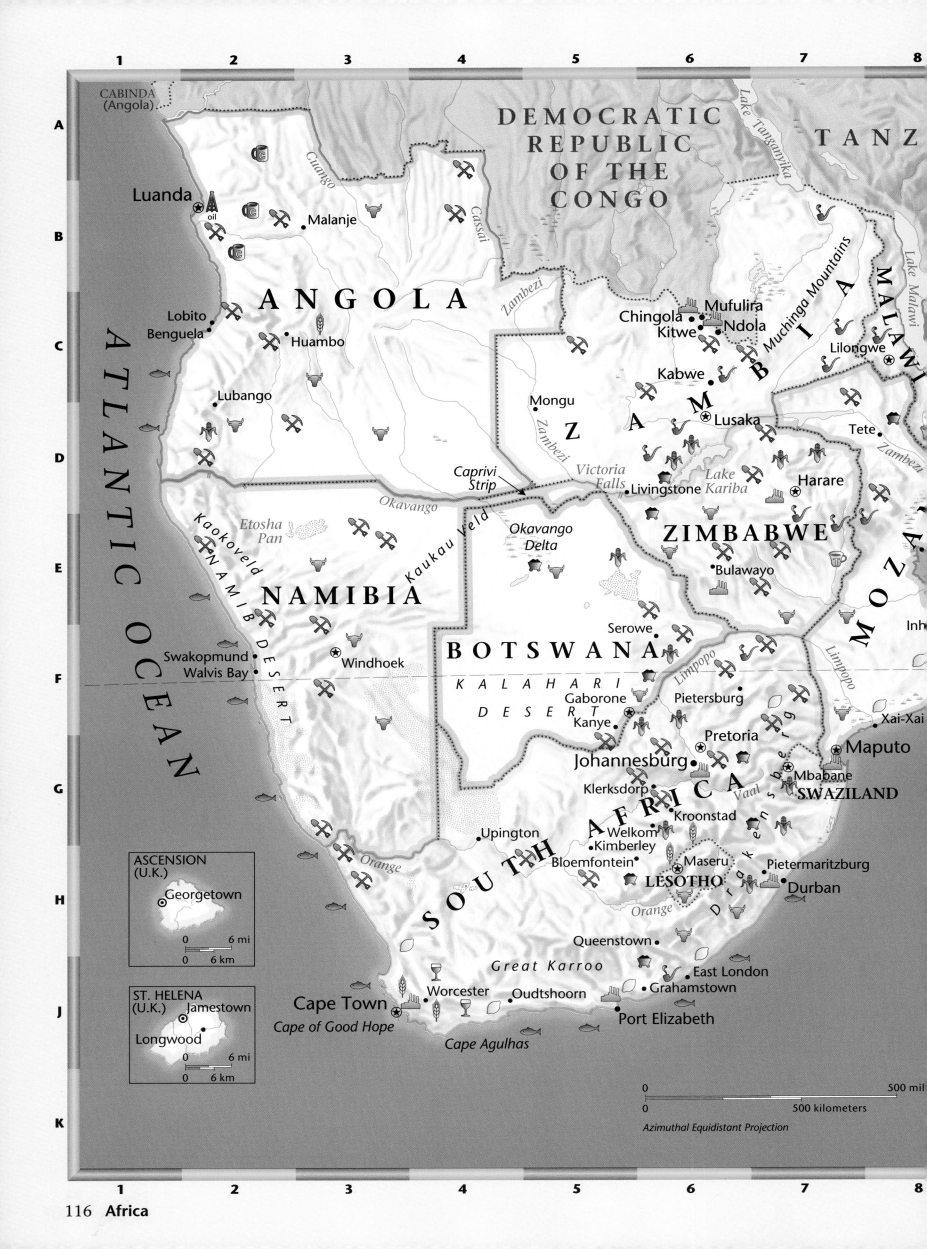

CABINDA
(Angola)

A

DEMOCRATIC
REPUBLIC
OF THE
CONGO

T A N Z

Lake Tanganyika

Luanda
oil

Cuango

B

Malanje

Cassai

Lobito
Benguela

ANGOLA

Zambezi

Chingola   Mufulira
Kitwe   Ndola

Muchinga Mountains

MALAWI

Lake Malawi

C

Huambo

Kabwe

Z A M B I A

Lilongwe

Lubango

Mongu

Zambezi

Lusaka

Tete

Zambezi

MOZA

D

Caprivi
Strip

Victoria
Falls

Livingstone

Lake
Kariba

Harare

Etosha
Pan

Okavango

ZIMBABWE

Kaokoveld

Okavango
Delta

E

NAMIBIA

Kaukau Veld

NAMIB DESERT

Bulawayo

Inh

ATLANTIC OCEAN

Serowe

B O T S W A N A

Limpopo

MOZA

Swakopmund
Walvis Bay

Windhoek

K A L A H A R I
D E S E R T

Gaborone
Kanye

Pietersburg

Limpopo

Xai-Xai

F

Pretoria

Johannesburg

Maputo

Mbabane
SWAZILAND

G

Klerksdorp

S O U T H   A F R I C A

Vaal

Kroonstad

Drakensberg

Upington

Orange

Welkom
Kimberley
Bloemfontein

Maseru

LESOTHO

Pietermaritzburg

Durban

H

Orange

Queenstown

Great Karroo

East London
Grahamstown

J

Cape Town
Cape of Good Hope

Worcester

Oudtshoorn

Port Elizabeth

Cape Agulhas

0   500 mil
0   500 kilometers

K

Azimuthal Equidistant Projection

INDIAN OCEAN

SEYCHELLES

MOZAMBIQUE CHANNEL

Moroni

COMOROS

Glorioso Is.
(France)

Cap d'Ambre
Antsiranana

Mayotte
(Fr.)

Pemba

Maromokotro
9,436 ft
2,876 m

Mozambique

Nampula

Mahajanga

MADAGASCAR

Juan de Nova
(Fr.)

nane

Toamasina

Antananarivo

Antsirabe

Bassas da India
(France)

Fianarantsoa

Île Europa
(France)

Toliara

'IC OF CAPRICORN

Cap Ste. Marie

Islands of Africa

MADEIRA IS.
(PORTUGAL)

CANARY IS.
(SPAIN)

CAPE
VERDE

AFRICA

EQUATORIAL GUINEA

EQUATOR 0°

SAO TOME
AND PRINCIPE

SEYCHELLES

ASCENSION
(UNITED KINGDOM)

COMOROS

ST. HELENA
(UNITED KINGDOM)

MAURITIUS

RÉUNION
(FRANCE)

Southern Africa

Rich in minerals and natural beauty, the countries of southern Africa range in size from Angola, on the Atlantic coast, to the Seychelles, a tiny country in the Indian Ocean.

Angola
Area: 481,354 sq mi
(1,246,700 sq km)
Population: 11,600,000
Capital: Luanda
Language: Portuguese

Botswana
Area: 231,805 sq mi
(600,372 sq km)
Population: 1,500,000
Capital: Gaborone
Language: English

Comoros
Area: 719 sq mi
(1,862 sq km)
Population: 600,000
Capital: Moroni
Languages: Arabic, French

Lesotho
Area: 11,720 sq mi
(30,355 sq km)
Population: 2,000,000
Capital: Maseru
Language: English

Madagascar
Area: 226,658 sq mi
(587,041 sq km)
Population: 14,100,000
Capital: Antananarivo
Language: French

Malawi
Area: 45,747 sq mi
(118,484 sq km)
Population: 9,600,000
Capital: Lilongwe
Languages: English, Chichewa

Mauritius
Area: 788 sq mi
(2,040 sq km)
Population: 1,100,000
Capital: Port Louis
Language: English

Mozambique
Area: 308,642 sq mi
(799,380 sq km)
Population: 18,400,000
Capital: Maputo
Language: Portuguese

Namibia
Area: 318,261 sq mi
(824,292 sq km)
Population: 1,700,000
Capital: Windhoek
Language: English

Seychelles
Area: 175 sq mi
(453 sq km)
Population: 100,000
Capital: Victoria
Languages: English, French

South Africa
Area: 471,445 sq mi
(1,221,037 sq km)
Population: 42,500,000
Capitals: Cape Town, Pretoria,
(Bloemfontein, judicial)
Languages: Afrikaans,
English, others

Swaziland
Area: 6,704 sq mi
(17,364 sq km)
Population: 1,000,000
Capital: Mbabane
Languages: English, siSwati

Zambia
Area: 290,586 sq mi
(752,614 sq km)
Population: 9,400,000
Capital: Lusaka
Language: English

Zimbabwe
Area: 150,804 sq mi
(390,580 sq km)
Population: 11,400,000
Capital: Harare
Language: English

Réunion (France)

St. Helena (United Kingdom)

Asia

From a great distance, the Zagros Mountains of Iran, in southwestern Asia, look like mere ripples of mud in a drying puddle. Yet the snowcapped northern peaks (bottom), reach 14,000 feet (4,267 meters). (In this image, south is at the top.) Land jutting in at the right pinches the Persian Gulf in two, forming the narrow Strait of Hormuz. Ships that pass through this strait carry much of the world's oil, pumped from under the sands around the Persian Gulf. The shallow waters north of the strait (far right) make up the Persian Gulf. South (top) lie the Gulf of Oman and the Arabian Sea. The world's largest continent, Asia occupies one-third of all the earth's landmass.

A Muslim prayer tower marks the skyline of Dubayy, a deepwater port on the Persian Gulf. A trading center, Dubayy belongs to the country known as the United Arab Emirates, or U.A.E.

CONNECTION: *You can find the Strait of Hormuz and Dubayy on the maps on pages 120–121 and 134–135.*

Asia

Land on a Grand Scale

Asia ranks as the world's biggest continent and almost everything here is on a grand scale. It boasts not just earth's highest peak, but the ten highest, in the colossal Himalaya. On Asia's Arabian Peninsula, in the southwest, lies the lowest place on earth's surface—the Dead Sea, too salty to support life. The world's largest expanse of tundra stretches across northern Asia. Southeast Asia offers a contrast: tropical forests drenched by monsoon rains. Rain water and snowmelt feed into major rivers such as the Yangtze (Chang) and Yellow (Huang).

The Land

Area
17,213,298 sq mi
(44,579,000 sq km)

Highest mountain
Everest: 29,028 ft (8,848 m)

Lowest point
Dead Sea: 1,339 ft (408 m)
below sea level

Longest river
Yangtze (Chang): 3,964 mi
(6,380 km)

Largest lake
Baikal: 12,163 sq mi
(31,500 sq km)

Largest island
Borneo: 280,137 sq mi
(725,500 sq km)

ATLANTIC OCEAN

EUROPE

RUSSIA

Europe-Asia Boundary

MEDITERRANEAN SEA

BLACK SEA

AEGEAN SEA

ANATOLIA

TURKEY

CYPRUS

LEBANON
ISRAEL

Suez Canal →

Sinai

JORDAN

SYRIA
Syrian Desert

TROPIC OF CANCER

Dead Sea
World's lowest point
-1,339 feet, -408 meters

RED SEA

AFRICA

KUWAIT

SAUDI ARABIA

BAHRAIN
QATAR

ARABIAN

UNITED ARAB EMIRATES

PENINSULA
Rub al Khali

YEMEN

OMAN

Gulf of Aden

Mesopotamia

Tigris

Euphrates

Zagros Mountains

Persian Gulf

Gulf of Oman

IRAQ

IRAN

CASPIAN SEA

Caspian Depression

Caucasus Mts.

GEORGIA

ARMENIA

AZERBAIJAN

ELBURZ MTS.

THE STE

KAZAKHS

Aral Sea

Syr Darya

UZBEKISTAN

Amu Darya

TURKMENISTAN

AFGHANISTAN

PAKISTAN

Indus

Volga

Ural

URAL M

Caspian

R

U

ARCTIC CIRCLE

ARABIAN SEA

LACCAD

MALDIVES

EQUATOR

INDIAN

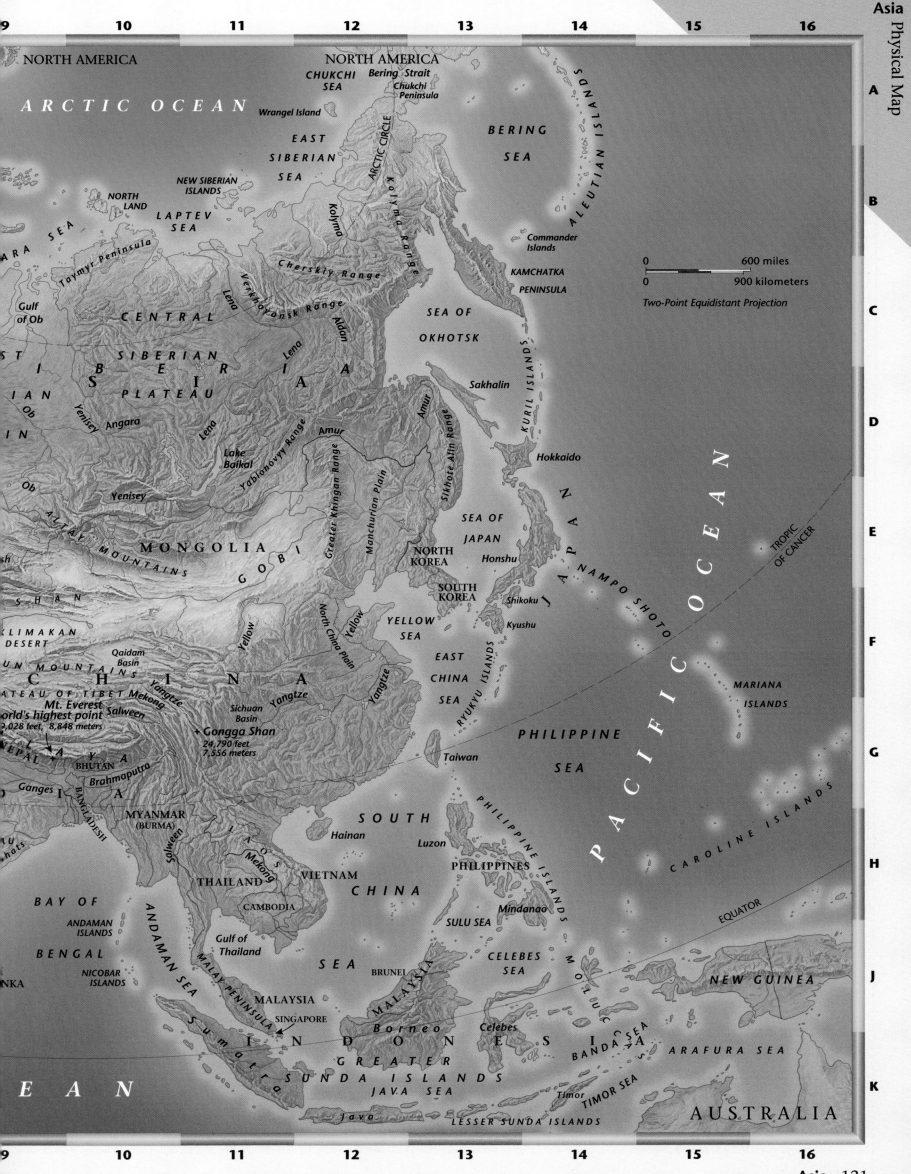

9 10 11 12 13 14 15 16

A
B
C
D
E
F
G
H
J
K

NORTH AMERICA

ARCTIC OCEAN

CHUKCHI
SEA
Bering Strait
Chukchi
Peninsula

NORTH AMERICA

Wrangel Island

BERING
SEA

EAST
SIBERIAN
SEA

NEW SIBERIAN
ISLANDS

NORTH
LAND

LAPTEV
SEA

ARA SEA

Taymyr Peninsula

ARCTIC CIRCLE

Kolyma Range

Cherskiy Range

Commander
Islands

KAMCHATKA
PENINSULA

ALEUTIAN ISLANDS

600 miles

900 kilometers

Two-Point Equidistant Projection

Gulf
of Ob

CENTRAL

SIBERIAN

PLATEAU

Verkhoyansk Range

Lena

Lena

Aldon

SEA OF
OKHOTSK

KURIL ISLANDS

Sakhalin

Yenisey

Angara

Lena

Lake
Baikal

Amur

Yablonovyy Range

Amur

Sikhote Alin Range

Hokkaido

Ob

Yenisey

ALTAY
MOUNTAINS

MONGOLIA

GOBI

Greater Khingan Range

Manchurian
Plain

SEA OF
JAPAN

SHAN

KLIMAKAN
DESERT

UN MOUNTAINS

CHINA

Qaidam
Basin

PLATEAU OF TIBET

Mt. Everest
World's highest point
29,028 feet, 8,848 meters

Mekong

Salween

HIMALAYA

NEPAL

BHUTAN

Ganges

Brahmaputra

BANGLADESH

INDIA

North China plain

Yellow

Yellow

Yangtze

Sichuan
Basin

Yangtze

Gongga Shan
24,790 feet
7,556 meters

NORTH
KOREA

SOUTH
KOREA

YELLOW
SEA

EAST
CHINA
SEA

Honshu

Shikoku

Kyushu

RYUKYU ISLANDS

JAPAN

NAMPO SHOTO

TROPIC OF CANCER

PACIFIC OCEAN

MARIANA
ISLANDS

PHILIPPINE
SEA

Taiwan

CAROLINE ISLANDS

MYANMAR
(BURMA)

Salween

LAOS

Mekong

THAILAND

VIETNAM

CAMBODIA

SOUTH

CHINA

Hainan

SEA

Luzon

PHILIPPINES

Mindanao

SULU SEA

PHILIPPINE ISLANDS

EQUATOR

BAY OF

ANDAMAN
ISLANDS

BENGAL

NICOBAR
ISLANDS

NKA

ANDAMAN SEA

MALAY PENINSULA

Gulf of
Thailand

MALAYSIA

SINGAPORE

SUMATRA

Borneo

CELEBES
SEA

Celebes

MOLUCCA

BANDA SEA

NEW GUINEA

ARAFURA SEA

BRUNEI

MALAYSIA

INDONESIA

GREATER

SUNDA ISLANDS

JAVA SEA

Java

Timor

TIMOR SEA

LESSER SUNDA ISLANDS

AUSTRALIA

EAN

9 10 11 12 13 14 15 16

Asia
Ancient and Modern

Biggest, highest, most populous; to the superlatives Asia can boast of, add another: oldest culturally. Archaeologists believe that the world's first city-based civilization arose in the wide plain between the Tigris and Euphrates Rivers 55 centuries ago. Here, people learned how to bring water to their lands and plant grain. Cities grew up. Over the centuries, civilizations arose in other river valleys across Asia. These ancient cultures gave us writing, the wheel, astronomy, and mechanical printing, as well as all of the world's major religions.

In many parts of Asia—especially remote areas—people still live lives very similar to those of their ancestors. They depend on herding and traditional farming methods. They practice age-old crafts to make tools, clothes, and basic necessities. Other parts of Asia have entered the modern world in a big way. Huge cities have grown up, with the pollution and crowding that so often come with industrialization. Asian governments face the challenge the whole world faces—how to provide for their people and still protect the environment.

▲ **THE TIGER'S** *terrifying pounce can't protect it from the double threat it faces: illegal hunting, or poaching, and loss of habitat. Tigers live only in Asia.*

◄ **HANDLING** *her test tubes with care, a researcher in South Korea helps to develop new medicines.*

► **SKYSCRAPERS** *loom behind Singapore's deep harbor. This small country off the tip of the Malay Peninsula provides a major port for ships traveling between the Indian and Pacific Oceans.*

▲ **SNAKING** *nearly 4,000 miles (6,437 kilometers) across China, the Great Wall once kept out invaders from the north. Today, 2,200 years after the wall was begun, the structure is a major tourist attraction for foreigners.*

▶ **A TRADITIONAL** *Arab headdress meets a high-tech tool—the cellular phone. A familiar sight in southwestern Asia, the traditional cloth called a kaffiyeh shields heads from the desert sun.*

▼ **STUDENTS** *attend a class taught in Hebrew at a Jewish school in Israel. Arab students attend separate schools where classes are taught in Arabic—Israel's other official language.*

▶ **MEMBERS OF EARTH'S** *most populous nation—China—commute on its most popular vehicle: the bicycle.*

▶ **A PERFECT CONE** *framed by cherry blossoms, Mount Fuji is sacred to followers of Shinto, a religion that has its origins in Japan. The volcanic mountain is the highest in Japan.*

▼ **ALL HER EGGS** *in two baskets, a woman in China shoulders a delicate burden. Most Asians live by farming or herding.*

▼ **EAST AND WEST MEET** *in Istanbul, Turkey, which straddles the Bosporus. It is the only major world city located on two continents—Europe and Asia. Although most of its people are Muslims, Turkey's laws, education, and politics show a strong European influence.*

▶ **A TOWERING** *gold-and-bronze Buddha fills a temple in Nara, a former capital of Japan. Buddhism arose in India and spread across much of Asia. It is practiced by millions today.*

▶ **DASHING THROUGH THE SNOW,** *a pair of reindeer pull a sled across the tundra of Siberia, in Russia. Reindeer play a central role in the lives of many people who are native to Russia's Arctic regions. They provide food, shelter, clothing, and transportation.*

Asia

Home to Half the World

Forty-six countries make up Asia. Two of them, China and India, contain two-thirds of the continent's population. Because so much of Asia is uninhabitable—too high, too dry, or too cold—a majority of the population lives in coastal areas and river valleys. Although most Asians make their living farming or fishing, a growing number are finding work in factories and service industries. Japan has been Asia's leader in developing a modern industrialized economy. Many other countries, especially along the Pacific Rim, are now following Japan's example.

The People

Population
3,604,000,000

Largest metropolitan area
Tokyo, Japan:
Pop. 27,200,000

Largest country
China: 3,705,407 sq mi
(9,596,961 sq km)

Most densely populated country
Singapore: 14,644 people
per sq mi

Economy
Farming: rice, wheat
Industry: petroleum, electronics

Life expectancy
65 years

A commonly accepted division between Asia and Europe–here marked by an orange line–is formed by the Ural Mountains, Ural River, Caspian Sea, Caucasus Mountains, and the Black Sea with its outlets, the Bosporus and the Dardanelles.

ATLANTIC OCEAN

Norwegian Sea

ARCTIC CIRCLE

Baltic Sea

Kaliningrad
(Russia)

Mu

Kola Penin

L. Ladoga
Lake Onega

St. Petersburg

Moscow

EU
BOU

R

Nizhniy Novgorod

Volga

Kazan

Perm'

Yekaterinburg

Samara

Ufa

URAL

Oral

Ma

Black Sea

Rostov

Volgograd

Ural

Istanbul

Izmir

Bursa

Ankara

T U R K E Y

Konya

GEORGIA

Caucasus Mts.

T'bilisi

ARMENIA

Caspian Depression

KAZAK

Kayseri

Nicosia

CYPRUS

LEBANON

Adana

Yerevan

AZERBAIJAN

Baku

Caspian Sea

Aral Sea

Qa

UZBEKISTAN

Beirut

Jerusalem

ISRAEL

Damascus

SYRIA

Syr Da

Amu Darya

Tashke

Dead Sea
-1,339 ft
-408 m

JORDAN

Amman

Euphrates

Tigris

Baghdad

Tehran

TURKMENISTAN

Ashgabat

M E D I T E R R A N E A N   S E A

TROPIC OF CANCER

Red Sea

IRAQ

Zagros Mts.

Kerman

Mashhad

Dushanbe

Basra

I R A N

AFGHANISTAN

Sa

Kuwait

KUWAIT

Persian Gulf

Kabul

Islamaba

Jeddah

Mecca

SAUDI

Manama

BAHRAIN

QATAR

Zahedan

Rawalpi

La

Riyadh

Doha

Abu Dhabi

Str. of Hormuz

PAKISTAN

Faisalaba

A R A B I A

UNITED ARAB EMIRATES

Gulf of Oman

Ne

Ja

Sanaa

Rub al Khali

Muscat

Karachi

Indus

In

BOUNDARY UNDEFINED

O M A N

Ahmadabad

Y E M E N

Vadodara

Aden

Gulf of Aden

Surat

Arabian Sea

Mumbai
(Bombay)

Socotra
(Yemen)

Bang

LAKSHADWEEP
(India)

My

0° EQUATOR

Coimba

M

MALDIVE ISLANDS

Ma
MA

INDIAN OC

| 0 | | 600 miles |
| 0 | | 900 kilometers |

Two-Point Equidistant Projection

CHAGOS AR
(British Te

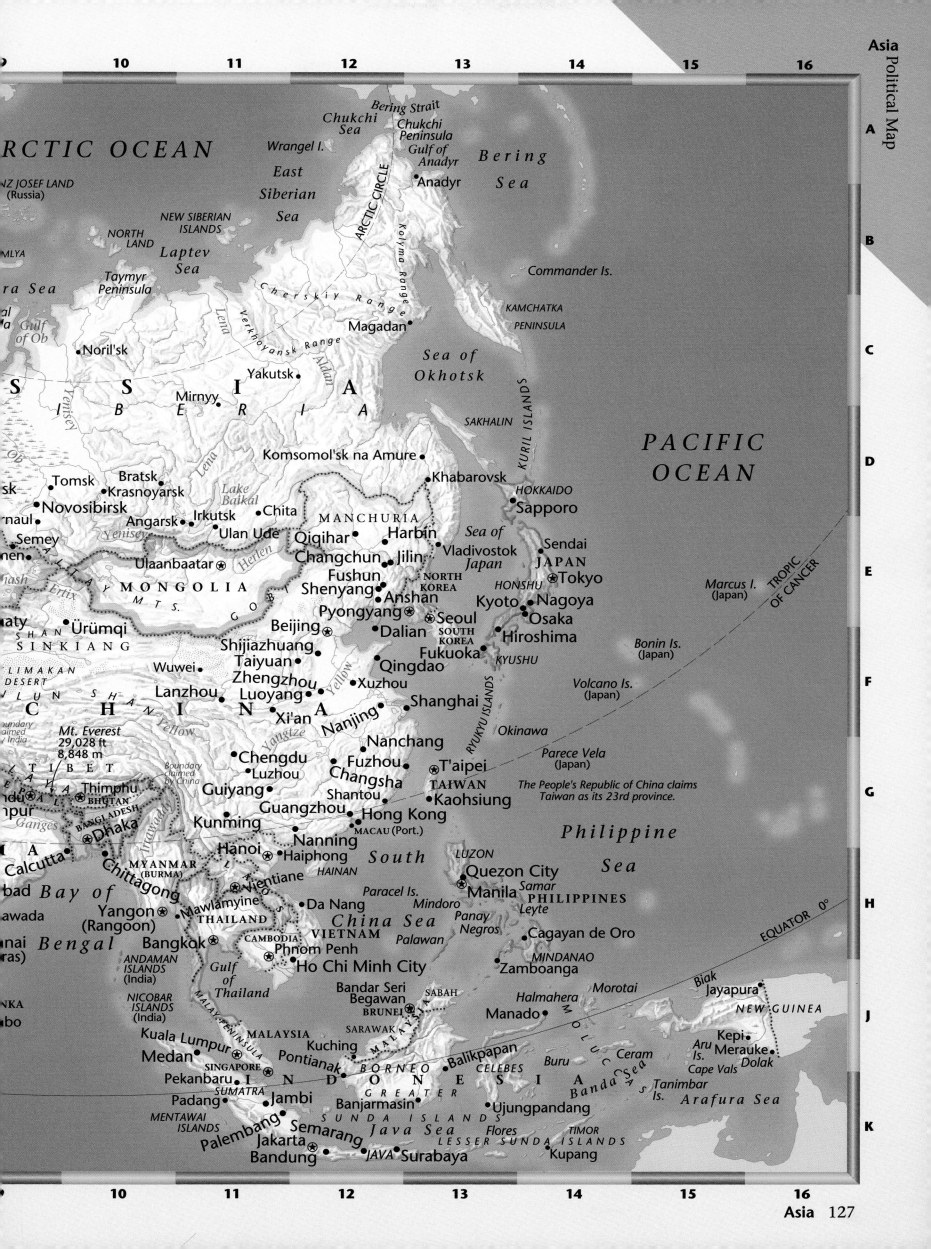

ARCTIC OCEAN

NZ JOSEF LAND
(Russia)

MLYA

ra Sea

al
Gulf
of Ob

NORTH
LAND

Taymyr
Peninsula

NEW SIBERIAN
ISLANDS

Laptev
Sea

East
Siberian
Sea

Wrangel I.

Chukchi
Sea

Bering Strait

Chukchi
Peninsula

Gulf of
Anadyr

• Anadyr

B e r i n g
Sea

Commander Is.

KAMCHATKA
PENINSULA

PACIFIC
OCEAN

ARCTIC CIRCLE

• Noril'sk

Magadan •

Sea of
Okhotsk

Kolyma Range

Cherskiy Range

Verkhoyansk Range

Lena

Yenisey

sk

• Tomsk
• Bratsk
• Krasnoyarsk
• Novosibirsk
• Angarsk • Irkutsk
• Semey
nen

naul

Ob

SIBERIA

• Yakutsk

Lake
Baikal

• Chita

Ulan Ude •

• Mirnyy

SAKHALIN

KURIL ISLANDS

Komsomol'sk na Amure •

• Khabarovsk

HOKKAIDO

• Sapporo

Sea of
Japan

TROPIC

OF CANCER

MANCHURIA

• Qiqihar
Harbin •
Changchun • • Jilin
Fushun •
Shenyang • Anshan •
Pyongyang ⊛

• Vladivostok

• Sendai

JAPAN

⊛ Tokyo

Marcus I.
(Japan)

ALTAY
M T S.

MONGOLIA

Ulaanbaatar ⊛

GOBI

Herlen

Ertix

nash

aty

SHAN

LIMAKAN
DESERT

• Ürümqi

SINKIANG

Wuwei •

NORTH
KOREA

HONSHU

Kyoto •
Osaka
• Nagoya

• Beijing ⊛

SOUTH
KOREA

Dalian •

Seoul

• Hiroshima

Fukuoka •

KYUSHU

Bonin Is.
(Japan)

• Shijiazhuang
Taiyuan •
Zhengzhou •
• Lanzhou Luoyang •
• Xuzhou

• Qingdao

LUN SHAN

Yellow

Yellow

• Xi'an
Nanjing •

• Shanghai

RYUKYU ISLANDS

Volcano Is.
(Japan)

undary
aimed
India

Mt. Everest
29,028 ft
8,848 m

• Nanchang

Okinawa

Parece Vela
(Japan)

HINA

TIBET

Boundary
claimed
by China

A L A

Thimphu
⊛ BHUTAN

• Chengdu
• Luzhou

Fuzhou •

• T'aipei ⊛

• Changsha

TAIWAN

mpur

ndu

BANGLADESH

Guiyang •

Shantou •

• Kaohsiung

The People's Republic of China claims
Taiwan as its 23rd province.

Ganges

⊛ Dhaka

Kunming •

• Guangzhou

Irrawaddy

• Hong Kong

MACAU (Port.)

Philippine

Calcutta •

A

Hanoi •

• Nanning

• Haiphong

South

LUZON

Sea

bad
awada

CHITTAGONG

MYANMAR
(BURMA)

Vientiane ⊛

HAINAN

• Quezon City

LUZON

China Sea

⊛ Manila

PHILIPPINES

Samar
Leyte

ras)

Yangon ⊛
(Rangoon)

• Mawlamyine

THAILAND

• Da Nang

Paracel Is.

Mindoro

VIETNAM

Panay
Negros

Palawan

nai
bo

Bay of
Bengal

Bangkok ⊛

CAMBODIA

Phnom Penh ⊛

Ho Chi Minh City •

• Cagayan de Oro

MINDANAO

NKA

ANDAMAN
ISLANDS
(India)

Gulf of
Thailand

• Zamboanga

EQUATOR 0°

NICOBAR
ISLANDS
(India)

Bandar Seri
Begawan ⊛

SABAH

Halmahera

Morotai

Biak

• Jayapura

MALAY PENINSULA

BRUNEI

• Manado

NEW GUINEA

Kuala Lumpur ⊛

MALAYSIA

• Kuching

SARAWAK

MALAYSIA

• Kepi

• Medan

Pontianak •

BORNEO

• Balikpapan

CELEBES

Buru

Ceram

Aru
Is.

Merauke •

SINGAPORE ⊛

I N D O N E S I A

GREATER

Cape Vals

Dolak

• Pekanbaru

SUMATRA

• Jambi

• Banjarmasin

Tanimbar
Is.

Arafura Sea

• Padang

MENTAWAI
ISLANDS

• Ujungpandang

Banda Sea

SUNDA ISLANDS

• Palembang
Semarang •

Java Sea

Flores

TIMOR

• Kupang

Jakarta ⊛

Bandung •

JAVA

• Surabaya

LESSER SUNDA ISLANDS

Central Asia

The countries of central Asia are marked by mountains and steppes. They also include some of Asia's biggest deserts, including the Gobi and the Kara Kum.

Kyrgyzstan
Area: 76,834 sq mi (199,000 sq km)
Population: 4,600,000
Capital: Bishkek
Languages: Kirghiz, Russian

Tajikistan
Area: 55,213 sq mi (143,000 sq km)
Population: 6,000,000
Capital: Dushanbe
Language: Tajik

Uzbekistan
Area: 172,588 sq mi (447,000 sq km)
Population: 23,700,000
Capital: Tashkent
Language: Uzbek

Kazakhstan
Area: 1,049,039 sq mi (2,717,000 sq km)
Population: 16,400,000
Capitals: Almaty, Astana
Languages: Kazakh, Russian

Mongolia
Area: 604,250 sq mi (1,565,000 sq km)
Population: 2,400,000
Capital: Ulaanbaatar
Language: Khalkha Mongolian

Turkmenistan
Area: 188,418 sq mi (488,000 sq km)
Population: 4,600,000
Capital: Ashgabat
Language: Turkmen

Asian Russia
Russia sprawls across the northern part of two continents: Europe and Asia. The Ural Mountains divide European Russia from Asian Russia. Statistics for Russia are found on page 99 in the Europe section.

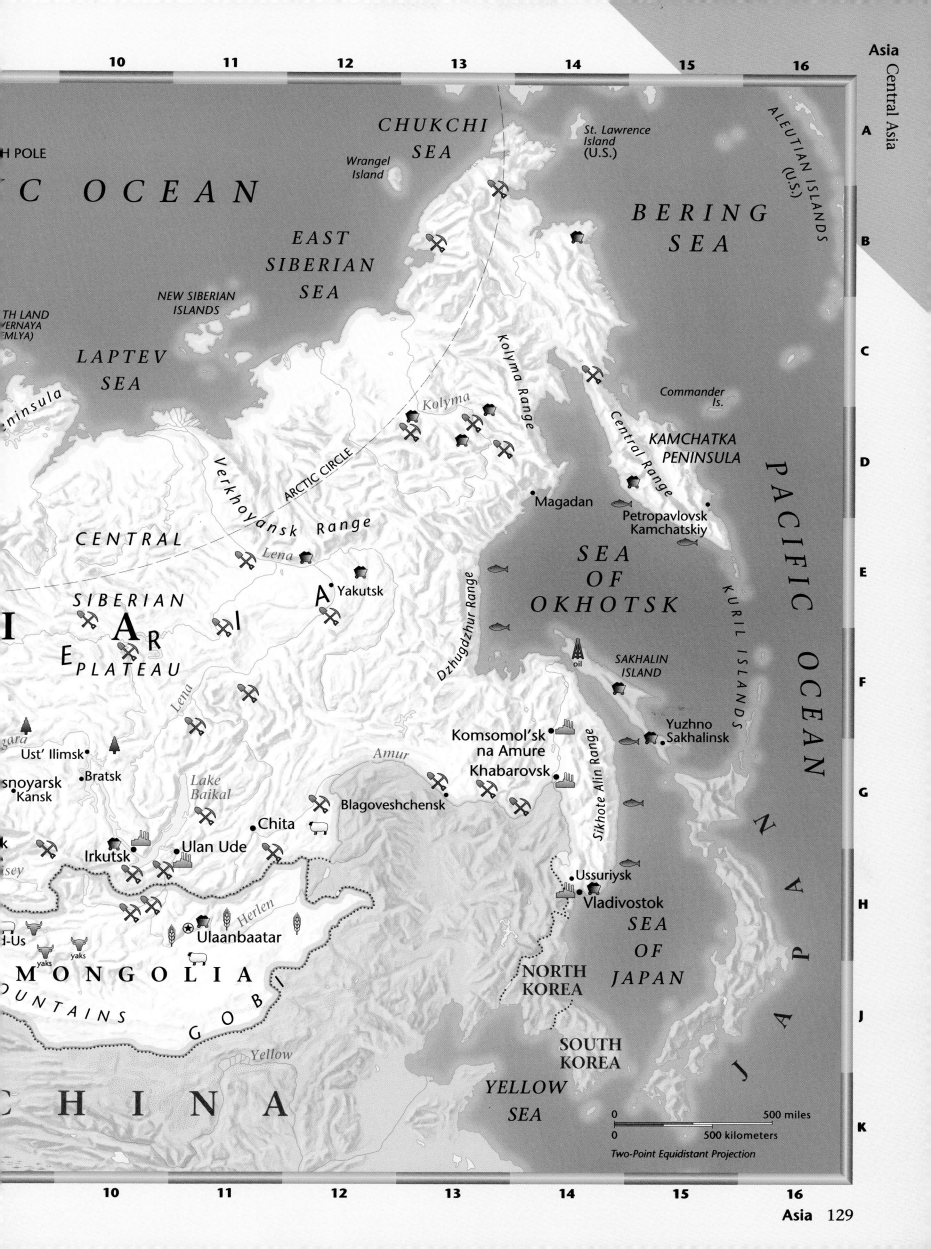

ARCTIC OCEAN

NORTH POLE

CHUKCHI
SEA

*Wrangel
Island*

St. Lawrence
Island
(U.S.)

BERING
SEA

ALEUTIAN ISLANDS
(U.S.)

EAST
SIBERIAN
SEA

*NEW SIBERIAN
ISLANDS*

NORTH LAND
(SEVERNAYA
ZEMLYA)

LAPTEV
SEA

Peninsula

Kolyma

Kolyma Range

Central Range

Commander
Is.

KAMCHATKA
PENINSULA

Verkhoyansk Range

ARCTIC CIRCLE

•Magadan

Petropavlovsk
Kamchatskiy

CENTRAL

SIBERIAN

Lena

•Yakutsk

A

I

A
R

PLATEAU

Dzhugdzhur Range

SEA
OF
OKHOTSK

KURIL ISLANDS

PACIFIC OCEAN

oil

SAKHALIN
ISLAND

Lena

Angara

•Ust' Ilimsk•

•Bratsk

•snoyarsk
Kansk

*Lake
Baikal*

Amur

Komsomol'sk
na Amure

Khabarovsk

Sikhote Alin Range

Yuzhno
Sakhalinsk

Blagoveshchensk

k•

Irkutsk•

•Chita

Ulan Ude

Herlen

•Ussuriysk

Vladivostok

SEA
OF
JAPAN

J
A
P
A
N

nisey

Ulaanbaatar

d-Us

yaks   yaks

MONGOLIA

OUNTAINS

GOBI

Yellow

NORTH
KOREA

SOUTH
KOREA

CHINA

YELLOW
SEA

0   500 miles

0   500 kilometers

Two-Point Equidistant Projection

East Asia

East Asia includes the world's most populous country. China's population has passed one billion and is still growing, although at a much slower rate than in the past. The area also encompasses the Korean Peninsula and the islands of Japan and Taiwan.

China
Area: 3,705,407 sq mi
(9,596,961 sq km)
Population: 1,236,700,000
Capital: Beijing
Language: Chinese

Taiwan
The People's Republic of China claims Taiwan as its 23rd province. Taiwan is a 230-mile-long island with an area of 13,900 square miles (36,000 square kilometers) and a population of 22 million people.

Japan
Area: 145,875 sq mi
(377,815 sq km)
Population: 126,100,000
Capital: Tokyo
Language: Japanese

North Korea
Area: 46,540 sq mi
(120,538 sq km)
Population: 24,300,000
Capital: Pyongyang
Language: Korean

South Korea
Area: 38,230 sq mi
(99,016 sq km)
Population: 45,900,000
Capital: Seoul
Language: Korean

Macau (Portugal)

R U

KAZAKHSTAN

Lake Balkhash

M

UZB. KYRGYZSTAN
TAJ.
AFGHAN.
PAK.

KASHMIR

H I M A L A Y A

NEPAL

BHUTAN

INDIA

BANGLADESH

TROPIC OF CANCER

Ganges

BAY OF BENGAL

MYANMAR
(BURMA)

THAILAND

A L T A Y   M T S

oil
oil

T I A N   S H A N
Ürümqi
Kashi
Tarim
SINKIANG
oil
TAKLIMAKAN DESERT
Turpan Depression
-505 ft
-154 m
Hami
Lop Nur
Yumen
oil
oil
oil
K U N   L U N   S H A N
Hotan
ALTUN SHAN
oil
Boundary claimed by India
Boundary claimed by China
PLATEAU OF TIBET
Qinghai Hu
Xinin

C H I

TIBET
Salween
Mt. Everest
29,028 ft
8,848m
yaks
Lhasa
yaks
Boundary claimed by China

Irrawaddy

Mekong

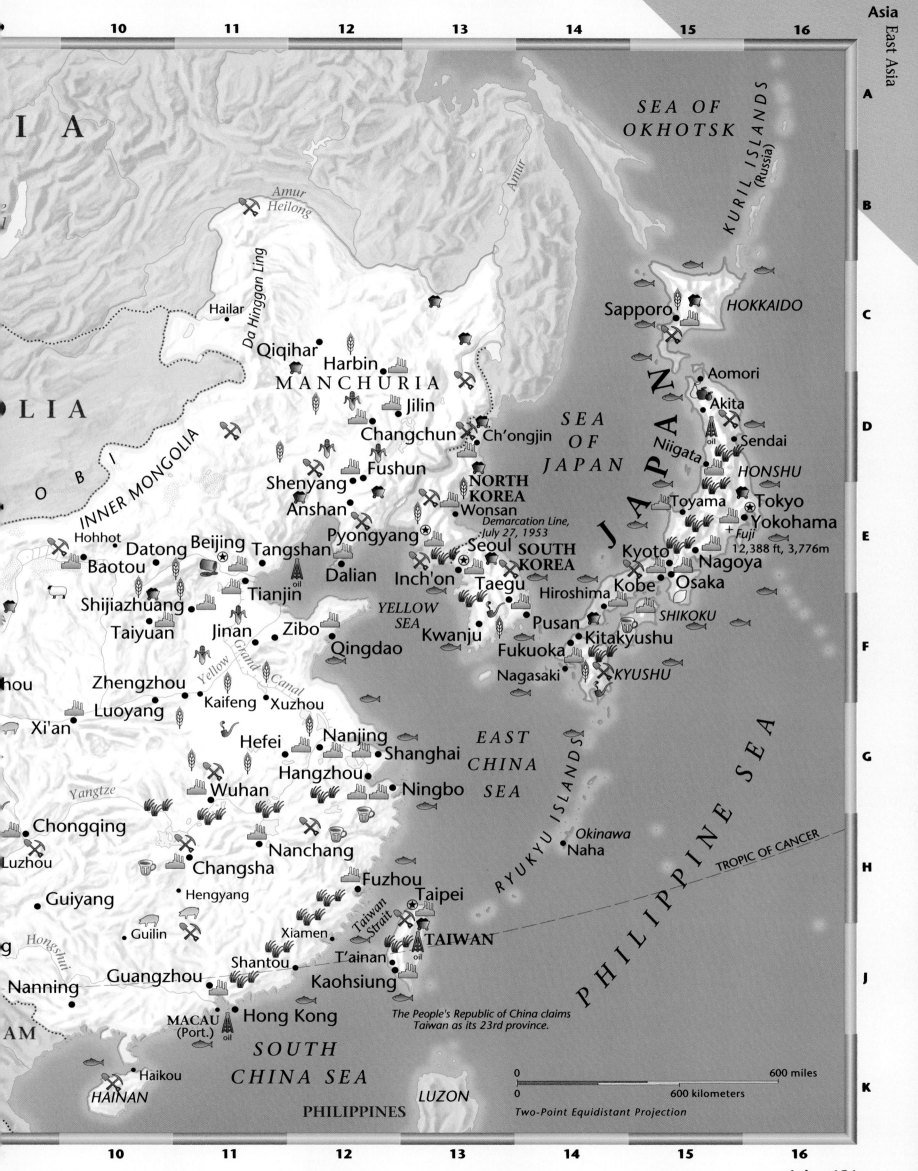

10   **11**   **12**   **13**   **14**   **15**   **16**

A

B

SEA OF
OKHOTSK

KURIL ISLANDS
(Russia)

Amur
Heilong

Amur

C

Hailar

HOKKAIDO

Sapporo

Qiqihar

Harbin

Aomori

M A N C H U R I A

Akita

Jilin

Changchun

Ch'ongjin

Niigata

Sendai

Fushun

oil

HONSHU

Shenyang

SEA
OF
JAPAN

Toyama

Tokyo

J
A
P
A
N

Yokohama

Anshan

NORTH
KOREA

Wonsan

+Fuji
12,388 ft, 3,776m

Pyongyang

Demarcation Line,
July 27, 1953

Kyoto

INNER MONGOLIA

Hohhot

Datong

Beijing

Tangshan

Seoul

SOUTH
KOREA

Nagoya

Baotou

Dalian

Inch'on

Kobe

Osaka

Taegu

SHIKOKU

Shijiazhuang

Tianjin

oil

Hiroshima

Taiyuan

Jinan

Zibo

YELLOW
SEA

Kwanju

Pusan

Fukuoka

Kitakyushu

Qingdao

Nagasaki

KYUSHU

Zhengzhou

Kaifeng

Xuzhou

Luoyang

Xi'an

EAST
CHINA
SEA

Hefei

Nanjing

RYUKYU ISLANDS

Wuhan

Shanghai

Hangzhou

Ningbo

Yangtze

Okinawa

Chongqing

Naha

TROPIC OF CANCER

Luzhou

Nanchang

Changsha

Fuzhou

*P
H
I
L
I
P
P
I
N
E
*
*S
E
A*

Guiyang

Hengyang

Taipei

Guilin

Xiamen

Taiwan
Strait

oil

TAIWAN

Shantou

T'ainan

Hongshui

Guangzhou

Kaohsiung

Nanning

MACAU
(Port.)

oil

Hong Kong

The People's Republic of China claims
Taiwan as its 23rd province.

SOUTH

Haikou

CHINA SEA

HAINAN

0   600 miles

PHILIPPINES

LUZON

0   600 kilometers

Two-Point Equidistant Projection

10   **11**   **12**   **13**   **14**   **15**   **16**

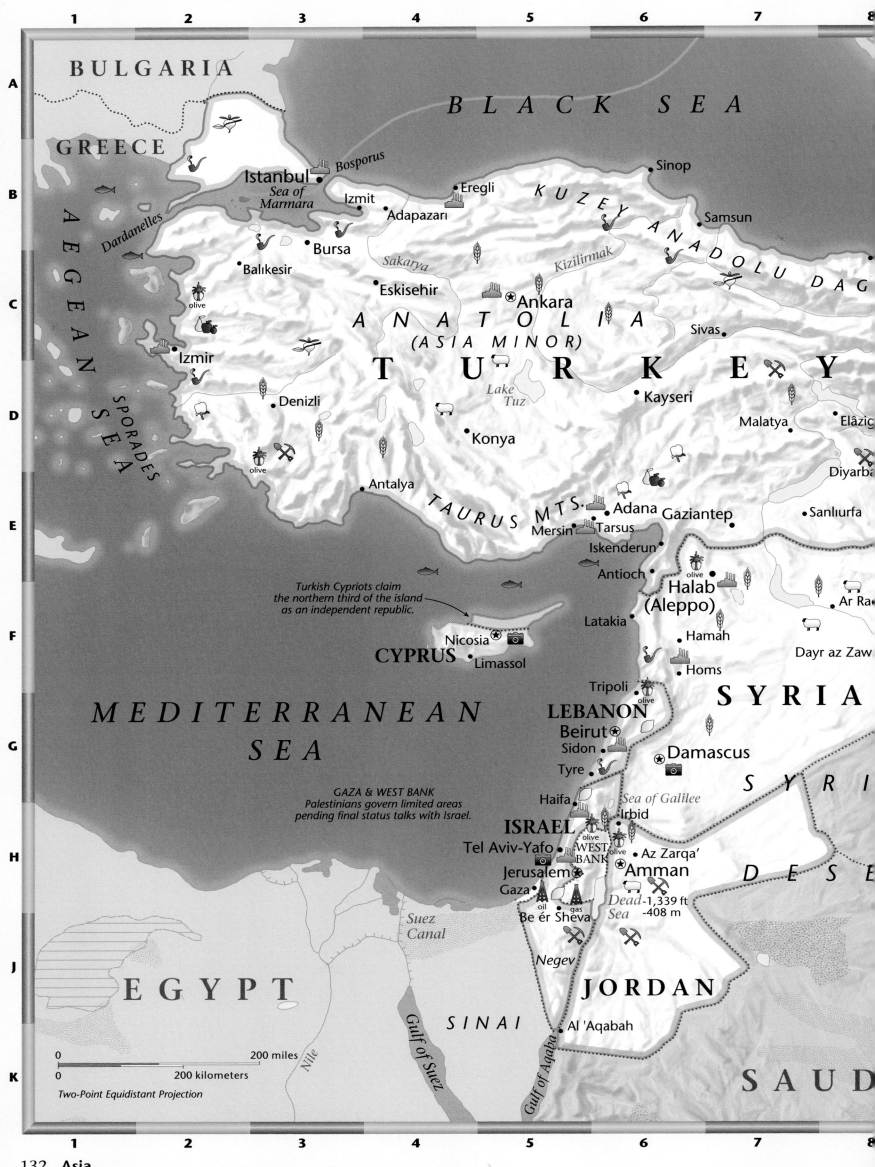

BULGARIA

GREECE

Dardanelles

AEGEAN SEA

SPORADES SEA

BLACK SEA

Istanbul
Sea of Marmara
Bosporus
Izmit • Adapazari •
• Eregli
• Sinop
Samsun •

• Bursa
• Balıkesir
Sakarya
Kizilirmak

KUZEY ANADOLU DAĞ

• Eskisehir
Ankara ⊛
ANATOLIA
(ASIA MINOR)

• Sivas

olive
• Izmir

T U R K E Y

• Kayseri
• Denizli
Lake Tuz
• Malatya
Elâziğ •
olive
• Konya
• Diyarba

TAURUS MTS.
• Antalya
• Adana Gaziantep •
• Şanlıurfa
Mersin • Tarsus
• Iskenderun
• Antioch
olive
Halab
(Aleppo)
Ar Ra

Turkish Cypriots claim
the northern third of the island
as an independent republic. →
• Latakia
• Hamah
Dayr az Zaw

Nicosia ⊛ 📷
CYPRUS
• Limassol
• Homs

S Y R I A

*MEDITERRANEAN
SEA*
• Tripoli
olive
LEBANON
Beirut ⊛
• Sidon
Damascus ⊛
📷
S Y R I
• Tyre

GAZA & WEST BANK
Palestinians govern limited areas
pending final status talks with Israel.
• Haifa
Sea of Galilee
• Irbid

ISRAEL
olive
Tel Aviv-Yafo •
**WEST
BANK**
olive
• Az Zarqa'
D E S E
📷
Jerusalem •
Amman ⊛
Gaza •
oil
gas
Dead -1,339 ft
Be ér Sheva
Sea -408 m

*Suez
Canal*

Negev
J O R D A N

E G Y P T

S I N A I
• Al 'Aqabah

0   200 miles
0   200 kilometers
Two-Point Equidistant Projection
Nile
Gulf of Suez
Gulf of Aqaba

S A U D

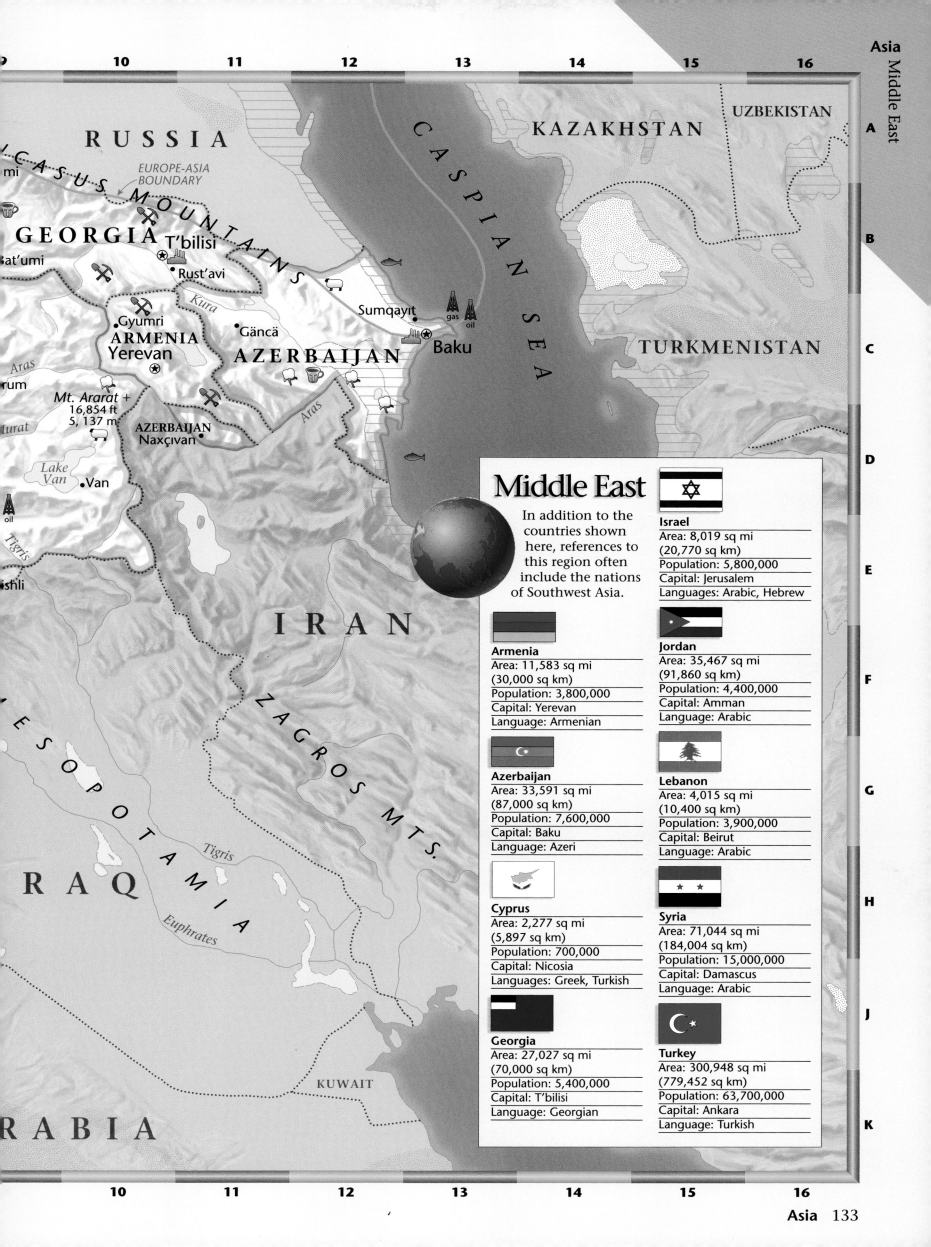

10 11 12 13 14 15 16

UZBEKISTAN

RUSSIA

KAZAKHSTAN

A

CAUCASUS MOUNTAINS

EUROPE-ASIA
BOUNDARY

GEORGIA
T'bilisi
Bat'umi
Rust'avi

C A S P I A N   S E A

B

Kura

Sumqayıt
gas oil
Gyumri
Gäncä
ARMENIA
Yerevan
AZERBAIJAN
Baku

TURKMENISTAN

C

Aras

rum
Mt. Ararat +
16,854 ft
5,137 m

AZERBAIJAN
Naxçıvan

Aras

D

Lake
Van

Van

urat

oil

Tigris

ishli

IRAN

E

Middle East

In addition to the
countries shown
here, references to
this region often
include the nations
of Southwest Asia.

Israel
Area: 8,019 sq mi
(20,770 sq km)
Population: 5,800,000
Capital: Jerusalem
Languages: Arabic, Hebrew

Armenia
Area: 11,583 sq mi
(30,000 sq km)
Population: 3,800,000
Capital: Yerevan
Language: Armenian

Jordan
Area: 35,467 sq mi
(91,860 sq km)
Population: 4,400,000
Capital: Amman
Language: Arabic

F

ZAGROS MTS.

Azerbaijan
Area: 33,591 sq mi
(87,000 sq km)
Population: 7,600,000
Capital: Baku
Language: Azeri

Lebanon
Area: 4,015 sq mi
(10,400 sq km)
Population: 3,900,000
Capital: Beirut
Language: Arabic

G

MESOPOTAMIA

Tigris

Cyprus
Area: 2,277 sq mi
(5,897 sq km)
Population: 700,000
Capital: Nicosia
Languages: Greek, Turkish

Syria
Area: 71,044 sq mi
(184,004 sq km)
Population: 15,000,000
Capital: Damascus
Language: Arabic

H

RAQ

Euphrates

Georgia
Area: 27,027 sq mi
(70,000 sq km)
Population: 5,400,000
Capital: T'bilisi
Language: Georgian

Turkey
Area: 300,948 sq mi
(779,452 sq km)
Population: 63,700,000
Capital: Ankara
Language: Turkish

J

KUWAIT

RABIA

K

10 11 12 13 14 15 16

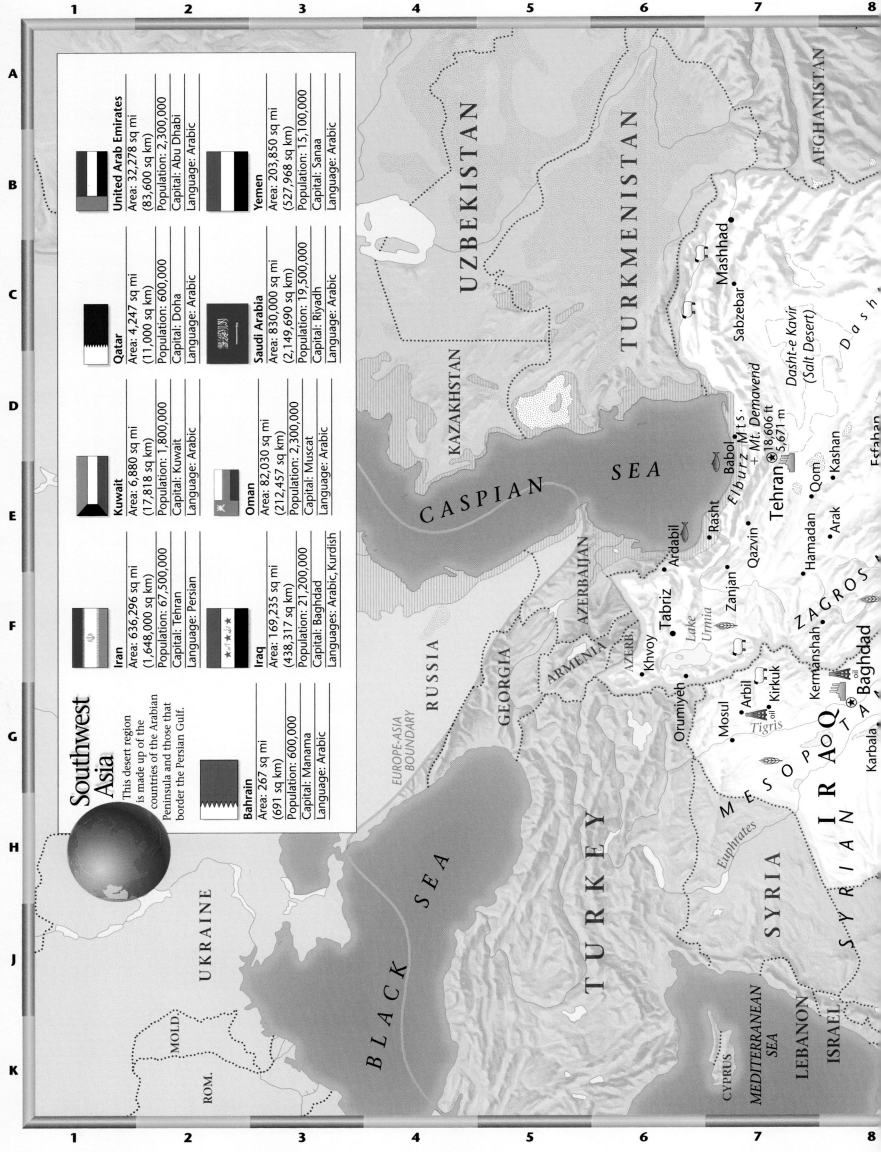

Southwest Asia

This desert region is made up of the countries of the Arabian Peninsula and those that border the Persian Gulf.

United Arab Emirates
Area: 32,278 sq mi (83,600 sq km)
Population: 2,300,000
Capital: Abu Dhabi
Language: Arabic

Yemen
Area: 203,850 sq mi (527,968 sq km)
Population: 15,100,000
Capital: Sanaa
Language: Arabic

Qatar
Area: 4,247 sq mi (11,000 sq km)
Population: 600,000
Capital: Doha
Language: Arabic

Saudi Arabia
Area: 830,000 sq mi (2,149,690 sq km)
Population: 19,500,000
Capital: Riyadh
Language: Arabic

Kuwait
Area: 6,880 sq mi (17,818 sq km)
Population: 1,800,000
Capital: Kuwait
Language: Arabic

Oman
Area: 82,030 sq mi (212,457 sq km)
Population: 2,300,000
Capital: Muscat
Language: Arabic

Iran
Area: 636,296 sq mi (1,648,000 sq km)
Population: 67,500,000
Capital: Tehran
Language: Persian

Iraq
Area: 169,235 sq mi (438,317 sq km)
Population: 21,200,000
Capital: Baghdad
Languages: Arabic, Kurdish

Bahrain
Area: 267 sq mi (691 sq km)
Population: 600,000
Capital: Manama
Language: Arabic

UZBEKISTAN

TURKMENISTAN

AFGHANISTAN

KAZAKHSTAN

Mashhad

Sabzebar

Dasht-e Kavir (Salt Desert)

Dasht

CASPIAN SEA

Babol

Elburz Mts.
+ Mt. Demavend
18,606 ft
5,671 m

Tehran

Qom · Kashan

Esfahan

Rasht

Qazvin

Arak

Hamadan

Ardabil

Zanjan

Tabriz

Lake Urmia

ZAGROS

AZERBAIJAN

ARMENIA

AZERB.

Khvoy

Orumiyeh

RUSSIA

GEORGIA

Kermanshah

Arbil · Kirkuk

Mosul

Tigris

I R A Q

Baghdad

Karbala

MESOPOTAMIA

I R A N

Euphrates

TURKEY

SYRIA

BLACK SEA

UKRAINE

MOLD

ROM.

S Y R I A N

LEBANON

ISRAEL

CYPRUS

MEDITERRANEAN SEA

EUROPE-ASIA BOUNDARY

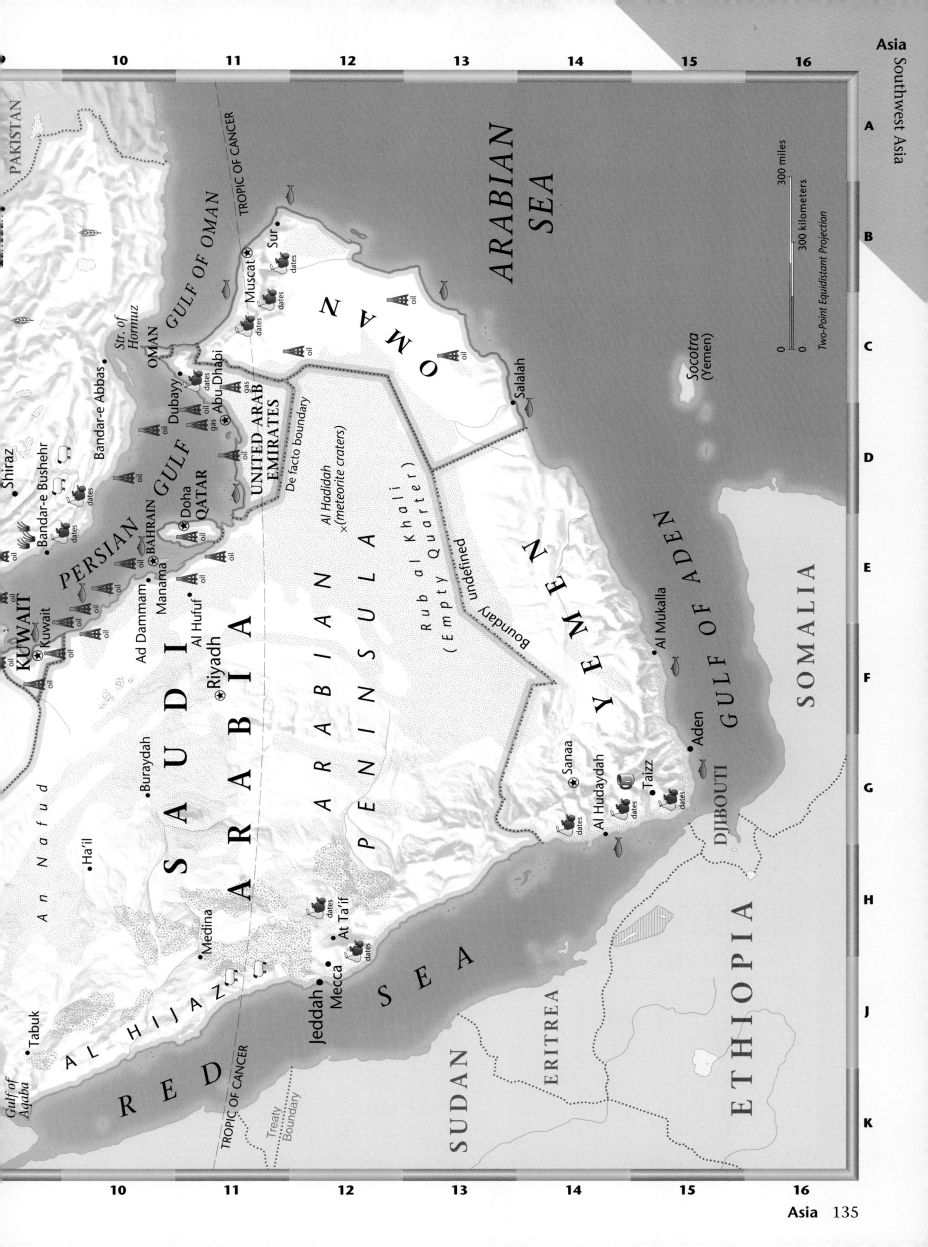

PAKISTAN

TROPIC OF CANCER

GULF OF OMAN

Str. of Hormuz

ARABIAN
SEA

Sur
dates
Muscat
dates
oil
OMAN
oil
oil

Shiraz
Bandar-e Bushehr
Bandar Abbas
OMAN
Dubayy
oil
dates
gas Abu Dhabi
gas
UNITED ARAB
EMIRATES
De facto boundary

Socotra
(Yemen)

Salalah

PERSIAN
dates
oil
BAHRAIN
Doha QATAR
oil
GULF
oil

Al Hadidah
x(meteorite craters)

Rub al Khali
(Empty Quarter)

YEMEN

GULF OF ADEN

Al Mukalla

KUWAIT
oil
Kuwait
oil
oil
oil
Ad Dammam
Manama
Al Hufuf
oil

SAUDIA
Riyadh

ARABIAN

PENINSULA

undefined
Boundary

Aden

DJIBOUTI

SOMALIA

An Nafud
Buraydah
Ha'il

ARABIA

Sanaa
Al Hudaydah
dates
Taizz
dates
dates

ETHIOPIA

Tabuk
Medina
Mecca At Ta'if
dates
dates
Jeddah

AL HIJAZ

RED
SEA

SUDAN
ERITREA

Gulf of Aqaba

TROPIC OF CANCER

Treaty
Boundary

300 miles
300 kilometers
0
0
Two-Point Equidistant Projection

A **1**

2 **3** **4** **5** **6** **7** **8**

TURKMENISTAN   UZB.

TAJIKISTAN

IRAQ

Mazar-e
Sharif

Herat   *Harirud*   HINDU KUSH

I R A N   Kabul   Islamabad

AFGHANISTAN   Peshawar
Rawalpindi
Sialkot
Gujranwala

KUWAIT   *Helmand*   Qandahar   Faisalabad

PERSIAN   Quetta   Multan   Lahore

BAHRAIN   **PAKISTAN**

QATAR   GULF   Sukkur   GREAT INDIAN DESERT

TROPIC OF
CANCER   *Indus*   Jaip

UNITED
ARAB
EMIRATES   GULF OF OMAN   Jodhpur   A

Karachi   Hyderabad   **I**

SAUDI
ARABIA   OMAN   *Mouths
of the
Indus*   Ahmadab
Ind

Jamnagar   Rajkot

YEMEN   A R A B I A N   *Narme*

S E A   Surat

Mumba
(Bombay

Pun

South Asia

This region's three
most populous
countries—India,
Pakistan, and
Bangladesh—make up
most of what is
commonly called the
Indian subcontinent.
The world's highest
mountains, the
Himalaya, form the
area's northern
boundary.

Afghanistan
Area: 251,773 sq mi
(652,090 sq km)
Population: 22,100,000
Capital: Kabul
Language: Afghan Persian

India
Area: 1,269,346 sq mi
(3,287,590 sq km)
Population: 969,700,000
Capital: New Delhi
Languages: Hindi, others

Nepal
Area: 54,362 sq mi
(140,797 sq km)
Population: 22,600,000
Capital: Kathmandu
Language: Nepali

Bangladesh
Area: 55,598 sq mi
(143,998 sq km)
Population: 122,200,000
Capital: Dhaka
Language: Bangla

Maldives
Area: 115 sq mi
(298 sq km)
Population: 300,000
Capital: Male
Language: Divehi

Pakistan
Area: 307,374 sq mi
(796,095 sq km)
Population: 137,800,000
Capital: Islamabad
Languages: English, Urdu

Bhutan
Area: 18,147 sq mi
(47,000 sq km)
Population: 800,000
Capital: Thimphu
Language: Dzongkha

Myanmar (Burma)
Area: 261,218 sq mi
(676,552 sq km)
Population: 46,800,000
Capital: Yangon
Language: Burmese

Sri Lanka
Area: 25,332 sq mi
(65,610 sq km)
Population: 18,700,000
Capital: Colombo
Languages: Sinhala, Tamil

Mangalore

(Calicut) Kozhi

Lakshadweep
(India)

**INDIAN
OCEAN**

coconuts   MALD

1 **2** **3** **4** **5** **6** **7** **8**

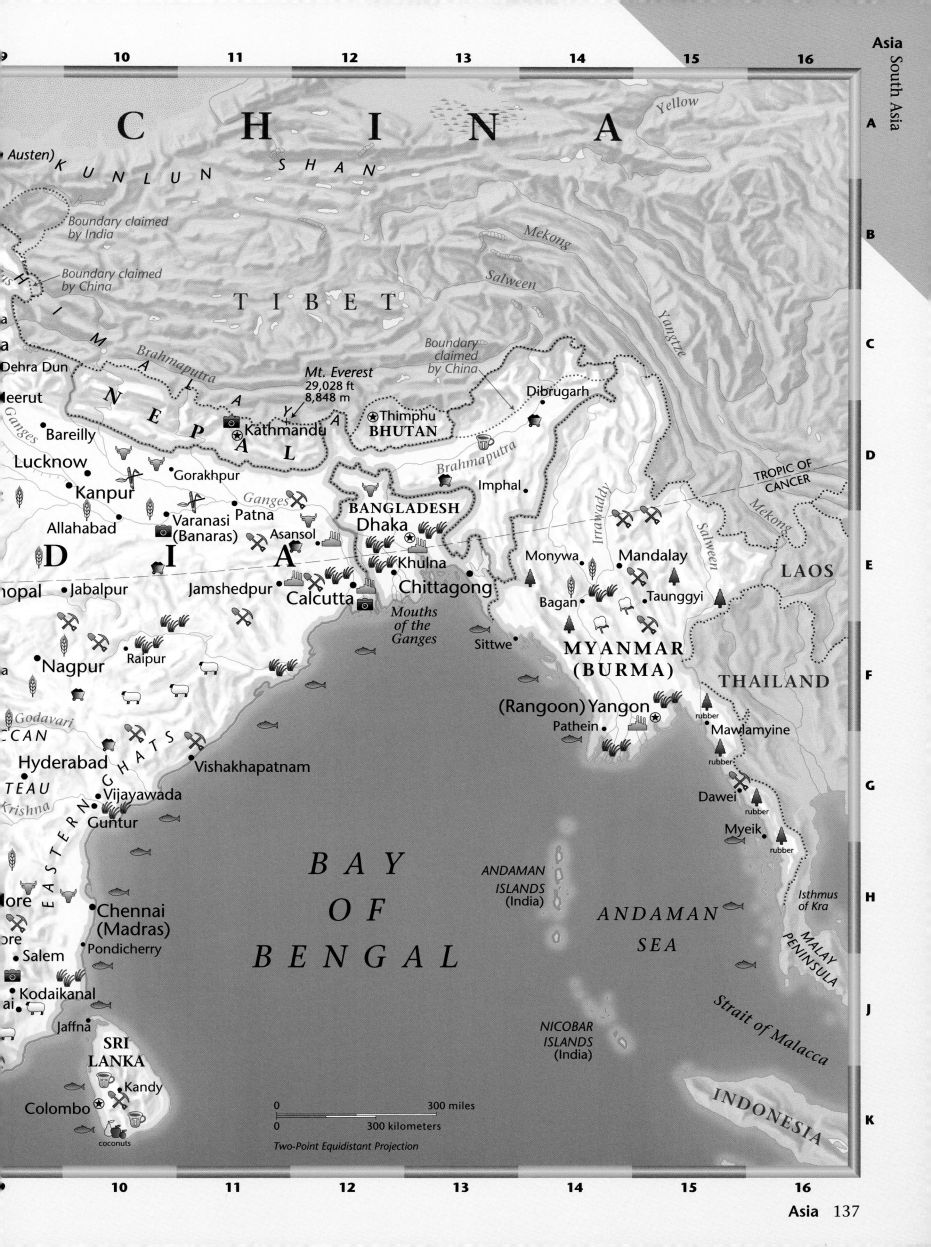

CHINA

Austen)

KUNLUN SHAN

Yellow

Boundary claimed by India

Boundary claimed by China

TIBET

Mekong

Salween

Yangtze

Brahmaputra

Dehra Dun

Meerut

NEPAL

Mt. Everest
29,028 ft
8,848 m

Kathmandu

Boundary claimed by China

Dibrugarh

★Thimphu
BHUTAN

Bareilly

Lucknow

Kanpur

Gorakhpur

Ganges

Brahmaputra

Imphal

TROPIC OF CANCER

Mekong

Varanasi
(Banaras)

Patna

BANGLADESH
Dhaka

Allahabad

Asansol

LAOS

I N D I A

Khulna

Monywa

Mandalay

hopal

Jabalpur

Jamshedpur

Calcutta

Chittagong

Bagan

Taunggyi

Mouths of the Ganges

Sittwe

MYANMAR
(BURMA)

THAILAND

Nagpur

Raipur

a

Godavari

CCAN

Hyderabad

Krishna

TEAU

Vijayawada

Guntur

Vishakhapatnam

(Rangoon) Yangon

Pathein

rubber

Mawlamyine

rubber

Dawei

rubber

Myeik

rubber

EASTERN GHATS

B A Y

O F

B E N G A L

ANDAMAN
ISLANDS
(India)

ANDAMAN

SEA

Isthmus of Kra

MALAY PENINSULA

ore

Chennai
(Madras)

ore

Pondicherry

Salem

Kodaikanal

ai

Jaffna

SRI
LANKA

Kandy

Colombo

coconuts

NICOBAR
ISLANDS
(India)

Strait of Malacca

INDONESIA

0   300 miles

0   300 kilometers

Two-Point Equidistant Projection

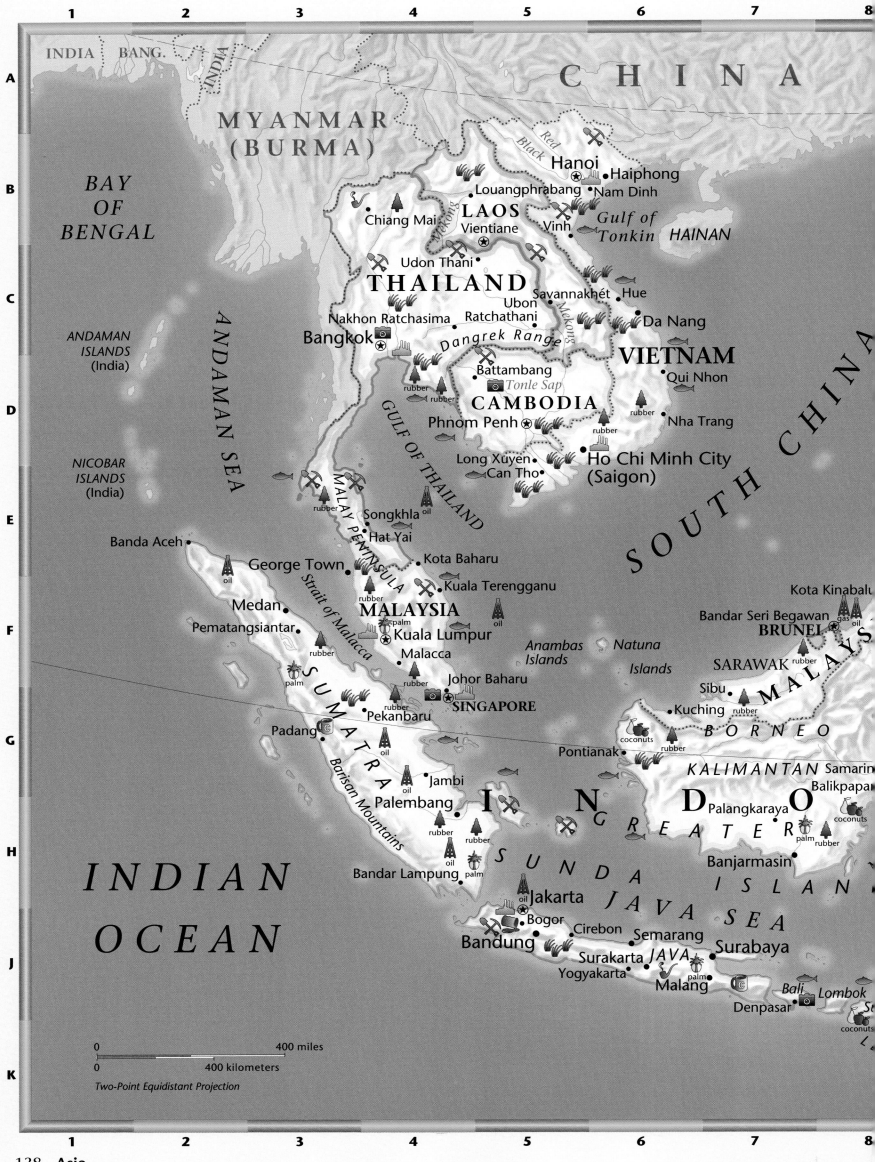

1 **2** **3** **4** **5** **6** **7** **8**

INDIA   BANG.   INDIA

C H I N A

**MYANMAR
(BURMA)**

*BAY
OF
BENGAL*

Hanoi   • Haiphong
• Louangphrabang   • Nam Dinh
Chiang Mai   **LAOS**
Vientiane   Vinh   *Gulf of
Tonkin*   HAINAN

Udon Thani
THAILAND   Savannakhét   Hue
Ubon   • Da Nang
Nakhon Ratchasima   Ratchathani
Bangkok   *Dangrek Range*   **VIETNAM**
rubber   Battambang   • Qui Nhon
rubber   *Tonle Sap*
CAMBODIA   rubber   Nha Trang
Phnom Penh   rubber

*ANDAMAN
ISLANDS*
(India)

ANDAMAN SEA

*NICOBAR
ISLANDS*
(India)

GULF OF THAILAND

Long Xuyen   Ho Chi Minh City
Can Tho   (Saigon)

S O U T H   C H I N A

rubber
Songkhla   oil
Hat Yai

Banda Aceh   *MALAY PENINSULA*   Kota Baharu
George Town   Kuala Terengganu
oil   rubber   **MALAYSIA**
Medan   palm   oil   Kota Kinabalu
Pematangsiantar   **Kuala Lumpur**   *Anambas
Islands*   *Natuna
Islands*   Bandar Seri Begawan
rubber   Malacca   **BRUNEI**   gas oil
Strait of Malacca   Johor Baharu   **SARAWAK**   **MALAYS**
S U M A T R A   rubber   **SINGAPORE**   rubber
Padang   Pekanbaru   Sibu   **BORNEO**
rubber   Kuching   rubber
coconuts   rubber
oil   Pontianak   *KALIMANTAN*   Samarin

Jambi   Balikpapa
oil   **I**   **N**   **D**   **O**
Palembang   Palangkaraya
rubber   rubber   *G R E A T E R*   coconuts
oil   palm   palm rubber

INDIAN   Banjarmasin
S U N D A   **I S L A N**

Bandar Lampung   palm
oil   Jakarta   *J A V A   S E A*
OCEAN   Bogor   Cirebon   Semarang   Surabaya
Bandung   Surakarta   *JAVA*
Yogyakarta   palm   *Bali*   Lombok
Malang   Denpasar   coconuts

0   400 miles
0   400 kilometers
Two-Point Equidistant Projection

A

B

C

D

E

F

G

H

J

K

TAIWAN

TROPIC OF CANCER

Batan Is.

Babuyan Is.

Laoag

LUZON

Baguio

PHILIPPINE

Manila

Quezon City

SEA

PHILIPPINES

Mindoro

Samar

coconuts

Panay

Tacloban

Iloilo

Cebu

Leyte

Bacolod

Cebu

PALAWAN

Negros

Bohol

coconuts

SULU

Cagayan de Oro

SEA

MINDANAO

Zamboanga

coconuts

Davao

Cotabato

kan

General Santos

SULU ARCHIPELAGO

Talaud Islands

C E L E B E S

S E A

PACIFIC OCEAN

EQUATOR 0°

Manado

Ternate

Halmahera

coconuts

Gorontalo

MOLUCCA SEA

oil

Sorong

Jayapura

M

Tomini

Bay

I R I A N   J A Y A

ber

Misool

M a o k e   M o u n t a i n s

oil

PAPUA

E

S

I

A

C E R A M   S E A

N E W

Puncak Jaya

NEW

GUINEA

coconuts

Sulu Islands

Ceram

16,499 ft

LAWESI

5,029 m

G U I N E A

Buru

Ambon

M

arepare

rubber

O

L

U

Tual

Aru Islands

ngpandang

Tukangbesi

Islands

C

C

Dolak

A

Barat Daya Islands

S

Tanimbar

Islands

es SEA

Dili

ARAFURA SEA

ba

Kupang

TIMOR

TIMOR

SEA

A   U   S   T   R   A   L   I   A

DA ISLANDS

Southeast Asia

Warm and wet, the countries of Southeast Asia extend far into the Pacific Ocean. Indonesia alone contains more than 13,000 islands. Tiny Singapore is the region's financial hub and trade center.

Brunei
Area: 2,226 sq mi
(5,765 sq km)
Population: 300,000
Capital: Bandar Seri Begawan
Language: Malay

Cambodia
Area: 69,898 sq mi
(181,035 sq km)
Population: 11,200,000
Capital: Phnom Penh
Language: Khmer

Indonesia
Area: 741,101 sq mi
(1,919,443 sq km)
Population: 204,300,000
Capital: Jakarta
Language: Bahasa Indonesia

Laos
Area: 91,429 sq mi
(236,800 sq km)
Population: 5,100,000
Capital: Vientiane
Language: Lao

Malaysia
Area: 127,317 sq mi
(329,749 sq km)
Population: 21,000,000
Capital: Kuala Lumpur
Language: Malay

Philippines
Area: 115,831 sq mi
(300,000 sq km)
Population: 73,400,000
Capital: Manila
Languages: Filipino, others

Singapore
Area: 239 sq mi
(618 sq km)
Population: 3,500,000
Languages: Chinese, others

Thailand
Area: 198,457 sq mi
(514,000 sq km)
Population: 60,100,000
Capital: Bangkok
Language: Thai

Vietnam
Area: 127,242 sq mi
(329,556 sq km)
Population: 75,100,000
Capital: Hanoi
Language: Vietnamese

Australia N

The low peaks of the Hamersley Range along the west coast of Australia form the starting point for arrowlike clouds (right). The Hamersley Range is typical of Australia's mountains—low and located near the coast. Deserts cover much of the continent's sparsely populated interior.

Unlike Australia, which is geologically stable, New Zealand stretches along a subduction zone. In the north its landscape is marked by hot springs and geysers. In the south rise the glacier-covered peaks of the Southern Alps.

Oceania is the name that geographers commonly use for the Pacific islands that make up the regions of Melanesia, Micronesia, and Polynesia. Australia and New Zealand are often included in Oceania.

The white sands of Cable Beach, along Australia's northwestern coast, are a popular destination for tourists, including these on camelback. Although camels are not native to Australia, they are well suited to the continent's dry climate.

CONNECTION: *You can find Australia's west coast on the maps on pages 142–143.*

w Zealand
eania

Australia

Down Under and Outback

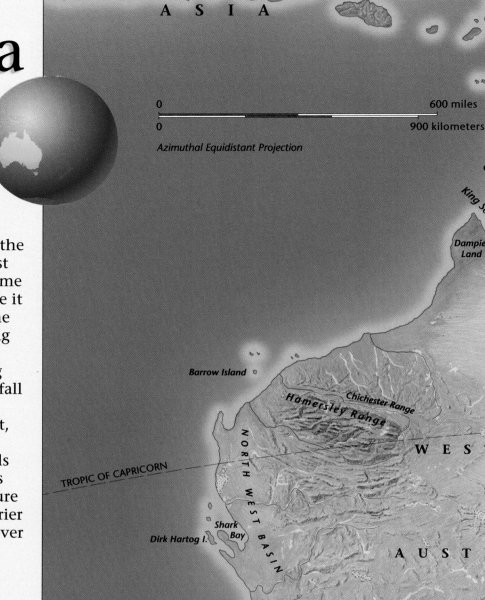

Just three times bigger than Greenland (the earth's largest island), Australia is the smallest of the continents—and the flattest as well. It earns the nickname "land down under" because it is located entirely below the Equator. The Great Dividing Range—low mountains running north-south along the east coast—blocks rainfall from the Pacific. Inland lie the dry scrublands and vast, hot deserts of central and western Australia that locals call the outback. Australia's most famous physical feature lies offshore: the Great Barrier Reef, the largest structure ever built by living creatures.

The Land

Area
2,966,368 sq mi
(7,682,300 sq km)

Highest mountain
Kosciuszko: 7,310 ft (2,228 m)

Lowest point
Lake Eyre: 52 ft (16 m)
below sea level

Longest river
Murray-Darling: 2,911 mi
(4,685 km)

Largest body of water
Lake Eyre: 3,430 sq mi
(8,884 sq km)

Largest island
Tasmania: 26,383 sq mi
(68,332 sq km)

ASIA

Timor Sea

Bonaparte Archipelego

Collier Bay

King Sound

Kimberley Plateau

Dampier Land

Great Sandy Desert

Barrow Island

Hamersley Range

Chichester Range

WESTERN

Gibson

AU

PLA

NORTH WEST BASIN

TROPIC OF CAPRICORN

Shark Bay

Dirk Hartog I.

AUSTRALIA

Lake Barlee

Great Vict

DARLING RANGE

EUCLA

N

Cape Naturaliste

Austr

INDIAN OCEAN

0   600 miles
0   900 kilometers
Azimuthal Equidistant Projection

10 **11** **12** **13** **14** **15** **16**

A R A F U R A   S E A

Torres Strait

Cape York

Great Barrier Reef

NEW
GUINEA

Van
Diemen Gulf

Cobourg
Peninsula

Wessel
Islands

A r n h e m

L a n d

Daly

Gulf of

Groote Eylandt

C a r p e n t a r i a

Sir Edward Pellew Group

Mornington
Island

Cape
York

Peninsula

Princess
Charlotte
Bay

C O R A L

S E A

Barkly Tableland

N O R T H E R N

Tanami
Desert

T E R R I T O R Y

N

Macdonnell Ranges

U

Depression

R A L I A

Simpson
Desert

Flinders

CLONCURRY

Georgina

PLATEAU

Diamantina

Q U E E N S L A N D

G R E A T

Channel Country

A R T E S I A N

Cooper Cr.

Barcoo

Great Barrier Reef

Capricorn Channel

TROPIC OF CAPRICORN

Fraser Island

L A K E   E Y R E
B A S I N

Lowest point
in Australia

Lake Eyre
-52 feet
-16 meters

Warrego

Balonne

DARLING
DOWNS

S O U T H

A U S T R A L I A

Lake Torrens

Lake
Frome

FLINDERS RANGES

L O W L A N D S

B A S I N

Barwon

in

L. Gairdner

Eyre
Peninsula

Darling

N E W   S O U T H

Macquarie

G R E A T   D I V I D I N G   R A N G E

Lord Howe Island

Ball's Pyramid

Spencer
Gulf

Yorke Pen.

M U R R A Y   R I V E R

Murray

W A L E S

Lachlan

Murrumbidgee

Gulf
St.
Vincent

M U R R A Y
B A S I N

R i v e r i n a

t

Kangaroo
Island

Murray

AUSTRALIAN
CAPITAL TERRITORY

T A S M A N

B i g h t

Highest point
in Australia

Mount Kosciuszko
7,310 feet, 2,228 meters

Cape Howe

VICTORIA

Australian
Alps

Wilsons Promontory

S E A

King
Island

Bass
Strait

FURNEAUX
GROUP

Mt. Ossa
5,305 feet, 1,617 meters

TASMANIA

10 **11** **12** **13** **14** **15** **16**

A

B

C

D

E

F

G

H

J

K

Australia
New Zealand, Oceania
Lands of Natural Wonder

When English explorers landed in Australia and caught their first glimpse of a kangaroo, words failed them. Captain James Cook wrote in 1770, "To compare it to any European animal would be impossible as it has not the least resemblance of any one I have seen."

Australia owes its odd animal life to the fact that the continent has been isolated from other land for millions of years. During that time, its animals evolved into strange and wonderful creatures. Australia is famous for its marsupials (pouched mammals)—kangaroos, koalas, wombats, and Tasmanian devils, to name a few.

Most of New Zealand's land animals have been introduced from other countries. The country has many native birds, including the flightless kiwi, whose name is a nickname for a New Zealander. Birds—especially long-distance fliers such as albatrosses and terns—are the most common kind of wildlife native to islands in Oceania.

▼**STRANGEST IN A STRANGE LAND:**
The poison-spurred, duck-billed platypus is a member of an unusual order of egg-laying mammals called monotremes.

▲ **KANGAROOS CROSSING!**
A uniquely Australian road sign greets visitors to Ayers Rock. Exposed by years of wind and weather, the rock is sacred to Aborigines, Australia's native people, who call it Uluru.

▶**BEACH MEETS CITY** *along Australia's Queensland coast. More than 80 percent of Australia's population lives in coastal cities.*

▲ **PULLING FOR ALL** *they're worth as they crash through the surf, an Aussie lifeboat crew competes in a race. Australia's long beaches are popular with surfers and swimmers alike.*

▶ **SNUGGLING CHEEK** *to cheek, an Aborigine child savors a quiet moment with a pet kangaroo. In 1976 Aborigines regained title to traditional lands that make up a third of Australia's Northern Territory.*

▲ **SAFE WITHIN** *the slender fingers of yellow coral, an anemonefish peers out from Australia's famous Great Barrier Reef.*

▶ **SHIMMERING** *colors make opals precious stones. Most of the world's gem opals come from fields in southeastern Australia.*

▲ **A KNACK** *for looking cute and cuddly makes the koala a worldwide symbol for Australia. Because koalas eat only leaves from eucalyptus trees, few zoos outside the continent manage to keep them.*

▲ **DRESSED TO SCARE,** *a tribesman from New Guinea's Asaro River Valley wears a clay mask in a ritual meant to ward off evil spirits. New Guinea is the largest island in Melanesia.*

◀ **RAINBOW LORIKEETS** *groom one another in a show of feathered friendship. Lorikeets and cockatoos are colorful parrots native to Australia and New Guinea.*

▲ **A SAILBOAT SCUDS** *across Sydney Harbor, its sails echoed by the arches of the city's famous Opera House. Once a giant British penal colony, Australia now boasts its own world-class music, theater, and architecture.*

◀ **SHEEPDOGS** *join their owner as he calls out across a New Zealand sheep station. Australia and New Zealand devote vast acreage to sheep and cattle ranching.*

▲ **STEAM RISING** *above the green waters of New Zealand's Emerald Lake hints at geothermal activity. North Island has many volcanoes and hot springs.*

Australia
Country and Continent

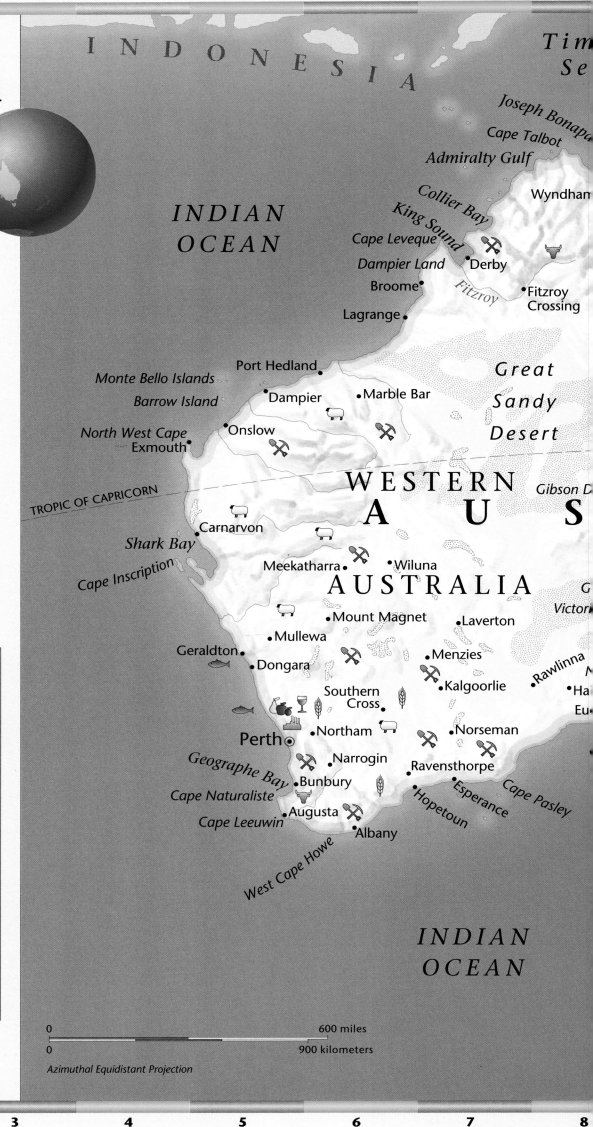

A political map of Australia highlights an unusual feature: The entire continent is one sparsely populated country. Aborigines, the first Australians, came from Asia 50,000 years ago. In 1770, England claimed Australia as a colony and British immigrants flowed in. Today, most Australians live in coastal cities such as Sydney and Melbourne, though hardy ranchers still work the country's dry interior lands. Independent and politically stable since 1901, Australia is a prosperous country. It is one of the world's largest exporters of coal and iron ore and a world leader in wool production.

The People

Population
18,700,000

Capital: Canberra

Language: English

Largest metropolitan areas
Sydney: Pop. 3,600,000
Melbourne: Pop. 3,100,000

Population density
6 people per sq mi

Economy
Farming: livestock, wheat, fruit
Industry: mining, wool, oil

Life expectancy
78 years

INDONESIA

Timor Sea

INDIAN OCEAN

Joseph Bonapa
Cape Talbot
Admiralty Gulf
Collier Bay
King Sound
Cape Leveque
Dampier Land
Broome
Lagrange
Wyndham
Derby
Fitzroy
Fitzroy Crossing

Monte Bello Islands
Barrow Island
North West Cape
Exmouth
Port Hedland
Dampier
Marble Bar
Onslow

Great Sandy Desert

TROPIC OF CAPRICORN

Carnarvon
Shark Bay
Cape Inscription

WESTERN AUSTRALIA

Gibson D

Meekatharra
Wiluna

Mount Magnet
Laverton
Mullewa
Menzies
Geraldton
Dongara
Kalgoorlie

Southern Cross
Rawlinna
Ha
Eu

Perth
Northam
Norseman

Geographe Bay
Narrogin
Ravensthorpe
Cape Pasley
Bunbury
Cape Naturaliste
Esperance
Hopetoun
Augusta
Cape Leeuwin
Albany
West Cape Howe

Victori
G

INDIAN OCEAN

0   600 miles
0   900 kilometers

Azimuthal Equidistant Projection

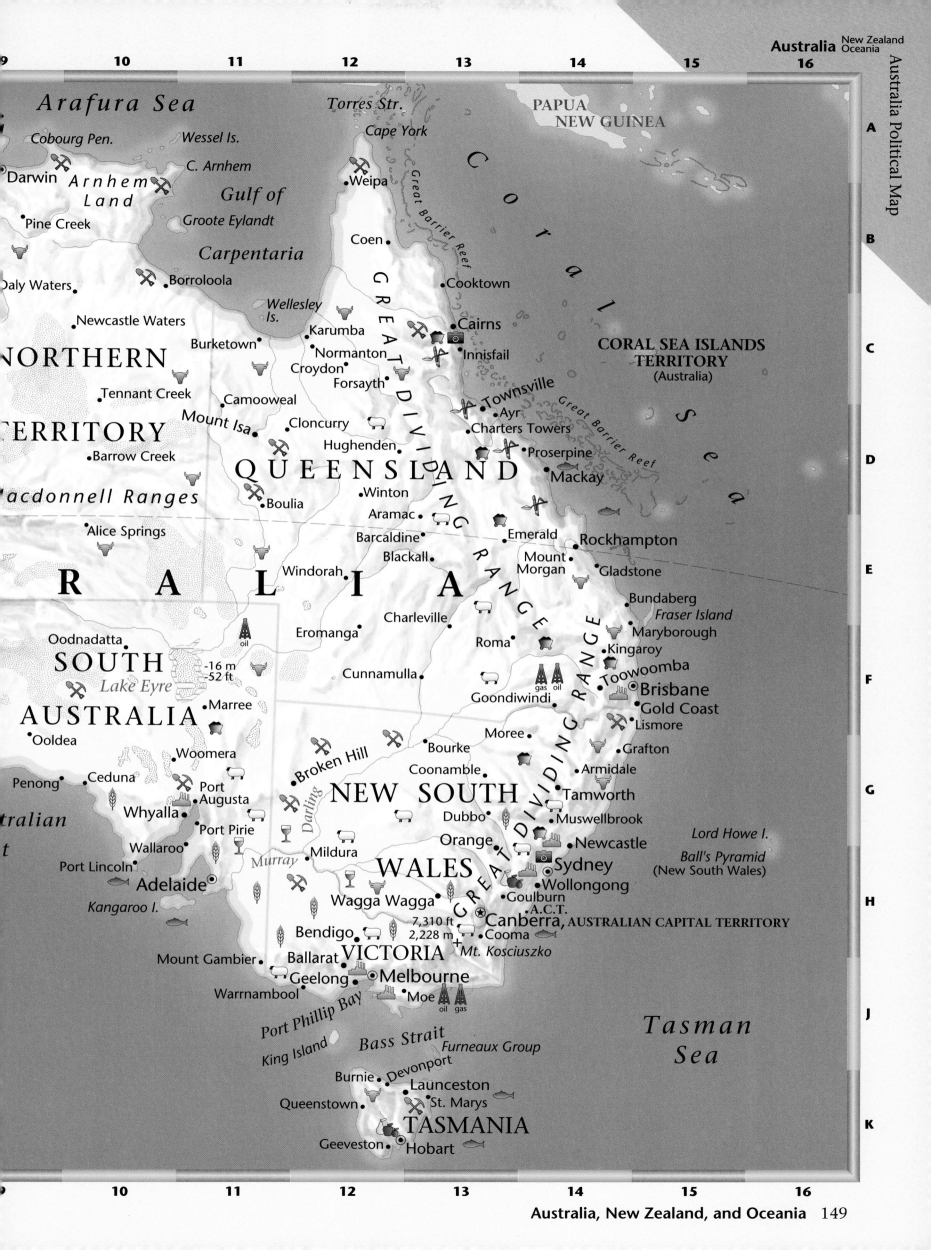

Arafura Sea

Torres Str.

PAPUA NEW GUINEA

Cobourg Pen.

Wessel Is.

Cape York

Darwin

C. Arnhem

Arnhem Land

Gulf of

Pine Creek

Groote Eylandt

•Weipa

C o r a l

CORAL SEA ISLANDS TERRITORY
(Australia)

Daly Waters

Borroloola

Wellesley Is.

Coen•

Newcastle Waters

Carpentaria

•Cooktown

NORTHERN

Karumba

•Cairns

Burketown•

Normanton

•Innisfail

Croydon

•Townsville

Tennant Creek

Camooweal

Forsayth

Ayr

S

Great Barrier Reef

TERRITORY

Mount Isa

Cloncurry

•Charters Towers

e

•Barrow Creek

Hughenden

•Proserpine

a

acdonnell Ranges

QUEENSLAND

•Mackay

•Alice Springs

•Boulia

•Winton

Aramac

G

Emerald

•Rockhampton

R   A   L   I   A

Barcaldine

R

Mount Morgan

•Gladstone

Blackall

E

A

Windorah

A

Bundaberg

Fraser Island

Charleville

N

•Maryborough

Oodnadatta

oil

Eromanga

D

Kingaroy

SOUTH

-16 m
-52 ft

Roma

I

•Toowoomba

•Brisbane

Lake Eyre

Cunnamulla

N

•Gold Coast

AUSTRALIA

Goondiwindi

gas oil

G

•Lismore

•Marree

R

Moree

A

•Grafton

•Ooldea

Bourke

N

•Armidale

Woomera

Coonamble

G

Tamworth

Penong

Ceduna

Broken Hill

NEW SOUTH

E

Muswellbrook

Whyalla

Port Augusta

Darling

Dubbo

R

•Newcastle

Lord Howe I.

Wallaroo

Port Pirie

Orange

A

•Sydney

Ball's Pyramid
(New South Wales)

Port Lincoln

Mildura

WALES

N

•Wollongong

Adelaide

Murray

Wagga Wagga

G

•Goulburn

Kangaroo I.

7,310 ft
2,228 m

•Canberra   **A.C.T.**

AUSTRALIAN CAPITAL TERRITORY

Bendigo

Mt. Kosciuszko

•Cooma

Mount Gambier

Ballarat

VICTORIA

Warrnambool

Geelong

•Melbourne

•Moe

Tasman Sea

Port Phillip Bay

oil gas

King Island

Bass Strait

Furneaux Group

Burnie

•Devonport

Launceston

Queenstown

St. Marys

TASMANIA

Geeveston

•Hobart

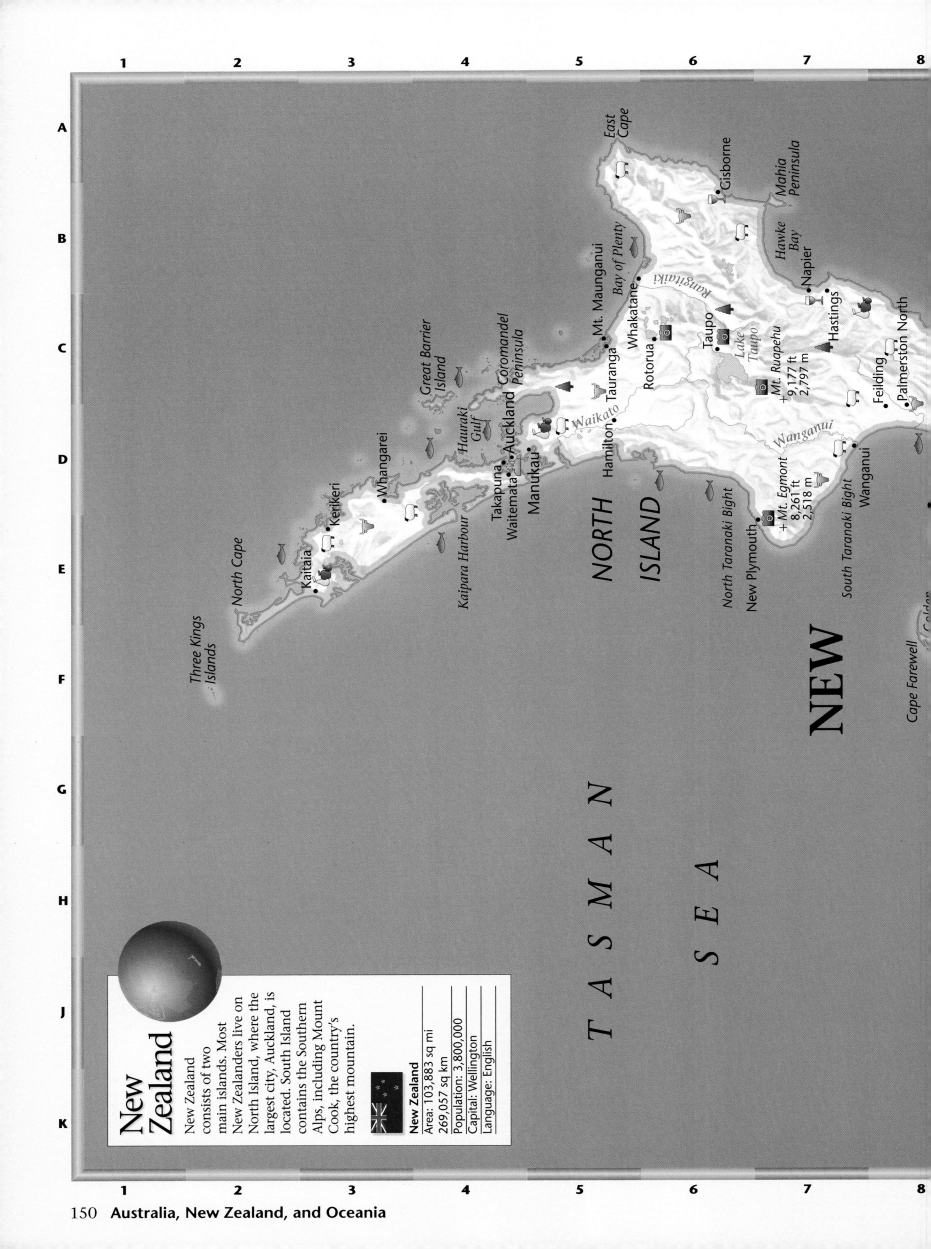

New Zealand

New Zealand consists of two main islands. Most New Zealanders live on North Island, where the largest city, Auckland, is located. South Island contains the Southern Alps, including Mount Cook, the country's highest mountain.

New Zealand

Area:	103,883 sq mi 269,057 sq km
Population:	3,800,000
Capital:	Wellington
Language:	English

East Cape

Gisborne

Mahia Peninsula

Hawke Bay

Napier

Hastings

Mt. Maunganui
Bay of Plenty
Whakatane

Rangitaiki

Tauranga
Rotorua
Taupo
Lake Taupo

Mt. Ruapehu
+ 9,177 ft
2,797 m

Feilding
Palmerston North

Great Barrier Island

Coromandel Peninsula

Hauraki Gulf

Auckland

Waikato

Hamilton

Wanganui

Whangarei

Kerikeri

Takapuna
Waitemata
Manukau

Kaipara Harbour

NORTH ISLAND

North Taranaki Bight

New Plymouth
+ Mt. Egmont
8,261 ft
2,518 m

South Taranaki Bight
Wanganui

Kaitaia

North Cape

Three Kings Islands

NEW

Cape Farewell

T A S M A N

S E A

9   10   11   12   13   14   15   16

A

B

C

D

E

F

G

H

J

K

Bounty Is.
(N.Z.)

100 miles

100 kilometers

Oblique Mercator Projection

P   A   C   I   F   I   C

O   C   E   A   N

Cape Palliser

ait

Blenheim

Kaikoura

Parnassus

Clarence

Christchurch
Lyttelton
Banks Peninsula

Ashburton

Canterbury Bight

SOUTH
ISLAND

Westport

Greymouth
Hokitika

Arthur's Pass

Timaru

Oamaru

Waitaki

Dunedin

ZEALAND

Franz Josef Glacier
Fox Glacier

S   O   U   T   H   E   R   N   A   L   P   S

Ex. Mt. Cook
12,316 ft
3,754 m

Balclutha

Haast

Jackson Head

Wanaka
Lake Wanaka

Queenstown
Lake Wakatipu

Clutha

Gore

Invercargill

Lake Te Anau

Milford
Sound

Foveaux Strait

STEWART
ISLAND

Puysegur Point

South West Cape

The Snares

A B C D E F G H J K

1 2 3 4 5 6 7 8

SEA OF JAPAN

JAPAN

NORTH PACIFIC

Bonin Islands
(Japan)

Midway Islands
(U.S.)

H

Volcano Islands
(Japan)

Minami Tori Shima
(Japan)

TROPIC OF CANCER

PHILIPPINE
SEA

NORTHERN
MARIANA
ISLANDS
(U.S.)
⊙ Saipan

Wake Island
(U.S.)

Johnston At
(U.

M I C R O N E S I A

Guam
(U.S.)

Enewetak
Atoll

Bikini
Atoll

Ratak Chain
Ralik Chain

MARSHALL
ISLANDS
coconuts
● Majuro

Yap Islands

coconuts

Senyavin
Is.
Palikir ⊛ Pohnpei

PALAU
Koror

CAROLINE ISLANDS

coconuts

FEDERATED STATES OF MICRONESIA

M E L

Kapingamarangi
Atoll

Gilbert Islands
● Tarawa

Howland Island
(U.S.) Baker Island

0° EQUATOR

Admiralty
Islands

Yaren

K I R I B A T I

coconuts

NEW GUINEA

Mt. Wilhelm
14,793 ft
4,509 m

Bismarck
Arch.

New Ireland

New
Britain

NAURU

coconuts

Bougainville

PHOENIX I

INDONESIA

Fly

coconuts

PAPUA NEW GUINEA

SOLOMON
ISLANDS

coconuts

● Honiara

M E L A N E S I A

TUVALU

● Funafuti

coconuts

coconuts

Port Moresby

ARAFURA SEA

CORAL

Guadalcanal

SANTA CRUZ
ISLANDS

coconuts

Rotuma
(Fiji)

Wallis &
Futuna
(France)

SAMOA

A

Apia

TOK
(N

SEA

coconuts

coconuts

VANUATU

Vanua
Levu

FIJI

Port-Vila ⊛ Éfaté

Viti Levu

● Suva

coconuts

CORAL SEA
ISLANDS
TERRITORY
(Australia)

Mt. Panié
5,341 ft
1,628 m

NEW
CALEDONIA
(France)

coconuts

TONGA

Nuku'alo

AUSTRALIA

● Nouméa

TROPIC OF CAPRICORN

SOUTH PA

Norfolk Island
(Australia) Phillip Island

Kermadec
Islands
(N.Z.)

1 2 3 4 5 6 7 8

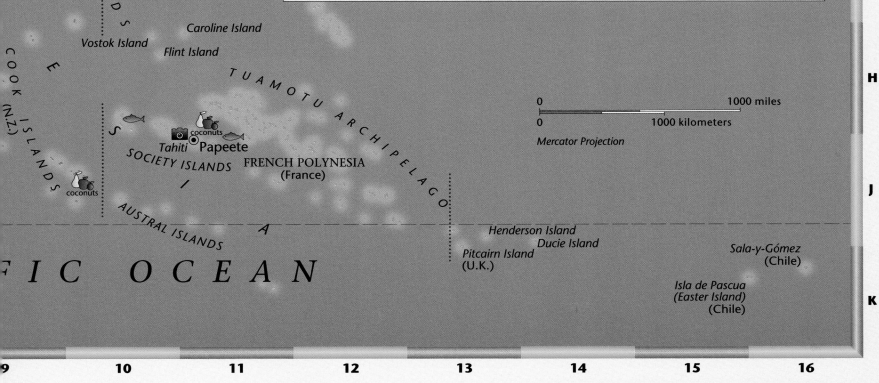

Oceania

More than 25,000 islands (not counting those belonging to Asia) spread across the Pacific Ocean. Together, these tropical islands are called Oceania. There are 12 independent countries within this island region.

Fiji
Area: 7,056 sq mi
(18,274 sq km)
Population: 80,000
Capital: Suva
Language: English

Kiribati
Area: 277 sq mi
(717 sq km)
Population: 79,000
Capital: Tarawa
Language: English

Marshall Islands
Area: 70 sq mi
(181 sq km)
Population: 10,000
Capital: Majuro
Language: English

Federated States of Micronesia
Area: 271 sq mi
(702 sq km)
Population: 102,300
Capital: Palikir
Language: English

Nauru
Area: 8 sq mi
(21 sq km)
Population: 10,000
Capital: Yaren
Language: English

Palau
Area: 188 sq mi
(487 sq km)
Population: 2,000
Capital: Koror
Languages: English, others

Papua New Guinea
Area: 178,260 sq mi
461,691 sq km
Population: 4,300,000
Capital: Port Moresby
Language: English

Samoa
Area: 1,093 sq mi
(2,831 sq km)
Population: 200,000
Capital: Apia
Languages: English, French

Solomon Islands
Area: 10,985 sq mi
(28,450 sq km)
Population: 400,000
Capital: Honiara
Languages: English, Melanesian

Tonga
Area : 270 sqmi
(699 sq km)
Population: 106,000
Capital: Nuku'alofa
Languages: English, Tongan

Tuvalu
Area: 10 sq mi
(26 sq km)
Population: 10,000
Capital: Funafuti
Languages: English, Tuvaluan

Vanuatu
Area: 5,700 sq mi
(14,760 sq km)
Population: 200,000
Capital: Port-Vila
Languages: English, French

American Samoa
(United States)

Baker Island (United States)

Cook Islands (New Zealand)

Easter Island (Chile)

French Polynesia (France)

Guam (United States)

Howland Island
(United States)

Jarvis Island (United States)

Johnston Atoll (United States)

Kingman Reef (United States)

Midway Islands
(United States)

New Caledonia (France)

Northern Mariana Islands
(United States)

Palmyra Atoll (United States)

Pitcairn Island
(United Kingdom)

Wake Island (United States)

Wallis and Futuna Islands
(France)

OCEAN

Honolulu

Oahu

Hawaii

Kingman Reef (U.S.)
Palmyra Atoll (U.S.)

Kiritimati
(Christmas I.)
coconuts

s Island
(U.S.)

Malden Island

Starbuck Island

Caroline Island

Vostok Island

Flint Island

TUAMOTU ARCHIPELAGO

COOK ISLANDS (NZ)

coconuts

Tahiti Papeete

SOCIETY ISLANDS

FRENCH POLYNESIA
(France)

AUSTRAL ISLANDS

Henderson Island
Ducie Island

Pitcairn Island
(U.K.)

Sala-y-Gómez
(Chile)

Isla de Pascua
(Easter Island)
(Chile)

IC OCEAN

0   1000 miles
0   1000 kilometers

Mercator Projection

Antarctica

Most people think ice-covered Antarctica is the end of the world, an expanse of white at the bottom of the map. This picture, put together from dozens of satellite images, shows the continent as it appears from space. The curving arm reaching into the sea (lower right) is the Antarctic Peninsula, more than 800 miles long. To the right of the peninsula, the rough peaks of the Transantarctic Mountains snake across the continent. Beyond them is the flat central area of Antarctica called the Polar Plateau. Surrounding the whole continent is a vast, floating sheet of ice. In the winter, this sea ice extends for 7,300,000 square miles (18,906,000 square kilometers).

Adélie penguins appear unfazed by a researcher's presence. Antarctica provides nesting sites for seven species of these flightless birds.

CONNECTION: *You can find the continent of Antarctica on the map on pages 156–157.*

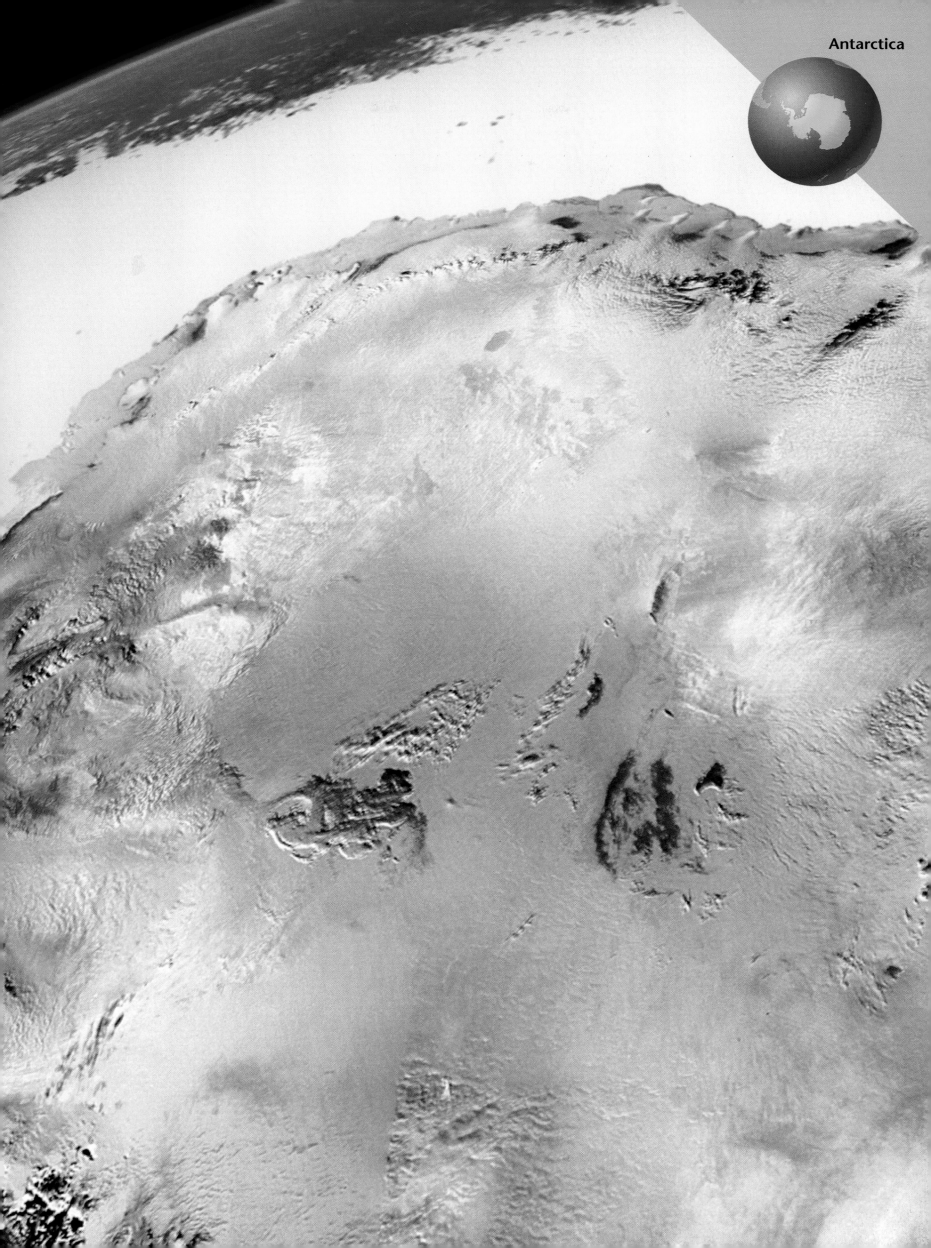

Antarctica

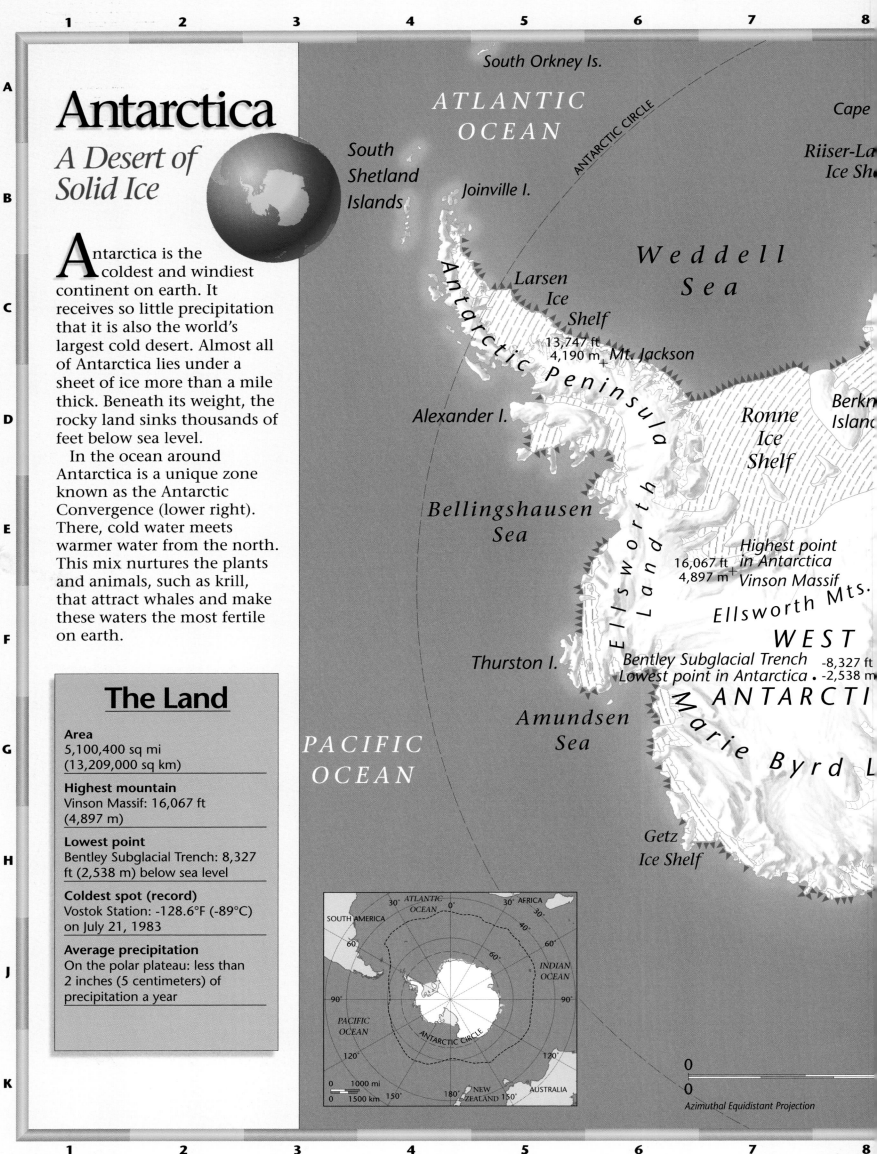

Antarctica
A Desert of Solid Ice

Antarctica is the coldest and windiest continent on earth. It receives so little precipitation that it is also the world's largest cold desert. Almost all of Antarctica lies under a sheet of ice more than a mile thick. Beneath its weight, the rocky land sinks thousands of feet below sea level.

In the ocean around Antarctica is a unique zone known as the Antarctic Convergence (lower right). There, cold water meets warmer water from the north. This mix nurtures the plants and animals, such as krill, that attract whales and make these waters the most fertile on earth.

The Land

Area
5,100,400 sq mi
(13,209,000 sq km)

Highest mountain
Vinson Massif: 16,067 ft
(4,897 m)

Lowest point
Bentley Subglacial Trench: 8,327 ft (2,538 m) below sea level

Coldest spot (record)
Vostok Station: -128.6°F (-89°C) on July 21, 1983

Average precipitation
On the polar plateau: less than 2 inches (5 centimeters) of precipitation a year

South Orkney Is.

ATLANTIC OCEAN

ANTARCTIC CIRCLE

Cape

Riiser-La
Ice Sh

South Shetland Islands

Joinville I.

Weddell Sea

Larsen Ice Shelf

13,747 ft
4,190 m Mt. Jackson

Alexander I.

Ronne Ice Shelf

Berk
Island

Antarctic Peninsula

Bellingshausen Sea

Highest point in Antarctica
16,067 ft
4,897 m Vinson Massif

Ellsworth Mts.

Ellsworth Land

Thurston I.

Bentley Subglacial Trench -8,327 ft
Lowest point in Antarctica -2,538 m

WEST

ANTARCTI

Amundsen Sea

PACIFIC OCEAN

Marie Byrd L

Getz Ice Shelf

ATLANTIC OCEAN
SOUTH AMERICA
30°
0°
30° AFRICA
60°
40°
30°
INDIAN OCEAN
90°
60°
90°
PACIFIC OCEAN
120°
120°
ANTARCTIC CIRCLE
150°
180°
NEW ZEALAND
150°
AUSTRALIA

0   1000 mi
0   1500 km

0
0
Azimuthal Equidistant Projection

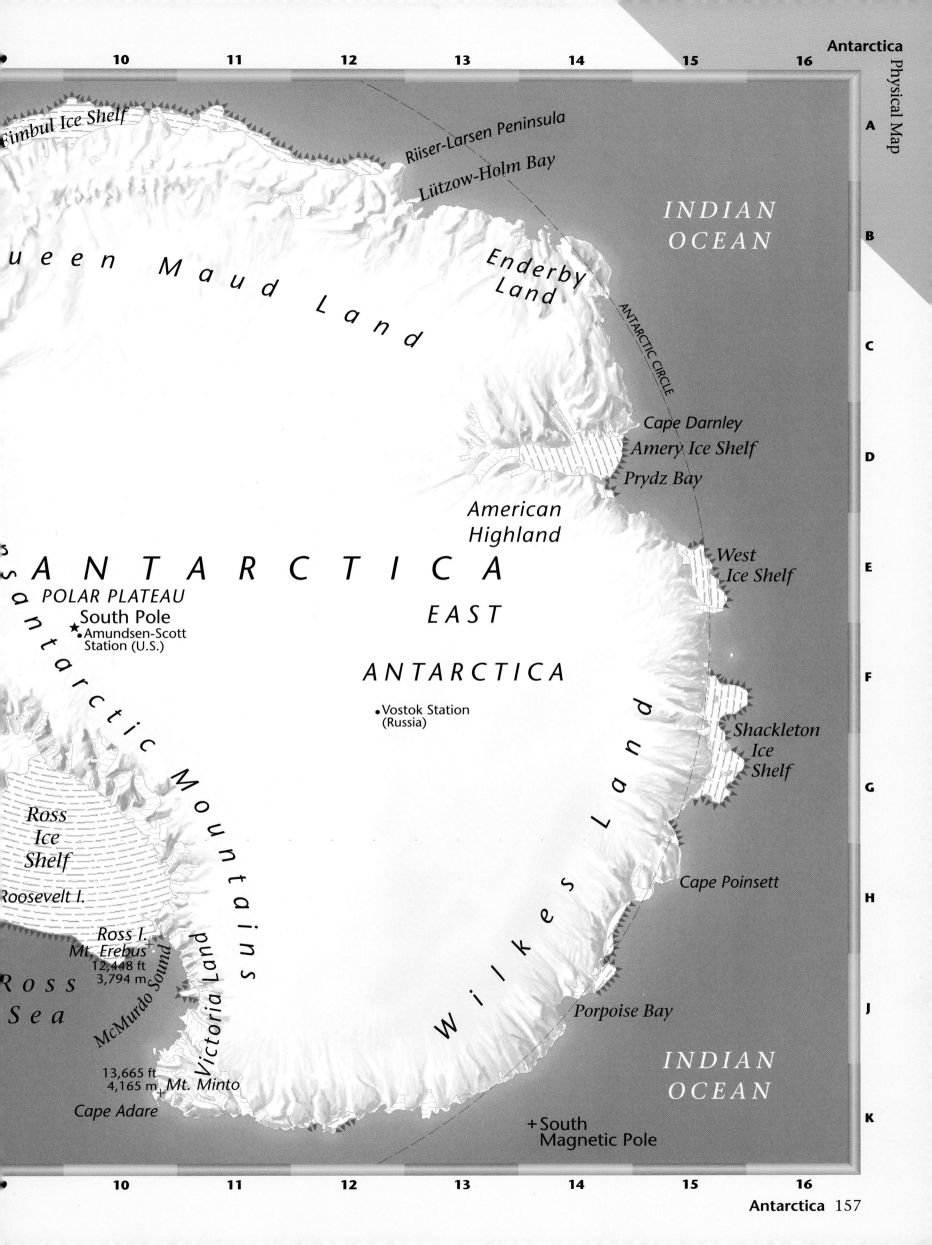

Fimbul Ice Shelf

Riiser-Larsen Peninsula

Lützow-Holm Bay

Queen Maud Land

Enderby Land

INDIAN OCEAN

ANTARCTIC CIRCLE

Cape Darnley

Amery Ice Shelf

Prydz Bay

American Highland

West Ice Shelf

ANTARCTICA

POLAR PLATEAU

South Pole

★ Amundsen-Scott Station (U.S.)

EAST

ANTARCTICA

• Vostok Station (Russia)

Shackleton Ice Shelf

Transantarctic Mountains

Wilkes Land

Ross Ice Shelf

Roosevelt I.

Cape Poinsett

Ross I.

Mt. Erebus

12,448 ft

3,794 m

McMurdo Sound

Ross Sea

Victoria Land

Porpoise Bay

INDIAN OCEAN

13,665 ft

4,165 m Mt. Minto

Cape Adare

+South Magnetic Pole

Antarctica
Continent Under Ice

Antarctica is like a living laboratory. More than 30 major research stations perch on the ice. Most are found along the coast, but a few exist even in the continent's interior, including one at the South Pole itself. Many are occupied year-round, and others only seasonally. Important research goes on in the intense cold. Scientists study the ice sheet for possible effects of global warming. Researchers monitor the hole in the ozone layer—the layer of gases in the atmosphere that shields the earth from the sun's ultraviolet rays. Others examine tiny marine organisms called plankton for changes caused by increased radiation. Paleontologists scour exposed rocks for fossils, evidence that the continent once lay farther north, attached to South America, Africa, and Australia. Because of Antarctica's importance to science, 43 member countries of the Antarctic Treaty agreed, in 1991, to ban all mining and oil exploration for 50 years, preserving this unusual continent for science.

▶ **TWO EMPEROR PENGUINS** *stand beak to beak over a fluffy chick. Emperors are the only native warm-blooded animals to spend the winter in Antarctica.*

▼ **STILL ACTIVE,** *Mount Erebus is one of the highest volcanoes in the world at 12,447 feet (3,794 meters).*

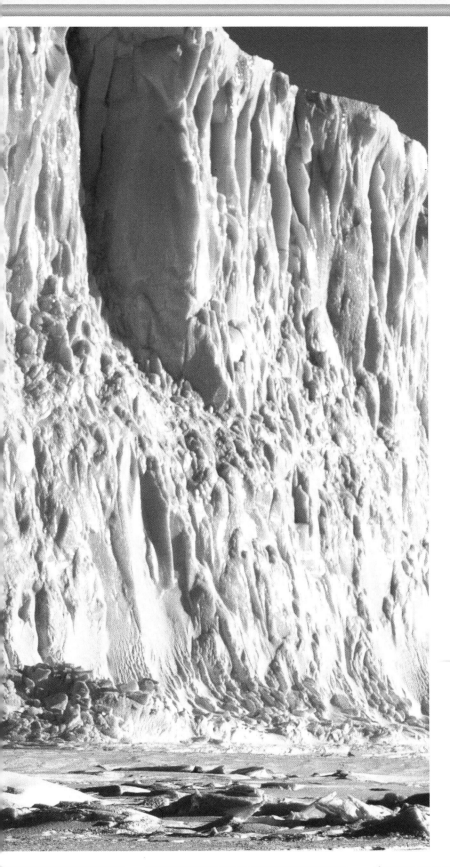

ICE CLIFFS *of Barne Glacier tower above a skier pulling a sledge. Once, polar explorers used dogsleds to cross the ice. Today, to protect wildlife, no dogs are allowed in Antarctica.*

BUILDINGS *stand abandoned at Grytviken whaling station on nearby South Georgia Island. Once hunted, whales are now protected in Antarctic waters.*

ANTARCTICA *is not a country, nor does it belong to any one country. Seven nations have claimed portions of the continent, as shown below. Since 1959, 43 countries have signed the Antarctic Treaty. In it, they agree to work with each other in their scientific research. They also agree to forbid military action and nuclear explosions.*

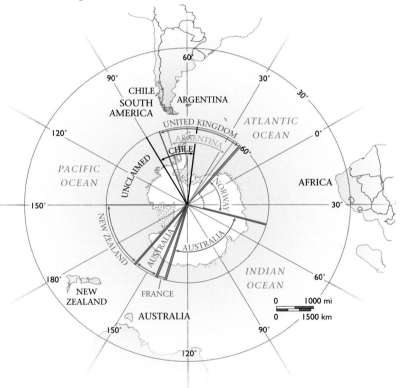

SURROUNDED *by flags and holding one of his own, a proud visitor stands next to the exact location of the South Pole. The Pole, at latitude 90° S, is the southern end of the earth's imaginary axis.*

THE ONLY MAMMALS *native to Antarctica are the whales and seals that live in the surrounding waters. The Weddell seal (below) can be found at 78° S—farther south than any other marine mammal.*

Facts & Figures

Planet Earth

Mass: 6,583,348,000,000,000,000,000,000 tons
(5,974,000,000,000,000,000,000,000 metric tons)
Distance around the Equator:
24,901 mi (40,073 km)
Area: 196,951,900 sq mi (510,066,000 sq km)
Land area: 57,313,000 sq mi (148,429,000 sq km)
Water area: 139,634,000 sq mi (361,637,000 sq km)

The Continents

Asia: 17,213,300 sq mi (44,579,000 sq km)
Africa: 11,609,000 sq mi (30,065,000 sq km)
North America: 9,366,000 sq mi
(24,256,000 sq km)
South America: 6,880,500 sq mi
(17,819,000 sq km)
Antarctica: 5,100,400 sq mi (13,209,000 sq km)
Europe: 3,837,400 sq mi (9,938,000 sq km)
Australia: 2,968,200 sq mi (7,687,000 sq km)

Highest Mountain on Each Continent

Everest, Asia: 29,028 ft (8,848 m)
Aconcagua, South America: 22,834 ft (6,960 m)
McKinley (Denali), North America:
20,320 ft (6,194 m)
Kilimanjaro, Africa: 19,340 ft (5,895 m)
El'brus, Europe: 18,510 ft (5,642 m)
Vinson Massif, Antarctica: 16,067 ft (4,897 m)
Kosciuszko, Australia: 7,310 ft (2,228 m)

Lowest Point on Each Continent

Antarctica: -8,327 ft (-2,538 m)
Dead Sea, Asia: -1,339 ft (-408 m)
Lake Assal, Africa: -512 ft (-156 m)
Death Valley, North America: -282 ft (-86 m)
Valdés Peninsula, South America: -131 ft (-40 m)
Caspian Sea, Europe: -92 ft (-28 m)
Lake Eyre, Australia: -52 ft (-16 m)

Longest Rivers

Nile, Africa: 4,241 mi (6,825 km)
Amazon, South America: 4,000 mi (6,437 km)
Yangtze (Chang), Asia: 3,964 mi (6,380 km)
Mississippi-Missouri, North America:
3,710 mi (5,971 km)
Yenisey-Angara, Asia: 3,440 mi (5,536 km)
Yellow (Huang), Asia: 3,395 mi (5,464 km)
Ob-Irtysh, Asia: 3,361 mi (5,410 km)
Congo (Zaire), Africa: 2,715 mi (4,370 km)
Amur, Asia: 2,744 mi (4,416 km)
Lena, Asia: 3,395 mi (5,464 km)

Major Islands

Greenland: 840,065 sq mi (2,175,600 sq km)
New Guinea: 306,008 sq mi (792,500 sq km)
Borneo: 280,137 sq mi (725,500 sq km)
Madagascar: 226,658 sq mi (587,000 sq km)
Baffin: 195,961 sq mi (507,500 sq km)
Sumatra: 164,993 sq mi (427,300 sq km)
Honshu: 87,806 sq mi (227,400 sq km)
Great Britain: 84,215 sq mi (218,100 sq km)
Victoria: 83,906 sq mi (217,300 sq km)
Ellesmere: 75,759 sq mi (196,200 sq km)

Major Lakes

Caspian Sea, Europe-Asia: 143,254 sq mi
(371,000 sq km)
Superior, North America: 31,701 sq mi
(82,100 sq km)
Victoria, Africa: 26,836 sq mi (69,500 sq km)
Huron, North America: 23,013 sq mi
(59,600 sq km)
Michigan, North America: 22,318 sq mi
(57,800 sq km)
Tanganyika, Africa: 12,704 sq mi (32,900 sq km)
Baikal, Asia: 12,163 sq mi (31,500 sq km)
Great Bear, North America: 12,086 sq mi
(31,300 sq km)
Aral Sea, Asia: 11,854 sq mi (30,700 sq km)
Malawi, Africa: 11,159 sq mi (28,900 sq km)

Oceans

Pacific: 64,190,671 sq mi (166,241,000 sq km)
Atlantic: 33,422,271 sq mi (86,557,000 sq km)
Indian: 28,352,382 sq mi (73,427,000 sq km)
Arctic: 3,662,445 sq mi (9,485,000 sq km)

Major Seas

South China: 1,148,583 sq mi (2,974,600 sq km)
Caribbean: 971,465 sq mi (2,515,900 sq km)
Mediterranean: 969,187 sq mi (2,510,000 sq km)
Bering: 873,079 sq mi (2,261,100 sq km)
Gulf of Mexico: 582,130 sq mi (1,507,600 sq km)
Sea of Okhotsk: 537,532 sq mi (1,392,100 sq km)
Sea of Japan: 391,111 sq mi (1,012,900 sq km)
Hudson Bay: 281,912 sq mi (730,100 sq km)
East China: 256,622 sq mi (664,600 sq km)
Andaman: 218,125 sq mi (564,900 sq km)

Geographic Extremes

Highest Mountain
Everest (Chomolungma), China/Nepal:
29,028 ft (8,848 m)

Deepest Point in the Ocean
Challenger Deep, Mariana Trench, Pacific:
-35,827 ft (-10,920 m)

Hottest Place
Dalol, Denakil Depression, Ethiopia:
annual average temperature 93° F (34° C)

Coldest Place
Plateau Station, Antarctica:
annual average temperature -70°F (-56.7° C)

Wettest Place
Mawsynram, Assam, India: annual average
rainfall 467 in (11,873 mm)

Driest Place
Atacama Desert, Chile: barely measurable rainfall

Largest Hot Desert
Sahara, Africa: 3,475,000 sq mi (9,000,000 sq km)

Largest Cold Desert
Antarctica: 5,100,400 sq mi (13,209,000 sq km)

People

Most People by Continent
Asia: 3,604,000,000

Least People by Continent
Antarctica: 2,000 (transient)
Australia: 18,700,000

Most Densely Populated Country
Monaco: 31,719 people in 0.6 sq mi

Least Densely Populated Country
Mongolia: 4 people per sq mi

Biggest Metropolitan Areas
Tokyo, Japan: 27,242,000
Mexico, Mexico: 16,908,000
São Paulo, Brazil: 16,792,000
New York, United States: 16,390,000
Bombay (Mumbai), India: 15,725,000
Shanghai, China: 13,659,000
Los Angeles, United States: 12,576,000
Calcutta, India: 12,118,000
Buenos Aires, Argentina: 11,931,000
Seoul, South Korea: 11,768,000
Beijing, China: 11,414,000
Lagos, Nigeria: 10,878,000
Osaka, Japan: 10,618,000
Delhi, India: 10,298,000
Rio de Janeiro, Brazil: 10,264,000

Countries with the Highest Life Expectancy
Iceland: 79 years
Japan: 79 years
Andorra: 78 years
Australia: 78 years
Canada: 78 years
Sweden: 78 years
Austria: 77 years

Countries with the Lowest Life Expectancy
Central African Republic: 41 years
Guinea: 44 years
Guinea-Bissau: 44 years
Burkina Faso: 45 years
Gambia: 45 years
Malawi: 45 years
Congo: 46 years

Countries with the Highest Annual Income per Person
Switzerland: $36,410
Luxembourg: $35,850
Japan: $31,450
Denmark: $26,510
Norway: $26,340
United States: $24,750

Countries with the Lowest Annual Income per Person
Mozambique: $80
Ethiopia: $100
Tanzania: $100
Sierra Leone: $140
Somalia: $150

Glossary

archipelago a group or chain of islands

bay a body of water, usually smaller than a gulf, that is partially surrounded by land

border the area on either side of a boundary

boundary most commonly, a line that has been established by people to mark the limit of one political unit, such as a country or state, and the beginning of another; geographical features such as mountains sometimes act as boundaries

breakwater a structure, such as a wall, that protects a harbor or beach from pounding waves

canal an artificial waterway that is used by ships or to carry water for irrigation

canyon a deep, narrow valley that has steep sides

cape a point of land that extends into an ocean, a lake, or a river

cliff a very steep rock face, usually along a coast but also on the side of a mountain

continent one of the seven main landmasses on the earth's surface

country a territory whose government is the highest legal authority over the land and people within its boundaries

delta lowland formed by silt, sand, and gravel deposited by a river at its mouth

desert a hot or cold region that receives 10 inches (25 centimeters) or less of rain or other kinds of precipitation a year

divide an elevated area drained by different river systems flowing in different directions

elevation distance above sea level, usually measured in feet or meters

escarpment a cliff that separates two nearly flat land areas that lie at different elevations

fault a break in the earth's crust along which movement up, down, or sideways occurs

fork in a river, the place where two streams come together

glacier a large, slow-moving mass of ice

gulf a portion of the ocean that cuts into the land; usually larger than a bay

harbor a body of water, sheltered by natural or artificial barriers, that is deep enough for ships

hemisphere literally half a sphere; the earth has four hemispheres: Northern, Southern, Eastern, and Western

highlands an elevated area or the more mountainous region of a country

inlet a narrow opening in the land that is filled with water flowing from an ocean, a lake, or a river

island a landmass, smaller than a continent, that is completely surrounded by water

isthmus a narrow strip of land that connects two larger landmasses and has water on two sides

lagoon a shallow body of water that is open to the sea but also protected from it by a reef or sandbar

lake a body of water that is surrounded by land; large lakes are sometimes called seas

landform a physical feature of the earth that is shaped by tectonic activity and weathering and erosion; the four major kinds are plains, mountains, plateaus, and hills

landmass a large area of the earth's crust that lies above sea level, such as a continent

large-scale map a map, such as a street map, that shows a small area in great detail

latitude distance north and south of the Equator, which is 0° latitude

longitude distance east and west of the prime meridian, which is 0° longitude

mesa an eroded plateau, broader than it is high, that is found in arid or semiarid regions

metropolitan area a city and its surrounding suburbs or communities

mountain a landform, higher than a hill, that rises at least 1,000 feet (300 meters) above the surrounding land and is wider at its base than at its top, or peak; a series of mountains is called a range

nation people who share a common culture; often used as another word for "country," although people within a country may be of many cultures

ocean the large body of saltwater that surrounds the continents and covers more than two-thirds of the earth's surface

peninsula a piece of land that is almost completely surrounded by water

plain a large area of relatively flat land that is often covered with grasses

plateau a relatively flat area, larger than a mesa, that rises above the surrounding landscape

point a narrow piece of land smaller than a cape that extends into a body of water

population density in a country, the number of people living on each square mile or kilometer of land (calculated by dividing population by land area)

prime meridian an imaginary line that runs through Greenwich, England, and is accepted as the line of 0° longitude

projection the process of representing the round earth on a flat surface, such as a map

reef an offshore ridge made of coral, rocks, or sand

Sahel a semiarid grassland immediately south of the Sahara in western and central Africa

savanna a tropical grassland with scattered trees

scale on a map, a means of explaining the relationship between distances on the map and actual distances on the earth's surface

sea the ocean or a partially enclosed body of saltwater that is connected to the ocean; completely enclosed bodies of saltwater, like the Dead Sea, are really lakes

small-scale map a map, such as a country map, that shows a large area without much detail

sound a long, broad inlet of the ocean that lies parallel to the coast and often separates an island and the mainland

spit a long, narrow strip of land, often of sand or silt, extending into a body of water from the land

strait a narrow passage of water that connects two larger bodies of water

territory land that is under the jurisdiction of a country but that is not a state or a province

tributary a stream that flows into a larger river

valley a long depression, usually created by a river, that is bordered by higher land

volcano an opening in the earth's crust through which molten rock erupts

Abbreviations

°C	degrees Celsius
°F	degrees Fahrenheit
ft	feet
I.	island
km	kilometers
L.	lake
m	meters
mi	miles
Mt.	mountain or mount
Pt.	point
R.	river
sq km	square kilometers
sq mi	square miles
Str.	strait
Vol.	volcano

Index

Map references are in boldface (**50**) type. Letters and numbers following in lightface (D12) locate the place-names using the map grid. (Refer to page 7 for more detail.) Illustrations appear in italic (*140*) type and text references are in lightface.

Prut (river), Moldova-Romania **95** J9, **97** B10
Prydz Bay, Antarctica **157** D14
Pskov, Russia **98** J7
Pucallpa, Peru **74** G8
Puebla, Mexico **60** E5
Pueblo, Colorado **44** F6, **51** C11
Puerto Barrios, Guatemala **62** C6
Puerto Cortés, Honduras **62** C7
Puerto La Cruz, Venezuela **74** C2
Puerto Montt, Chile **73** H11, **79** H10
Puerto Rico **41** B11, **61** E14
Puerto Vallarta, Mexico **60** E3
Puget Sound, Washington **48** G2
Pullman, Washington **48** D3
Puncak Jaya (mountain), Indonesia **139** H15
Pune, India **136** G8
Punta Arenas, Chile **73** H13, **79** G14
Purus (river), Brazil **72** G5, **74** D8, **76** D7
Pusan, South Korea **131** F14
Putumayo (river), South America **74** G5, **76** C5
Puysegur Point, New Zealand **151** K14
Pyongyang, North Korea **131** E13
Pyramid Lake, Nevada **49** E9
Pyrenees (mountains), France-Spain **88** H6, **93** G9

Q

Qaidam Basin, China **121** F10
Qandahar, Afghanistan **136** C6
Qaraghandy, Kazakhstan **128** H6
Qatar **126**, **134**, **135**
Qattara Depression, Egypt **112** J6
Qazvin, Iran **134** E7
Qeqertarsuaq (island), Greenland **40** E3
Qingdao, China **131** F11
Qinghai Hu (river), China **130** F8
Qiqihar, China **131** C12
Qom, Iran **134** E7
Quebec (province), Canada **40** D6, **43** H13
Québec, Canada 39, *39*, **40** D7, 42, **43** J13
Queen Charlotte Islands, British Columbia **34** J5, **40** J5, **42** F5
Queen Elizabeth Islands, Northwest Territories **34** F2, **40** F2, **43** B9
Queen Maud Land, Antarctica **157** B9
Queensland (state), Australia 144, **149** D12
Queenstown, Australia **149** K11
Queenstown, New Zealand **151** H12
Queenstown, South Africa **116** H6
Quelimane, Mozambique **117** D9
Querétaro, Mexico **60** E5
Quetta, Pakistan **136** C6
Quetzaltenango, Guatemala **62** D4
Quezon City, Philippines **139** C10
Qui Nhon, Vietnam **138** D6
Quincy, Illinois **54** G7
Quito, Ecuador **72** J4, **74** H6

R

Raba, Indonesia **139** J9
Rabat, Morocco **108** H3, **110** B5
Racine, Wisconsin **55** E9
Rainier, Mount, Washington **48** G3
Rainy Lake, Minnesota-Ontario **54** B7
Raipur, India **137** F10
Rajkot, India **136** E7
Raleigh, North Carolina **45** F14, **57** D13
Ralik Chain (islands), Marshall Islands **152** E5
Rangitaiki (river), New Zealand **150** B6
Rankin Inlet, Northwest Territories **43** F10
Rapid City, South Dakota **44** D7, **54** D2
Rasht, Iran **134** E7
Rat Islands, Alaska **46** J2
Ratak Chain (islands), Marshall Islands **152** E5
Raton, New Mexico **52** A8
Ravensthorpe, Australia **148** G6
Rawalpindi, Pakistan **136** B8
Rawlinna, Australia **148** G7
Rawlins, Wyoming **50** D8
Reading, Pennsylvania **58** J6
Recife, Brazil **72** A5, **77** E14
Red (river), U.S. **44** H10, **53** C12, **57** F6
Red (river), Vietnam **138** B5
Red River of the North, Minnesota **54** A5
Red Sea 100, *100-101*, **102**, **108**, **112**, **120**, **135**
Red Wing, Minnesota **54** D7
Redding, California **44** D2, **49** G9
Redwood City, California **49** G12
Redwood N.P., California **48** H8
Regina, Saskatchewan **40** G7, **42** H8
Reindeer Lake, Manitoba-Saskatchewan **43** G9
Rennes, France **88** F6
Reno, Nevada **40** H8, **44** D2, **49** E10
Republican (river), Nebraska **54** G3
Resistencia, Argentina **72** F8, **78** D5
Resita, Romania **96** C8
Resolute, Northwest Territories **43** C10
Réunion (island), Indian Ocean **117** K12
Reykjavík, Iceland **88** B5, **90** E2
Rhine (river), Europe 82, **88** F8, **92** E7
Rhode Island (state), U.S. **45**, 59, **59**
Rhodes (island), Greece **89** K11, **97** J11
Rhodope Mountains, Bulgaria **96** E8
Rhône (river), France-Switzerland 82, **92** E8
Ribeirão Prêto, Brazil **72** D7, **77** G11
Richfield, Utah **51** G10
Richland, Washington **48** E4
Richmond, Kentucky **57** C10
Richmond, Virginia **45** E14, **57** C13
Ridgecrest, California **49** D13
Rift Valley, Democratic Republic of the Congo **115** B12
Riga, Gulf of, Estonia-Latvia **91** C13
Riga, Latvia **89** E10, **91** C14
Riiser-Larsen Ice Shelf, Antarctica **156** B7
Riiser-Larsen Peninsula, Antarctica **157** A13
Rijeka, Croatia **96** C4
Rimouski, Quebec **43** H14

Río Azul (ruin), Guatemala **62** B6
Rio Branco, Brazil **72** G5, **76** E7
Rio de Janeiro, Brazil **72** C8, **77** H12
Río Gallegos, Argentina **73** G13, **79** G14
Rio Grande (Rio Bravo del Norte) (river), Mexico-U.S. 35, G10, **41** G10, **44** J7, **51** D13, **52** C7, **60** B4
Rio Grande City, Texas **53** K13
Río Muni (province), Equatorial Guinea **108** F8, **115** H10
Riverina (region), Australia **143** H13
Riverside, California **44** G3, **49** D15
Riverton, Wyoming **50** E7
Rivne, Ukraine **94** F8
Riyadh, Saudi Arabia **135** F11
Roanne, France *87*
Roanoke (river), Virginia **57** C13
Roanoke, Virginia **57** C12
Rochester, Minnesota **54** E7
Rochester, New York **45** D13, **58** F5
Rock Hill, South Carolina **57** D11
Rock Island, Illinois **54** F7
Rock Springs, Wyoming **50** F8
Rockall (island), U.K. **88** D5, **92** K2
Rockford, Illinois **45** D11, **54** F8
Rockhampton, Australia **149** E14
Rocky Mountain N.P., Colorado **51** D9
Rocky Mountains, Canada-U.S. **34**, **40**, **42**, **44**, **50**, 51
Rolla, Missouri **54** J7
Roma, Australia **149** F13
Romania **89**, **96**, 97
Rome, Georgia **57** E10
Rome, Italy **88** J8, **93** C9
Rome, New York **58** F7
Ronne Ice Shelf, Antarctica **156** D7
Roosevelt Island, Antarctica **157** H9
Roraima, Mount, Venezuela **74** B4
Rosario, Argentina **73** F9, **78** E7
Roseau, Dominica **61** F15
Roseburg, Oregon **48** H6
Ross Ice Shelf, Antarctica **157** G9
Ross Island, Antarctica **157** H10
Ross Sea, Antarctica **157** J9
Rostock, Germany **92** D4
Rostov, Russia **89** G13, **99** G12
Roswell, New Mexico **44** G6, **52** D8
Rotorua, New Zealand **150** C6
Rotterdam, Netherlands **92** E5
Rotuma (island), Fiji **152** H7
Rouen, France **92** F6
Rouyn-Noranda, Quebec **40** E7
Rovaniemi, Finland **90** C7
Ruapehu, Mount, New Zealand **150** C7
Rub al Khali (desert), Saudia Arabia **120** D5
Rubtsovsk, Russia **128** H7
Ruby Mountains, Nevada **49** B9
Ruse, Bulgaria **97** D10
Russia 85, *85*, **89**, **94**, **98**, 99, 120, 125, *125*, **126**, **128**
Rust'avi, Georgia **133** B11
Ruston, Louisiana **56** E6

Rutland, Vermont **58** E8
Rwanda **108**, 109, 112, **113**
Ryazan', Russia **89** E13, **99** G9
Rybinsk Reservoir, Russia **98** G7
Rybinsk, Russia **98** G7
Ryukyu Islands, Japan **121** G13, **131** H13
Rzeszów, Poland **94** F6

S

Saaremaa (island), Estonia **91** D13
Saba (island), Lesser Antilles **61** E14
Sabah (region), Malaysia **138** F9
Sabha, Libya **111** D9
Sabine (river), Louisiana-Texas **53** F16, **56** G5
Sabzebar, Iran **134** C7
Sacramento (river), California **49** G9
Sacramento Valley, California **49** G9
Sacramento, California **40** J8, **44** E2, **48** F11
Safford, Arizona **52** E5
Saginaw Bay, Michigan **55** E11
Saginaw, Michigan **55** E11
Saguaro N.P., Arizona **52** E4
Sahara (desert), Africa **102**, 103, 106, *106–107*, **108**, 109, **110**
Sahel (region), Africa **102** H6, 106, **110** F6, **114** G5
Saimaa, Lake, Finland **91** B10
Saint Augustine, Florida **57** G11
Saint Charles, Missouri **54** H8
Saint Clair, Lake, Michigan-Ontario **55** E12
Saint Cloud, Minnesota **54** D6
Saint Croix (river), Wisconsin **54** D6
Sainte Marie, Cap (cape), Madagascar, **117**, G11
Saint Eustatius (island), Lesser Antilles **61** E15
Saint Francis (river), Missouri-Arkansas **56** B7
Saint George's, Grenada **61** G15
Saint George, Utah **51** H12
Saint Helena (island), South Atlantic Ocean **116** J1, 117
Saint Helens, Mount, Washington **48** G4
Saint John (river), Maine **59** B11
Saint John's, Antigua and Barbuda **61** E15
Saint John's, Newfoundland **40** B6
Saint Joseph, Missouri **54** G5
Saint Kitts and Nevis, 41, **41** B10, 60, **61** F14
Saint Lawrence (river), Canada-U.S. **45** B14
Saint Lawrence Island, Alaska **34** K2, **40** K2, **46** E6 **129** A14
Saint Lawrence, Gulf of, Canada **34** C6, **40** C6
Saint Louis, Missouri **40** F8, **45** E10, **54** H8
Saint Lucia **41** A11, 60, **61** F16
Saint Martin (island), Lesser Antilles **61** E15
Saint Marys, Australia **149** K13
Saint Matthew Island, Alaska **46** F6
Saint Paul, Minnesota **40** F7, **45** C9, **54** D6
Saint Petersburg, Florida **45** J13, **57** H11

Saint Petersburg, Russia **89** D11, **98** H6
Saint Vincent and the Grenadines **41** A11, 60, **61** F15
Saint Vincent, Gulf, Australia **143** H11
Saint-Pierre and Miquelon (islands), North Atlantic Ocean **40** B6, 42
Saipan, Northern Mariana Islands **152** E3
Sakakawea, Lake, North Dakota **54** B2
Sakarya (river), Turkey **132** C4
Sakhalin Island, Russia **121** D13, **129** F15
Sala-y-Gómez (island) South Pacific Ocean **153** K16
Salalah, Oman **135** C14
Salamanca, Spain **93** J9
Salar de Uyuni (river), Bolivia **72** G7
Salem, India **137** J9
Salem, Oregon **44** C2, **48** G5
Salina, Kansas **54** H4
Salinas, California **49** G12
Salisbury, Maryland **57** B14
Salmon (river), Idaho **50** J5
Salmon River Mountains, Idaho **50** J5
Salt Lake City, Utah **40** H8, **44** E4, 51, **51** G9
Salta, Argentina **72** G8, **78** F4
Saltillo, Mexico **60** D4
Salto, Uruguay **78** D7
Salton Sea, California **44** G3, **49** B15
Salvador (Bahia), Brazil **72** B6, **77** F13
Salween (river), Asia **121** H10, **130** G7, **137** E15
Salzburg, Austria **92** C7
Samar (island), Philippines **139** D11
Samara, Russia **89** E14, **99** C9
Samarinda, Indonesia **138** G8
Samarqand, Uzbekistan **128** K5
Samoa **152**, 153
Samsun, Turkey **89** J12, **132** B7
San Ambrosio Island, Chile **72** J8
San Angelo, Texas **53** F11
San Antonio, Texas **41** F10, **44** J8, **53** G13
San Bernardino, California **44** G3, **49** C15
San Cristóbal, Venezuela **72** H2, **74** F3
San Diego, California **41** J9, **44** G2, **49** C16
San Félix Island, Chile **72** K8
San Francisco, California **40** J8, **44** E1, **49** G11
San Joaquin (river), California **48** G11
San Joaquin Valley, California **48** F11
San Jorge, Golfo, Argentina **73** G12, **79** F12
San José del Guaviare, Colombia **74** F5
San Jose, California **44** E2, **49** G12
San José, Costa Rica **41** D13, **63** H10
San Juan (river), Costa Rica-Nicaragua **63** G9
San Juan Island, Washington **48** G1
San Juan Mountains, Colorado-New Mexico **51** E11
San Juan, Argentina **78** G6
San Juan, Puerto Rico **41** B11, **61** E14
San Lucas, Cabo (cape), Mexico **41** H10, **60** D2

National Geographic Society

John M. Fahey, Jr.
President and Chief Executive Officer

Gilbert M. Grosvenor
Chairman of the Board

Nina D. Hoffman
Senior Vice President

William R. Gray
Vice President and Director of the Book Division

Staff for this book

Barbara Lalicki
Director of Children's Publishing

Patricia Daniels
Project Editor

Marianne R. Koszorus
Art Director

Dorrit Green
Designer

Carl Mehler
Director of Maps

Susan McGrath
Writer

Suzanne Patrick Fonda
Editor

Marilyn Mofford Gibbons
Illustrations Editor

Jennifer Emmett
Assistant Editor

Kristin Edmonds
Sean M. Groom
Jocelyn Lindsay
Keith R. Moore
Text Research

Thomas L. Gray
Map Editor

Jehan Aziz
John S. Ballay
George Bounelis
Geosystems Gobal Corp.
James Huckenpahler
Mapping Specialists, Ltd.
Martin S. Walz
Beth N. Weisenborn
Scott Zillmer
Map Production

Tibor G. Tóth
Map Relief

Stuart Armstrong
Map Illustration

Judith Klein
Copy Editor

Ellen Teguis
Assistant Vice President Marketing, Publications

Mark Caraluzzi
Director of Direct Response Marketing

Ruth Chamblee
Marketing Manager

Vincent P. Ryan
Manufacturing Manager

Gary Colbert
Production Director

Lewis Bassford
Production Manager

National Geographic Maps

Allen Carroll
Managing Director National Geographic Maps

Richard W. Bullington
Project Manager

Neal J. Edwards
Senior Pre-Press Cartographer

Eric Lindstrom
Edit Cartographer

Dianne C. Hunt
Production Cartographer

Sally Summerall
Senior Design Cartographer

Alfred L. Zebarth
Senior Production Cartographer

Consultants

Geography Education Consultants

Billie Kapp
Teacher Consultant Connecticut Geographic Alliance

Lydia Lewis
Geography Education National Geographic Society

Martha Sharma
National Cathedral School Washington, D.C.

Jackie Vawter
Educational Consulant Alexandria, VA

Regional Consultants

Africa
Dr. C. Gregory Knight
Pennsylvania State University

Antarctica
Dr. Deneb Karentz
University of San Francisco

Asia
Dr. Clifton Pannell
University of Georgia

Australia/Oceania
Dr. Michael Brown
University of Washington

Europe
Dr. Craig ZumBrunnen
University of Washington

South America
Dr. Stephen Frenkel
University of Washington

North America
Dr. Stephen Birdsall
University of North Carolina

Acknowledgements

We are grateful for the assistance of John Agnone, Anne Marie Houppert, Joe Ochlak, Lyle Rosbotham, and Meredith Wilcox of the National Geographic Book Division

Illustrations Credits

Photographs are primarily from Tony Stone Images.

Abbreviations for terms appearing below: (t)-top; (b)-bottom; (l)-left; (r)-right; (c)-center; NGP-National Geographic Photographer; NGS-National Geographic Staff.

Cover, art digitally created by Douglas Stern.
Back Cover (l–r), (art) Shusei Nagaoka; Paul Souders; (art) Robert Cremins; Bruno De Hogues.

All locator globes created by Theophilus Britt Griswold

2–3 Original NASA photograph printed from digital image © 1996 Corbis; (l–r) Hiroyuki Matsumoto; David Levy; Masa Vemusi; John Beatty; Chris Shinn; Suzanne & Nick Geary; Art Wolfe.
4–5 (tl–r) (art) Shusei Nagaoka; A. Hyde; Art Wolfe; Penny Tweedie; (bl-r) (art) John D. Dawson; Ed Simpson; Christopher Arnesen; Phil Cole.

How to Use This Atlas
6 (t) Original NASA photograph printed from digital image © 1996 Corbis; (b) Doug Armand.

Understanding Maps
8 (art) © 1998 Sally J. Bensusen/Visual Science Studio. 10 (art) Shusei Nagaoka. 10–11 Lockheed Martin. 11 Mark O. Thiessen/NGP. 12–13 (art) Shusei Nagaoka. 14 (bl and br) (art) Shusei Nagaoka. 14–15 (art) Ron Miller. 15 (tr) Robert Hynes; (cr) John Pervet; (br) (art) Shusei Nagaoka.

Planet Earth
16 (t) (art) Shusei Nagaoka; (b) (art) Christopher R. Scotese/PALEOMAP Project, U. TX, Arlington. 17 (t) (art) Shusei Nagaoka; (b) (art) Susan Sanford. 18 (b) (art) NG Maps. 18–19 (art) Shusei Nagaoka. 19 (l–r) Robert Frerck; Jason Hawkes; Art Wolfe; Ron Sanford.

The World
23 (b) NOAA/NESDIS. 24 (t) Raymond Gehman; (l–r) (art) John D. Dawson; Freddy Storheil; Tim Davis. 25 (l) Ed Pritchard; (tr) Chris Baker; (br) Michael K. Nichols/NGP; (art) Stuart Armstrong. 24–25 Desertification data UNEP. 28 (bl) Hansen Planetarium Publications. 29 (art) Theophilus Britt Griswold. 30 (t) Roger Tully; (b) Paul Chesley. 31 (l) Doug Armand; (r) (art) Theophilus Britt Griswold.

North America
32 Bert Sagara. 32–33 Original NASA photograph printed from digital image © 1996 Corbis. 36 (l) Robert Frerck; (r) Hiroyuki Matsumoto. 36–37 Paul Souders. 37 (art) Tony Chen. 38 (tl) Gary John Norman; (cl) Chad Ehlers; (bl) (art) Tony Chen. 38–39 (t) A. Hyde; (b) Rosemary Calvert. 39 (tl) Glen Allison; (tr) Yves Marcoux; (c) Sarah Stone; (b) Paul Chesley.

South America
64 William J. Hebert. 64–65 Original NASA photograph printed from digital image © 1996 Corbis. 68 (l) Erik Svenson; (r) Richard T. Nowitz/NGS Image Collection. 68–69 Ed Simpson. 69 (l) (art) Tony Chen; (r) Kevin Schafer. 70 (tl) (art) Richard Schlect; (bl) Robert Frerck; (br) (art) Richard Schlecht. 70–71 David Levy. 71 (l) Jacques Jangoux; (r) Ken Fisher.

Europe
80 Nicholas DeVore. 80–81 Original NASA photograph printed from digital image © 1996 Corbis. 84 (l) Phil Cole. 84–85 Masa Vemusi. 85 (t–b) Bail and Spiegel; Martine Mouchy; Steven Weinberg. 86 (tl) Richard Elliot; (bl) (art) Harry Bliss; (br) Guy Marche. 86–87 Bob Handelman. 87 (tl) Anthony Cassidy; (tr) Will & Deni McIntyre; (cl) Vince Streano; (cr) James L. Stanfield; (b) Rob Talbot.

Africa
100 Marc Chamberlain. 100–101 Original NASA photograph printed from digital image © 1996 Corbis. 104 (l) (art) John D. Dawson; (r) Ian Murphy. 104–105 (t) Ed Collacott; (b) Bruno De Hogues. 105 Art Wolfe. 106 (tl) (art) John D. Dawson; (cl) Penny Tweedie. 106–107 (t) John Beatty; (b) Bruno De Hogues. 107 (tl) Bruce Dale; (tr) Nicholas DeVore; (br) (art) Christopher Klein/NGS.

Asia
118 Doug Armand. 118–119 Original NASA photograph printed from digital image © 1996 Corbis. 122 (l) (art) Robert Cremins; (r) Terry Vine. 122–123 (t) Christopher Arnesen; (b) Steven Raymer. 123 Sylvain Grandadam. 124 (t–b) Erica Lansner; Orion Press; Keren Su. 124–125 (t) Chris Shinn; (b) Robert Frerck. 125 (t) (art) Kinuko Y. Craft; (c) Paul Harris.

Australia, New Zealand and Oceania
140 R. Ian Lloyd/Productions Pte. Ltd. 140–141 Original NASA photograph printed from digital image © 1996 Corbis. 144 (bl) (art) Tony Chen; (br) Hideo Kurihara. 144–145 Doug Armand. 145 (bl) Robin Smith; (br) Penny Tweedie. 146 (tl) Paul McKelvey; (cl) Christopher Arnesen; (bl) Fritz Prenzel; (tr) Stuart Westmorland; (cr) J. Scherschel. 146–147 John Eascott/Yva Momatiuk. 147 (t) Suzanne & Nick Geary; (b) William J. Hebert.

Antarctica
154-155 National Remote Sensing Centre, Farnsborough, England, and NOAA, Suitland, Maryland; digital composition created by Theophilus Britt Griswold. 154 Art Wolfe. 158 Art Wolfe. 158–159 (t) Roger Mear; (b) Kim Westerskov. 159 (t) Joel Bennett; (bl) Gordon Wiltsie; (br) (art) Richard Ellis.

Library of Congress Cataloging-in-Publication Data

National Geographic world atlas for young explorers.
   p. cm.
   Includes index.
   Summary: Presents world, regional, and thematic maps as well as photographic essays on each continent.
   ISBN 0-7922-7341-9   98-18366
   1. Children's atlases. [1. Atlases.]   CIP
G1021 .N43 1998 <G&M>   MAPS
912—DC21

150°   120°   90°   60°   30°W

60°

**N O R T H
A M E R I C A**
32-63

30°N

30°N

EQUATOR
0°

**S O U T H
A M E R I C A**
64-79

30°S

60°